במדבר | NUMBERS

A PARSHA COMPANION

במדבר | NUMBERS

A PARSHA COMPANION

Rabbi David Fohrman

Numbers: A Parsha Companion
First edition, 2025

Aleph Beta Press
Email info@alephbeta.org
Website www.alephbeta.org

Maggid Books
An imprint of Koren Publishers Jerusalem Ltd.
PO Box 8531, New Milford, CT 06776-8531, USA
& PO Box 4044, Jerusalem 9104001, Israel
www.korenpub.com

Book design by Cory Rockliff

Image credits:
Jackson Pollock, *Autumn Rhythm (No. 30)*, 1950, © ROBERT / Alamy Stock Vector
Georges Seurat, *A Sunday Afternoon on the Island of La Grande Jatte*, 1859–1891, © Universal Art Archive / Alamy Stock Photo
Claude Monet, *The Japanese Footbridge*, 1899, © Martin Shields / Alamy Stock Photo

The publication of this book was made possible through the generous support of *The Jewish Book Trust*.

ISBN 978-1-59264-698-2 (hardcover)

Printed and bound in the United States

The *Parsha Companion* series
is reverently dedicated by

Ronny & Toby Hersh

in memory of their parents

אברהם בן אהרן הלוי ז״ל
אסתר בת אברהם יהושע ז״ל

Abraham & Esther Hersh *z"l*

שמואל משה בן פסח יוסף ז״ל
חיה רבקה בת צירל ז״ל

Moshe & Rivka Zytelny *z"l*

and the many among their family
who perished in the Shoah

About Our Parents

Our parents surmounted great tragedy and hardship to live exemplary lives. They loved us, nourished us, and sacrificed much to help us flourish and become committed Jews. In their example, we saw sacred values of the Torah brought to life. We live in the shadow of their deeds.

ABRAHAM AND ESTHER HERSH hailed originally from the Carpathian Mountains. They were both survivors of Auschwitz, and they met after the war in a displaced persons camp in Germany. Shortly thereafter, they made their way from the ashes of Europe to the Land of Israel, where Abraham fought in Israel's War of Independence. He was a fierce lover of both the land and the Torah of Israel. Together, Abraham and Esther lived difficult lives but, through it all, somehow always maintained a deep faith in Hashem. Their strong values — commitment to family and to Judaism, and an abiding love of the State of Israel and the Jewish people — made powerful impressions upon their children.

RABBI MOSHE AND RIVKA ZYTELNY made their way from Europe to America. Toby's father was, in his younger years, a *yeshivah bachur* in Kletzk. Before Lakewood was a gleam in the eye of history, he became a close student of Rabbi Aharon Kotler, and a *chavruta* of his son, Rabbi Shneur. He escaped the ravages of war by heading, with his yeshivah, first to Siberia and then to Kazakhstan, where he met his wife, Rivka. The couple moved from Kazakhstan to France — and all this time, despite war and constant upheaval, Rabbi Aharon remained like a father to him. To this day, Ronny and Toby cherish letters in their possession that Rabbi Aharon sent to Rabbi Moshe in France, advising him on major life decisions. Eventually, Rabbi Moshe and Rivka came to America, where he rejoined his rebbe and yeshivah in Lakewood. There, he became part of an unlikely success story, as he helped reestablish a vibrant center of Torah on new and distant shores. All in all, Moshe was the only one in his entire immediate family to survive the war. Together, he and Rivka raised seven children.

Our parents lived through harrowing times and emerged with a steely, strengthened faith; they sacrificed much to pass on their vibrant heritage. We remember them with love, and are honored to carry their legacy forward.

Ronny & Toby Hersh

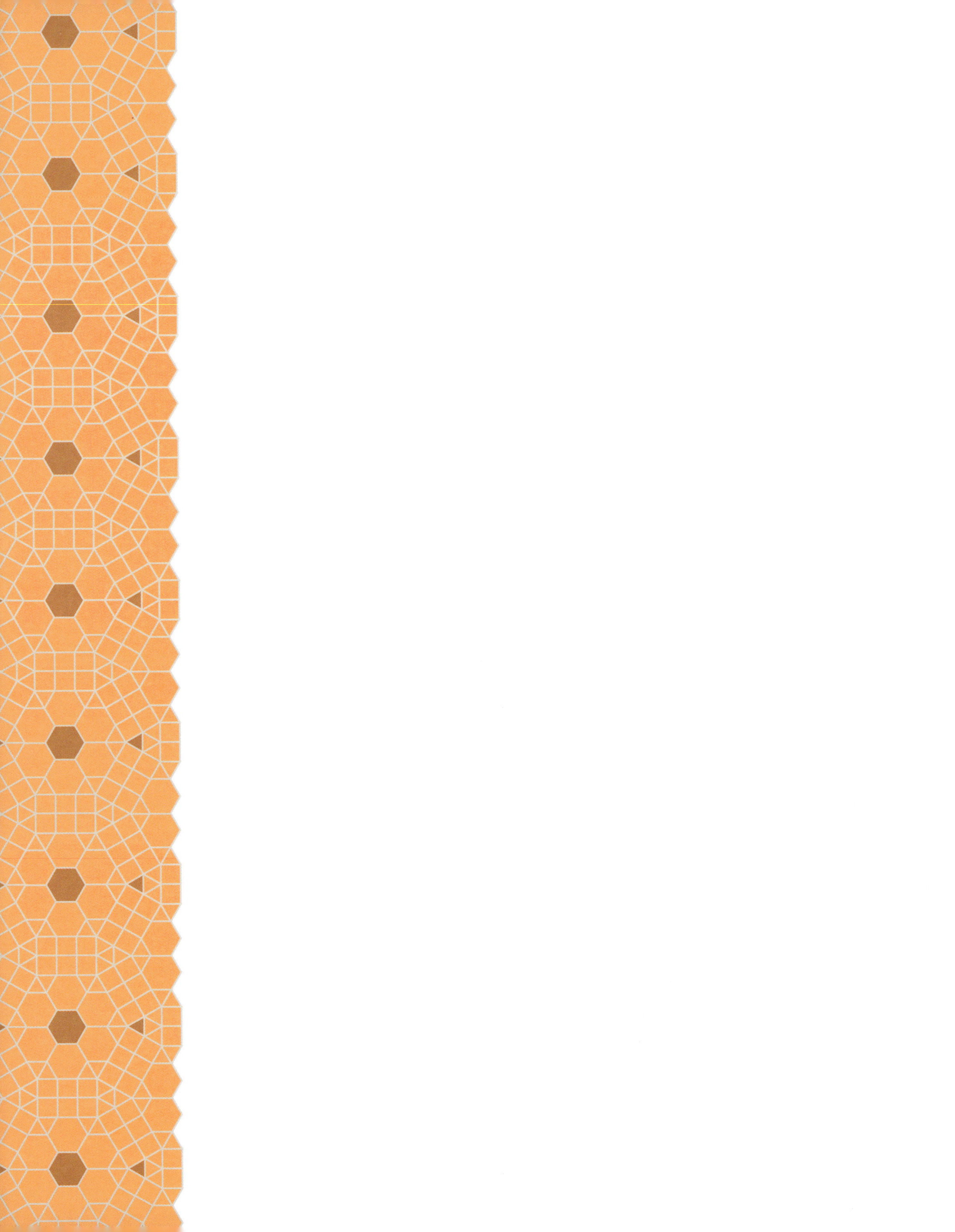

The Numbers volume of the
Parsha Companion is dedicated by

Dr. Bruce Wayne Greenstein

& Ms. Monica Patricia Martinez

in honor of

Dr. Melvyn and Irene Greenstein

Our family's association with Rabbi Fohrman and Aleph Beta stems from recognizing the magic of combining challenging Torah concepts and compelling insights with animation that appeals to both young and old. In a world that so often seems increasingly distant from the eternal values espoused by our sages and our Torah, this publication of a treatise on Bamidbar — a defining moment in history when the Israelites wavered from revolution to dedication to all that Hashem taught them — is most appropriate. We are deeply honored to have the Greenstein name associated with this incredible work.

Dr. Bruce Greenstein

We gratefully acknowledge the following patrons who, with generosity and vision, have dedicated individual volumes of this *Parsha Companion* series:

BEREISHIT

Tuvia Levkovich *a"h* & Barbara Levkovich

SHEMOT

Daniel & Jamie Schwartz

VAYIKRA

Alan and Fran Broder

Dr. Hillel and Chayi Cohen

Avram M. Cooperman MD,
the Cooperman and Weiss Families

Mark and Erica Gerson

Chaim and Livia Jacobs and Family

Harry and Eta Klaristenfeld

Yaron and Lisa Reich

Donny and Arielle Rosenberg

Yanky and Aliza Safier

BAMIDBAR

Dr. Bruce Wayne Greenstein
& Ms. Monica Patricia Martinez

DEVARIM

Andrew & Terri Herenstein

We also wish to acknowledge the

Legacy Heritage Fund

for its generous support to help
make this series of books possible.

LEGACY HERITAGE FUND

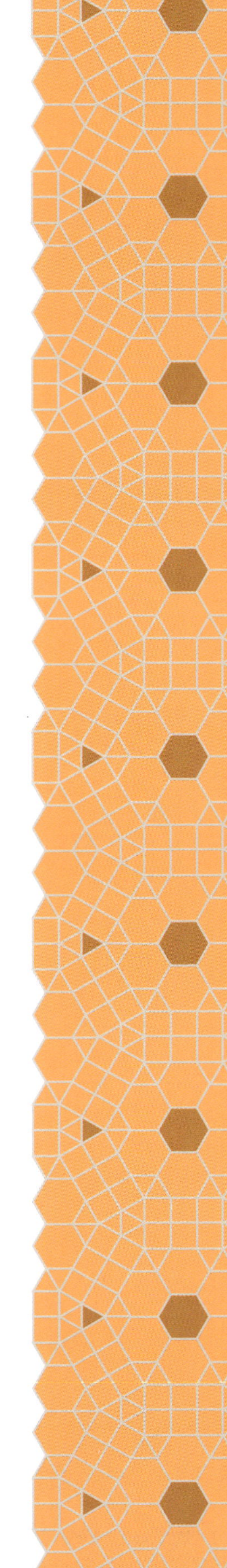

Contents

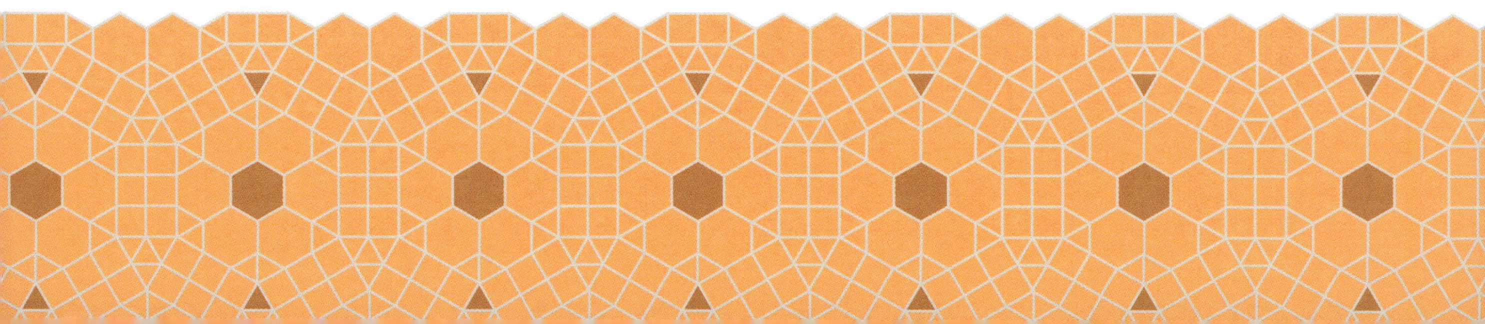

Some Words of Appreciation

THE BOOK OF NUMBERS chronicles Israel's sojourn in the wilderness. And, I must say, writing this volume of *Parsha Companion, Numbers*, would have felt like a sojourn alone in the wilderness for *me* — were it not for the companionship of a hearty band of collaborators. I'd like to take a moment to thank them and acknowledge their contributions to this shared endeavor.

Ronny and Toby Hersh are the patrons of this five-volume series of *Parsha Companions*. I have spent many memorable afternoons learning parsha with Ronny and Toby and their extended family, and it feels especially fitting for this series of books to bear their names. They have dedicated the series to the memory of their parents, Abraham and Esther Hersh *z"l* and Moshe and Rivka Zytelny *z"l*.

I would also like to acknowledge the Legacy Heritage Fund for its generous support in making this series of books possible. The foundation focuses much of its effort on supporting Jewish education. I am honored that the Legacy Heritage Fund has included this series of books among the many worthy projects they've chosen to champion.

This "Numbers" volume of the series has been generously sponsored by Dr. Bruce Greenstein and Monica Martinez, in honor of Bruce's parents, Dr. Melvyn and Irene Greenstein. Bruce is an avid enthusiast of my work, and I'm proud to call him a friend. Bruce's parents, Dr. Melvin and Irene, were innovators, founders, and supporters of Jewish education in many forms, and it is an honor to have their names associated with my work.

I also want to acknowledge those who have dedicated other volumes in the *Parsha Companion* series: Tuvia Levkovich *z"l* and Barbara; Dan and Jamie Schwartz; and Andrew and Terri Herenstein, along with the many dedicators of the Leviticus volume. Sadly, Tuvia, patron of the Genesis volume, has passed away since the publication of the volume that bears his name. May the thanks of those who've benefited from his generosity continue to nourish his soul in the Land of the Living.

* * *

A number of folks have helped shepherd the ideas in this book into the essays that you now hold in your hands. I'd like to offer them my thanks and tribute.

Among them are Mathew Miller and Rabbi Reuven Ziegler, of Koren Publishers Jerusalem. They have been assisted by Caryn Meltz, Estie Dishon, Rachelle Emanuel, and Debbie Ismailoff, as well as other mem-bers of the Koren team. All have been great to work with. The people at Koren are proudly bringing a new generation of original Jewish thought to the public, one beautiful book at a time. We are all enriched by their efforts.

On the Aleph Beta side, the principal editing of this volume was done by Shoshana Brody. She has an eye for beauty, a sensitivity to spirituality, and a mind that will not tolerate fuzziness or redundancy. She has brought all of these qualities to bear in editing these essays will love, skill, and care. She's also designed the graphics and charts that grace these pages. Adina Blaustein managed all the moving parts and pieces — and there were many of them! — in her role as project manager. She also provided valuable feedback and background research on many of the essays. Immanuel Shalev was invaluable as a *chavruta* partner working through many of these ideas; and his advice on issues of structure and presentation was invaluable. I want to thank, as well, Rabbis Eliyahu Raful and Elinatan Kupferberg, whose research skills, judgment, and stature as *talmidei chachamim* I relied on throughout the manuscript. My thanks also go to Cory Rockliff, who designed the series' overall aesthetic.

Many of the ideas in this book on Numbers had their *own* genesis, as it were, in parsha videos I created with the help and support of the amazing team at Aleph Beta (you can find those videos at www.alephbeta.org). I want to take this opportunity to acknowledge, with gratitude, those behind the scenes who have, over the years, helped to transform Aleph Beta from a mere idea, to a fledgling start-up, to a viable, going concern: its founders, board of directors, and officers. They are Etta Brandman, Alan Broder, David Hamburger, Jeff Haskell, Josh Malin, David Pollack, Donny Rosenberg, Robbie Rothenberg, Dan Schwartz, Kuty Shalev, and Steve Wagner. I want to thank, as well, the manifold subscribers of Aleph Beta, who each support our work in ways great and small, and provide us with meaningful feedback, appreciation, as well as a dose of constructive criticism. Having you by our side gives us the drive and motivation to continue. I also want to mention that a few of those subscribers — Laura Burdick; Eliakim and Nechama Pessil; and the entire Bang family; Scott and Shari Norvell; the Hackett family; Nat, Ayesha, Aliyah, Caleb, and Zach Schuster; Neal Gittelman, MD & Associates — made special donations to help shepherd this book through its production. I am grateful to them as well.

The *Parsha Companion* series, not to mention the rest of my work — none of it would have been possible were it not for three men, each of whom is no longer with us. All three played an outsized role in nurturing my development over the years. My father, Moshe Fohrman *z"l*, passed away when I was quite young, but he taught me so much about life, people, and relationships in the short years we had together; his love and influence continue to pervade my work. My stepfather, Zev Wolfson *z"l*, a man of towering accomplishments, took me under his wing, believed in me, and helped me thrive. LeRoy Hoffberger *z"l*, a bulwark of the Baltimore Jewish community, became a dear friend and mentor. LeRoy and I first met when he attended a class that I taught at Johns Hopkins University; he took a keen interest in my work and ultimately helped give it life by creating the Hoffberger Foundation for Torah Studies. The love of all three I shall carry with me as long as the One Above deigns that I walk the earth.

Finally, I want to acknowledge my family. My wife, Reena, has given me her unfailing love and support, and has partnered with me in the greatest endeavor of my life — raising seven delightful children: Moshe, Shalva, Avigail, Shana, Yael, Ariella, and Avichai. All have helped shape this book in ways great and small, for they, together with my four sons-in-law, Yosef, Boruch, Moshe, and Chaim Dovid, really are *my* "parsha companions." Many of the ideas contained in these pages were born, shaped, or refined in animated discussions with them around the Shabbos table. I treasure those moments: Learning Torah with my family is a constant opportunity to talk about things that matter deeply with people I care about the most — and what could be better than that?

Rabbi David Fohrman

Woodmere, NY
January 2025

INTRODUCTION

What Is the Book of Numbers About?

THE BOOK OF NUMBERS — what is it really about?

In Hebrew, Numbers is *Bamidbar,* literally "in the wilderness."[1] At some level, the book seems to reflect its name both literally and metaphorically.

Let's start with the literal. Having left Egypt, but having not yet arrived in the Land of Israel, the book of Numbers really *is* about the Israelites' journey through the wilderness.

Although in the beginning of Bamidbar, the journey begins with great hope and anticipation — the people are only eleven days away from the Promised Land, and it seems they will soon triumphantly enter — in no time those hopes come crashing down with the catastrophic sin of the spies. In response to that failing, God decrees that this generation will not enter the Promised Land; rather, they will wander for forty years in the desert, until the generation dies out and a new generation grows up, in the wilderness, to take their place. The people *will* enter the land, but that will be a dream deferred. For now, it will just be ... wilderness.

On the literal level, *Sefer Bamidbar* is about wandering through a desert — being in no-man's-land — in a very tangible, physical sense. But I would argue that the book is also about a more metaphorical desert journey. It's a story about losing the anchors that help us feel at home, even as we journey physically through no-man's-land. But it's not just that; it is about what happens when we enter no-man's-land, not just physically but *spiritually* as well.

The anchors I'm talking about are our parents.

---

1 The English name for the fourth book of the Torah, Numbers, derives from the Greek translation of the rabbinic term "The Book of Counting," reflecting the census taken at both the beginning and end of the book. However, in Hebrew, it is called *Bamidbar,* meaning "in the wilderness." This name was chosen partly because *bamidbar* is the fifth word in the text, but it also encapsulates the book's central theme, as I demonstrate in this introductory essay.

A Book About Parents?

While parenthood might not seem like the first theme that comes to mind when considering Numbers, I make the argument in this volume that the priestly blessing found early on in the book of Numbers is, in fact, a kind of incredibly concise parenting manual. Its three brief sentences provide guidance on how to shepherd a child through three critical phases of life. The priestly blessing teaches parents how to keep a child safe and warm. It teaches parents how to love. And it teaches them the hardest of lessons, too: how to ultimately let go.

As it turns out, this theme — how parents let go of children, and children let go of parents — is not just of theoretical interest in the book of Numbers. It becomes a matter of practical reality soon enough. There are several examples of these bittersweet partings in the book of Numbers — Moses' loss of Yitro comes to mind[2] — but none quite as momentous as that which occurs toward the end of the book, where we encounter the mysterious story of Moses hitting the rock. Moses finds himself barred from entering the Land of Israel as a result — but in truth, that story is not *just* about how the people lose Moses as their leader; it is a story about the loss of an entire family of leaders, an entire family of "national parental figures."

---

2 In **Parshat Beha'alotecha**, Yitro, Moses' father-in-law and advisor, decides it is time for him to leave and go home. Moses pleads with him to stay. He tells his father-in-law that God has good things in store for the people, and Yitro will share in that goodness. But Yitro declines. In words that echo — almost like a reverse image — the call of Abraham to leave his homeland, Yitro tells Moses (Num. 10:30):

וַיֹּאמֶר אֵלָיו, לֹא אֵלֵךְ, כִּי אִם אֶל אַרְצִי וְאֶל מוֹלַדְתִּי אֵלֵךְ.

And he said to him, "No, I will not go with you; rather, I will return to my land and my birthplace."

In some ways, Moses has been through this before. This is Moses' *third* parental loss. First, he lost Yocheved and Amram, his birth parents. That happened in the reeds at the Nile, where Moses' mother placed him in a basket in a desperate attempt to preserve his life. Years later, Moses lost his adoptive mother, the daughter of Pharaoh, when he fled Egypt to escape the wrath of Pharaoh. Then, when he married Tzippora, her father Yitro entered Moses' world, and became the only parent left in his life. Yitro advised him and cared for his welfare. But now, in the book of Numbers, Yitro would leave too.

After all, it is not just Moses, but — for reasons I discuss in the essay on **Parshat Chukat** — Aaron, too, who is destined to die for that act of hitting the rock. Moreover, this very same story begins by letting the reader know that Miriam, Moses' sister, had just died. Within a mere few lines, this one story seals the fates of all three major leaders of that first generation. None of them will be there to usher this newly born nation into its land.

Four Events

Then, just after we encounter the fateful story of Moses striking the rock, we read of several events that take place in quick succession:

1. Israel is attacked by surprise. The aggressor is the Canaanite king of Arad, identified by the Sages as a disguised version of Israel's ancient nemesis, Amalek.[3]
2. The people become travel weary and speak disparagingly about the manna.
3. They come upon a wellspring of fresh water in the desert.
4. Thankful for this well, the people burst out in song to God. The Torah relates this by telling us:

אָז יָשִׁיר יִשְׂרָאֵל אֶת־הַשִּׁירָה הַזֹּאת	Then Israel sang this song.	Numbers 21:17

So, dear reader, I have a question for you: *Does that list sound familiar to you at all?* Is there, perchance, another moment in the Torah when we encounter all of these elements?

There is. All four elements do appear earlier. They come in quick succession, just like here. And they come in precisely the same order — only *backward.*

It all happens way back in the book of Exodus.

The Four Events, Backward

***Az Yashir*: A Song of Thanksgiving.** Back in Exodus, you will recall, the Israelites sing a triumphant song at the sea. Remarkably, that song begins

---

3 See Rashi on Numbers 21:1.

with the very same words we just saw toward the end of the book of Numbers, *az yashir*:

Exodus 15:1	אָז יָשִׁיר־מֹשֶׁה וּבְנֵי יִשְׂרָאֵל אֶת־הַשִּׁירָה הַזֹּאת	Then Moses and the Children of Israel sang this song

The Advent of Wells. Shortly after that, in the very same chapter, the people thirsted for water. God leads them to an oasis at Marah, whose bitter water miraculously turns sweet when Moses casts a branch into it. Shortly after *that*, at the very end of chapter 15, the people find twelve wellsprings in the desert.

The Advent of Manna — But the People Don't Do Right by the Manna. Just after the discovery of the wells, in Exodus chapter 15, God gives the people manna for the very first time in chapter 16. Along with the manna, God gives them some very simple instructions as to how they are to treat it. For example, the manna will not fall on Saturdays, and no one should go out in the fields on Saturday to try to collect it; instead, they will receive a double portion on Friday. Nevertheless, some of the people *do* go out on Saturday looking for the manna. They fail to properly abide by God's instructions.

An Attack by Amalek. And what happens immediately after this manna crisis? The people are set upon by Amalek. God tells Moses to ascend with Aaron to the top of a hill, where he can overlook the battle. So long as Moses keeps his hands raised skyward, Israel prevails. Aaron and Hur support Moses' hands, and Amalek is vanquished, at least for the time being.

So, there it is. Four events from Exodus are replayed here, at the end of the book of Numbers, in backward order:

IN EXODUS

1. An *Az Yashir* Song. The song of thanksgiving for the victory at the sea.
2. Advent of Water. Search for water and the finding of wellsprings.
3. Manna. The advent of manna, and the crisis that ensues when the people fail to abide by God's instructions as to how to treat the manna.
4. Amalek. The attack by Amalek.

IN NUMBERS

1. Amalek. The attack by the Canaanite king of Arad, who the Sages say is in fact Amalek in disguise.
2. Manna. People speak disparagingly about the manna.
3. Advent of Water. Search for water and the finding of the well.
4. An *Az Yashir* Song. The song of thanksgiving for the well.

A Forty-Year Chiasm

If you've read some of the other volumes of this series, you are probably familiar with this literary structure. It's a chiasm — an ABCD-DCBA pattern, sometimes known as an *atbash* pattern in the world of Jewish mystical texts. Our case, though, is a remarkable version of an *atbash* pattern: It is a pattern that spans vast tracts of text, linking verses in Exodus to those in Numbers. Forty years separate the events in this chiasm: the four events in Exodus took place just as Israel was beginning its journey from Egypt to the Promised Land, and the four events in Numbers occur forty years later, as Israel nears the end of its long, winding journey.

So, what is the meaning of our chiasm? What is it that the Torah wants us to understand, once we've managed to pick up on this elegant series of inverted parallels?

Of Parallels and Contrasts

The important clues to answer that question, I think, come from noticing that the parallels are not just parallels, but are also contrasts. The most blatant contrast comes, perhaps, in who it is that sings the great song of thanksgiving at each bookend of these forty years:

NUMBERS: THE SONG AT THE WELL (21:17)	**EXODUS: THE SONG AT THE SEA (15:1)**
אָז יָשִׁיר **יִשְׂרָאֵל** אֶת־הַשִּׁירָה הַזֹּאת Then **Israel** sang this song.	אָז יָשִׁיר־**מֹשֶׁה וּבְנֵי יִשְׂרָאֵל** אֶת־הַשִּׁירָה הַזֹּאת Then **Moses and the Children of Israel** sang this song.

In the first song, in the book of Exodus, Moses leads the Children of Israel in song. In the second song, in the book of Numbers, it is the people of Israel who lead *themselves* in song.[4]

A similar thread seems to wind itself through the other events of the chiasm, too. Back in Exodus, the people thirsted for water, and Moses miraculously turned the bitter pool of water into a fresh, sweet oasis. The people themselves, back in Exodus, didn't do anything. They were passive. They thirsted and complained that the water was bitter. When the water was sweetened for them, they drank, but did not offer thanks or break into song. All of that changes in the book of Numbers. There, the people dig the well, as they themselves acknowledge in their words of thanksgiving:

Numbers 21:18

בְּאֵר חֲפָרוּהָ שָׂרִים כָּרוּהָ נְדִיבֵי הָעָם	The well, which the princes dug, which the nobles of the people dug.

Moreover, in Numbers, the people sing joyously in response to the appearance of the well. Even though they are the ones who dug the well, they still see fit to sing in gratitude. They attribute their ability to find the well to God.

And what of Moses, the great leader who sweetened the water the first time around, back in the book of Exodus? In the book of Numbers, his

4 Cf. *Ba'al HaTurim* (Ex. 15:1), citing *Midrash Tanchuma.*

role with respect to the wells fades into the background. It is the people who find the well, and it is the people who sing about it.[5]

And now let's talk about the manna. In both Exodus and Numbers, there is a crisis involving the manna. In both cases, the people do wrong by this wondrous gift from God. In the book of Exodus, they violate the rules that God gave them as to how and when they should collect it. In the book of Numbers, they speak disparagingly about the food granted them from Heaven. In both cases, they, in some way, shape, or form, take the manna for granted. But what's different about these episodes is what happens afterward. In the book of Exodus … *nothing* happens afterward. The people are silent in the face of God's displeasure. In the book of Numbers, though, they respond to God's anger with an apology:

וַיָּבֹא הָעָם אֶל־מֹשֶׁה וַיֹּאמְרוּ, חָטָאנוּ כִּי דִבַּרְנוּ בַיקֹוָה וָבָךְ.	The people came to Moses, and said, "We have sinned, for we have spoken against God and against you."	Numbers 21:7

And finally, let's consider the battle against Amalek in each instance. In both cases, the people of Israel fend off the threat from the marauders. In the book of Exodus, however, Israel does so through the agency of Moses. Moses takes the initiative: He ascends a hill, accompanied by Aaron and Hur, and by raising his hands heavenward, controls the destiny of the war. In the book of Numbers, Moses is not part of the story. The people of Israel *themselves* take the initiative. The people address God directly and make a vow to Him:

---

5 Cf. Rashi and Bamidbar Rabbah on Numbers 21:18. According to some interpretations, the people are alluding to wells that Moses had revealed to the people forty years earlier, that stayed with them miraculously. He is one of the "nobles of the nation" acknowledged in the song. Even so, though, the explicit role of Moses fades into the background in the book of Numbers. The people are in direct conversation with God about the wells. And they are acknowledging that whatever human endeavors allowed for the wells' revelation, the ultimate thanks for their beneficence rightfully goes to the Almighty.

Numbers 21:2

וַיִּדַּר יִשְׂרָאֵל נֶדֶר לַיקֹוָה
וַיֹּאמַר, אִם נָתֹן תִּתֵּן אֶת הָעָם
הַזֶּה בְּיָדִי, וְהַחֲרַמְתִּי אֶת
עָרֵיהֶם

Israel vowed a vow to God, and said, "If You will indeed deliver this people into my hand, then I will utterly destroy their cities."

This unilateral initiative by Israel, without mediation from Moses, is not only acknowledged but directly answered by God, as we see in the very next verse:

Numbers 21:3

וַיִּשְׁמַע יְקֹוָה **בְּקוֹל יִשְׂרָאֵל**
וַיִּתֵּן אֶת הַכְּנַעֲנִי

God listened **to the voice of Israel** and delivered up the Canaanites.

God didn't listen to the voice of Moses, pleading on behalf of the people. God listened to *Israel*. Directly.

The Three Faces of *Hoda'ah*

In the book of Numbers, the same four events happen as in Exodus — but the role of Israel in each of them changes dramatically. In Exodus, the people are largely silent. Events *happen* to them. In the book of Numbers, the people are active. They transform themselves, ever so cautiously, from object to subject.

And, in the book of Numbers, what the people *do* as they transform themselves in this way is also notable: They thank God. They praise Him. And they admit wrongdoing.

Thanks, praise, and admission. It turns out that there's a common denominator in these three things. You see it in the Hebrew language itself. In English, thanks, praise, and admission are each separate words. In Hebrew, though, there is a single word for all three. That word is *hoda'ah*.[6]

6 When I want to say "thank you," I say "***todah***," from the root *yod-dalet-heh* (*yadah*). When I admit something to you, such as acknowledging the truth of your position rather than mine, I can say "*ani* ***modeh*** *lecha*," from the very same root. And when

Why would the Hebrew language have a single word for three different ideas? Clearly, Hebrew does not consider these to be three different ideas, but three facets of the same idea. Let's endeavor to understand why.

What do thanks, praise, and admission all have in common?

It turns out that all three of these are marvelous relationship savers. I once heard it quoted in the name of Rabbi Dr. Abraham Twerski that you really need to know only three phrases to have a successful marriage: "Thank you," "I'm sorry," and "I admire you." These three phrases are powerful because they reset relationships in a very basic way. They rehabilitate relationships on the verge of withering.

How do they do this?

The Great Threat to Relationships: Imbalance

It turns out that relationships abhor imbalance. Any relationship, we might say, starts out naturally in a state of balance. When I begin to be friends with you, our relationship with one another is on equal footing. But that equality in our relationship can quickly change. Let's say I do you a favor. Now I'm up here, and you're down there. Our relationship is, at least temporarily, out of balance.

And that's just the *nice* way that our relationship can get out of balance. Our relationship can get out of balance in not-so-nice ways, too. Let's say I do something terrible to you. Now I'm down here, and you're up there. You have the moral high ground, and I have sinned against you. A gulf separates us. Things are uncomfortable.

When a relationship gets out of balance, a force begins to silently assert itself, trying to nudge the relationship back into balance. Let's say I graciously do you a favor. You move into my neighborhood, and my kids and I come over that night with some wonderful, fresh-baked muffins in hand. My kids sit down with your kids and help them with their homework. How do you feel? What do you want to do? You want to reciprocate the favor. With a simple act of reciprocity, our relationship can get back into balance.

---

we extol and praise God in our prayers, we once again concoct a word out of that same root — for example (Ps. 105:1):

הוֹדוּ לַיקוָה קִרְאוּ בִּשְׁמוֹ.

Praise God; call in His name.

The power of this dynamic should not be underestimated. Here's a tip: When you enter a car dealership and sit down with the salesperson to talk about what cars might work best for you, don't take the Coke he offers you from his personal little refrigerator underneath the desk. Why? Because if you do, you've just accepted a favor — and you will feel a need to reciprocate. But you don't have any easy way to reciprocate ... except by buying his car. I'm not kidding here: You're going to feel psychological pressure to buy that car, a $50,000 investment — all because of a $0.35 can of Coke. The urge to repay a favor — to seek balance in relationships — is extremely compelling.

Alternatives to Reciprocation

Here is the rub, though: It is not always advisable to reciprocate. Sometimes you just can't; not every favor can be repaid. Sometimes you can ... but you don't want to go that route. Reciprocation, after all, may come with a whole boatload of problems. Let's say we turn to the not-so-nice way that relationships get out of balance: Bob has done something to harm you. There's a part of you that wants to reciprocate, a part of you that wants to take revenge against Bob. Not for nothing do they say that revenge is sweet. But another part of you puts the brakes on that impulse. You feel there must be another way to rebalance this relationship. But what is it?

That's where *hoda'ah* comes in.

Thank you, and *I'm sorry*. They seem to be different things, but at the core, they are very similar. How do you convey gratitude without saying the words "thank you"? You say, "I appreciate what you've done." The word "appreciate" means to recognize the value of something. When I recognize the value of what it is that you've done for me and communicate that recognition to you — and then you accept that recognition — all of a sudden, our relationship resets itself and is in balance again. Likewise, how do you express regret without saying "I'm sorry"? That, too, involves recognition. You say, "I understand the terrible thing I've done to you, and I feel awful about it." When you make that recognition and it is accepted by the other person, your relationship can become whole again.

Thanks, praise, and admission. What these things have in common is that they're all about the recognition of imbalance as a way of resetting a relationship. While an act of *hoda'ah* may seem like a simple thing, actually making the recognition at the heart of *hoda'ah* is hard to do. Instinctively, when we intuit that an important relationship of ours has gotten out of balance, we want to avert our eyes from that truth. We would prefer to sweep the problem under a rug. But if you have the courage to fully and unflinchingly say that you're sorry, or say "thank you" — that radical act of recognition sets a wondrous paradox in motion. By recognizing and expressing the imbalance in your relationship — with that, somehow, the imbalance can resolve. The relationship can reset itself.

Because the way *hoda'ah* works is so counterintuitive — because it seems to make no sense at all that recognizing an imbalance can restore balance — true *hoda'ah* can be hard to come by in this world. People instinctively avoid it. But, if we muster up the courage to perform *hoda'ah*, a kind of miracle takes place. Our relationship can be rehabilitated, even when reciprocation is not available to us.

When the Children of Israel...Are No Longer Children

Perhaps here lies some of the meaning of the forty-year chiasm that we noticed before.

Something has changed over these forty years. In the beginning, the Children of Israel really were...children, at least in a sense. They were a just-born nation, getting their bearings in the no-man's-land of the wilderness. Like any just-born entity, they had parents, those who helped usher them into existence — a heavenly Parent, but also earthly ones like Moses, Aaron, and Miriam. These "parents" — the earthly ones, at least — would try to teach them how to behave, and would help them out of fixes they somehow managed to get themselves into. Miriam and Moses would teach them how to sing in *hoda'ah*. Moses would instruct them. Aaron would help hold up Moses' hands, to miraculously defeat the Amalekites.

But earthly parents aren't around forever. Over time, children need to grow up. Thus, the end of the book of Numbers tells us of the impending deaths of these three luminaries. Miriam dies, setting off a chain reaction. The Well of Miriam dries up (see Rashi on Num. 20:1, and the essay on **Parshat Chukat** in this volume), and Moses hits the rock. Moses is told by God that he and Aaron too will die before entering the land. And, just a few verses later, that process starts to get underway. At the very end of Numbers chapter 20, Moses takes Aaron up a mountain, and there, Aaron is laid to rest.

And it is right then that the second half of the chiasm begins. It is right at this moment, in Numbers chapter 21, that Amalek attacks, that the manna crisis befalls the people, that wells are found, that the people sing. And it is at this moment ... that the people begin to discover the secret of *hoda'ah*.

Hoda'ah: It's How We Grow Up

Learning to say "thank you," learning to admit I'm wrong and say "I'm sorry," learning to admit to myself, and to you, that I admire you — these are the things we teach our children to do. We teach them these things because they are the fundamental skills necessary to be an adult in this world, to be someone capable of independently cultivating relationships. If we are to have any hope of properly managing our incipient relationships, we must learn to do these things, or else those relationships will collapse in a heap around us. Perhaps it is not a coincidence that, just as Israel's earthly parents begin to leave them, it is these three things that Israel learns how to do.

What the Book of Numbers Is About

What is the book of Numbers about, then? It is a book about parents and children. It's a book about losing parents. But it's also a book about growing up as our parents begin to leave us. I mentioned earlier that in Exodus, the first time Israel sang a song to God, they were led by Moses, and the second time, the people initiated the song on their own. But there is another difference between these two *az yashir* episodes — a more subtle difference, perhaps. Look at how the people are characterized in each:

NUMBERS: THE SONG AT THE WELL (21:17)	EXODUS: THE SONG AT THE SEA (15:1)
אָז יָשִׁיר **יִשְׂרָאֵל** אֶת־הַשִּׁירָה הַזֹּאת Then **Israel** sang this song.	אָז יָשִׁיר־מֹשֶׁה **וּבְנֵי יִשְׂרָאֵל** אֶת־הַשִּׁירָה הַזֹּאת Then Moses **and the Children of Israel** sang this song.

Back in Exodus, the people were "the Children of Israel." But here, in the book of Numbers, as they sing this song on their own, they are called just…"Israel." The word "children" has somehow been dropped. Perhaps that is not a coincidence.

The book of Numbers is perhaps aptly named. As I mentioned before, in Hebrew, *bamidbar* literally means "in the wilderness." And that's an accurate description of the book in all sorts of ways beyond the obvious. This is a book about losing one's earthly parents and confronting the fear of being left alone in a barren and austere world. But it's also about a nation's struggle to transcend childhood, to claim, however tentatively, a certain spiritual independence — and part of that independence is the realization that they are not *really* alone, as harsh as the world out there can seem. Yes, it's a wilderness. But the gifts of our Heavenly Parent — bread from the heavens, wells of water from the earth, protection from the marauders that threaten us — remain with us. They are constant reminders that our Parent in Heaven may be invisible, but He is present in our world nevertheless — and it is up to us to build a lasting relationship with Him.

Let's begin to read this book together.

BAMIDBAR

Why We Count

שְׂאוּ אֶת־רֹאשׁ כָּל־עֲדַת
בְּנֵי־יִשְׂרָאֵל לְמִשְׁפְּחֹתָם
לְבֵית אֲבֹתָם בְּמִסְפַּר
שֵׁמוֹת כָּל־זָכָר לְגֻלְגְּלֹתָם׃

Count the heads of all the congregation of the Children of Israel by the clans of its ancestral houses, listing the names, every male, head by head.

NUMBERS 1:2

BAMIDBAR

Why We Count

AS WE CRACK OPEN *Sefer Bamidbar,* I'd like to explore one of life's big questions with you — the question of how we find meaning in life. I'd like to do that from a bit of an unconventional perspective: using **Parshat Bamidbar**, along with the work of three artists — Jackson Pollock, Claude Monet and Georges Seurat — as a lens. If that sounds disjointed, or unduly challenging, just hang on and let's see where this goes.

What's Love Got to Do with It?

Parshat Bamidbar is all about counting. The beginning of the book devotes scores of verses to the counting of the Israelites. It seems fair to ask: What's with all this counting? The emphasis on counting feels inordinate — especially since the one who requests a census here is actually... the Almighty Himself. One wonders why such a count was even necessary. Surely God knows how many Israelites there are without having to count them.

As it happens, we're not the first ones to wonder about this. Rashi implicitly addresses the issue with the following, enigmatic comment:

מִתּוֹךְ חִבָּתָן לְפָנָיו מוֹנֶה אוֹתָם כָּל שָׁעָה	Because of God's love for [Israel], He counts them all the time.	Rashi, Numbers 1:1

Rashi suggests that counting is an expression of love. As such, it serves more than a utilitarian purpose. It isn't just about knowing numbers. The process matters, too. There is something about the *act* of counting, Rashi is suggesting, that conveys care and regard. Counting conveys love.

Why does the act of counting carry such overtones?

Two Words

We find a clue, I think, in two key phrases, each of which conveys the idea of counting. In **Parshat Bamidbar**, when the Torah discusses God's command to Moses to conduct this census, the text uses two verbs in particular: נשא (*nasa*) and פקד (*pakad*). What is interesting about these two terms is that not only does each mean "to count," but each also has *another* meaning, too. The interplay between the two secondary meanings of each word is intriguing — and, I believe, instructive.

You can actually watch the secondary meanings of each word come into play if you pay close attention to the verses in our parsha. Indeed, no sooner does the Torah, in **Parshat Bamidbar**, use both נשא and פקד to mean "count," than it immediately employs the very same word to express its secondary meaning.

Let me show you what I'm talking about. Here is a verse in our parsha. With just a glance, you'll notice the verse contains forms of both roots:

Numbers 1:49

אַךְ אֶת־מַטֵּה לֵוִי לֹא **תִפְקֹד**, וְאֶת־רֹאשָׁם לֹא **תִשָּׂא** בְּתוֹךְ בְּנֵי יִשְׂרָאֵל:	However, do not **count** the tribe of Levi. Do not **count** their heads among the Children of Israel.

But now look at the very *next* verse. Once again, you'll find words that derive from the very same roots, but this time, neither term means "count":

Numbers 1:50

וְאַתָּה **הַפְקֵד** אֶת־הַלְוִיִּם עַל־מִשְׁכַּן הָעֵדֻת...הֵמָּה **יִשְׂאוּ** אֶת־הַמִּשְׁכָּן וְאֶת־כָּל־כֵּלָיו	You should **appoint** the Levites over the Tabernacle...they will **carry** the Tabernacle and all its utensils.

Now, all of a sudden, פקד means "to appoint": The Levites are *to be appointed* in charge of the Tabernacle and all its utensils; and now, all of a sudden, נשא here means "to carry," or even more literally perhaps, "to lift up":

הֵמָּה **יִשְׂאוּ** אֶת־הַמִּשְׁכָּן	They will **lift up** the Tabernacle.

It seems as if the text wants us to perceive some kind of connection between counting and appointing and between counting and lifting. So let's ponder that together: How might appointing and lifting, respectively, be conceptually connected to…counting?

How Counting Matters

Let's start with **נשא**, the word that means alternately "to count" or "to lift up." Consider the following verse, which seems to be instructive:

שְׂאוּ אֶת־רֹאשׁ כָּל־עֲדַת בְּנֵי־יִשְׂרָאֵל	**Count the heads** of all the congregation of the Children of Israel.	Numbers 1:2

Perhaps the verse doesn't just mean "count the heads" of the Children of Israel. It could also be translated as "lift up the heads of the Children of Israel." And maybe, indeed, the two ideas are connected. That is, perhaps God's counting the people has something to do with lifting up their heads. In other words, it seems that there's something affirming about God having us counted. It's almost like, through the act of counting, someone who previously felt downcast is now able to hold their head high.[1]

To Count and to Be Entrusted

And now let's talk about that other Hebrew word for counting, פקד. Besides meaning "to count," *pakad* also means to "**appoint**" or "**entrust**" with some sort of mission or task. In fact, the related Hebrew word פיקדון, *pikadon*, denotes an object that is entrusted for safekeeping. In a way, when you are appointed to carry out some sort of responsibility, you've been entrusted with a kind of *pikadon* to watch over, to safeguard. Someone

---

1 Interestingly, it isn't just in Hebrew that the word "count" holds such connotations. If we take the English phrase "to count," we find that it, too, has a similar double meaning. On the one hand, "to count" means to take stock of things numerically. But the other meaning of "to count" is inextricably tied to self-worth. When someone feels like they *count*, they feel like they matter, like their existence is meaningful for the world.

else is now counting on you, is trusting you, to do the task they need done — and it is yours to do for them.

I wonder if these secondary meanings of *pakad* and *nasa* — entrust and lift up — somehow connect with one another to give us a better sense of why being counted by God can be seen as an act of love. Counting is something you do when you enumerate the individuals in a larger community, of which each is a part. In a way, being counted by God's command perhaps affirms the place that each individual has in that community. Indeed, we might well say: *When can I "lift up my head"* (*nasa*)? *When I find myself "entrusted"* (*pakad*). When I play a unique role in a community, when I am charged with carrying out a piece of a shared mission much larger than myself, I really *do* feel like I count. When, on the other hand, I live only for my own self-preservation, what's really the point?

Community and Meaning

The relationship between the individual and the community, however, does not always recognize the value of the individual. This special combination of *pakad* and *nasa* that we've been talking about is unique to communities that somehow manage to celebrate the individual, even as they organize themselves to achieve noble tasks no individual could possibly achieve on their own. But that kind of relationship between one and many can't be taken for granted. One might imagine two other kinds of relationships between the individual and the community, each of which fails by veering dangerously toward one extreme or the other.

At one end: What if a community has a sense of cohesion that is so dramatic, so pronounced, that it squashes all sense of individuality among its members? Totalitarianism can create faceless communities. There remains no room for individuality in a community that swallows everything.

At the opposite extreme, one can imagine enthroning the role of the rugged individual so profoundly that individuals living in proximity to one another, who comprise a neighborhood, a city, or even a nation, never really cohere to form a group in a meaningful way. Sure, they may share a common postal code. But they are really nothing more than a whole bunch of people living near each other. There is no sense of shared "why"; no sense that I am contributing to a well-articulated, or even implicitly clear, overarching goal or set of principles. This is another kind of failed community.

What we aim to be a part of is the "*nasa* riding on *pakad*" sweet spot: a model of community wherein an individual can find a real sense of sustaining meaning, without getting squashed; a community in which each individual can become deeply part of something larger than him- or herself. In this third model, not only do we have a group that is pledged to some overarching, noble ideal, but the individuals who comprise the group have carved out what we might call a carefully crafted dual identity. Each person, we might say, is both an individual and a part of a community that transcends them. Each person has a vital role to play in actualizing the mission of the whole.

Three Painters: Pollock, Monet, and Seurat

I promised you we'd look at this question of "meaning" in the context of Pollock, Monet, and Seurat, and now we've finally arrived at the point where we can do that, looking at the styles of these three painters as symbols representing the three different interactions between individual and community that we outlined above.

Take a look at any painting by Jackson Pollock. Every individual element within the painting is recognizable, but there's no sense that it's coming together in any way that makes this painting a cohesive whole. I'll add a bit of a caveat here: To my untrained eye, his paintings seem random. Perhaps some art connoisseurs will see things differently. But I imagine there are plenty of respected art critics who see randomness and

disconnection as the whole point of a Jackson Pollock painting. One way or the other, for the purpose of my illustration here, let's call a Jackson Pollock painting a pictorial version of one of those failed communities we were talking about, where each individual is present but the group is bereft of a real sense of shared purpose.

At the other extreme, take a painter like Claude Monet, one of the early giants of the Impressionist movement. In any Monet painting, you get the sense you're looking at a very beautiful scene. But that's true only when you stand back and look at the painting as a whole. When you stand up close and try to identify the individual elements in the painting, you find that, astonishingly, they're not really there. When viewed from afar, the work gives the viewer the impression of a crowd of a bridge over flowers, but upon closer inspection, it just looks like broad, indistinguishable brushstrokes of paint. There is no individually carved-out identity; there is merely an impression (hence, the name for this style of art: Impressionist). Monet's paintings offer a pictorial representation of one of the failed communities we talked about above: the community that swallows the individual and leaves him or her without any distinguishing identity at all.

But then there's a middle path, where whole and part live in careful, balanced tension with one another. Welcome to the work of Georges Seurat, the painter who founded the technique of Pointillism. When you look at Seurat's paintings from afar, you can discern a grand scheme. It all comes together. But in his work, the grand scheme does not require the sacrifice of the individual. If you zoom in on a Seurat painting, you will find that, even at the most detailed level, not only does the individual exist, but every little mark of paint is its own individual dot. In a Seurat painting, the painting works because the dots come together to make something grand. All dots "count." All find themselves entrusted with the sacred purpose of the whole.

From Painting to Biology

It's not just in human societies that this middle path indicates a kind of flourishing. Something like this middle of the road sweet spot in the relationship between one and many seems to happen at the biological level as well, with the cells that make up our body. For on the one hand, each of our cells is self-sufficient, containing everything it needs to function: a cell membrane to keep it together, mitochondria to produce energy, and lysosomes to get rid of waste. But each of these almost infinitesimally small cells is no Marlboro Man, operating on its own with no connection to community. Rather, each cell is entrusted with a larger mission. Each has a role in supporting the function of the organs, which in turn support the workings of the body. Emblematic of this truth is what's contained in the tiniest little center of that cell — the nucleus, in which resides a DNA blueprint so detailed, wondrous, and complete that it can be used as a schematic from which to construct the entire body to which the cell belongs, with all its billions of differentiated cells. As much as the human cell is an individual being, entrusted with a role that may seem almost miniscule, it also, in some visceral way, shares deeply in the vision and mission of the whole.

What is it like to be part of the "Seurat" kind of community — the community where individuality is prized, and communal purpose is sacred? It is a deep privilege to be included — by God, no less, through a divinely ordained act of counting — in such a community. The act of counting that symbolizes the individual being entrusted with a larger purpose is truly an act of love.

In God's counting, and in the implicit stewardship that it engenders, we find a connection to a larger meaning that would be impossible to attain as a mere individual. In being counted by the Divine, we find that we truly *do* count.

NASO

Does the Torah Contain a Parenting Manual?

וַיְדַבֵּר יְקוָה אֶל מֹשֶׁה לֵּאמֹר, דַּבֵּר אֶל אַהֲרֹן וְאֶל בָּנָיו לֵאמֹר, כֹּה תְבָרְכוּ אֶת בְּנֵי יִשְׂרָאֵל

And God spoke to Moses, saying: "Speak to Aaron and his sons, saying, 'Thus shall you bless the people of Israel.'"

NUMBERS 6:22–23

NASO

Does the Torah Contain a Parenting Manual?

ONE OF THE PROBLEMS with having children is that they don't come with instruction manuals. But if we intuit that the Torah is, at some level, a grand instruction manual for life, we might find ourselves wondering: Is there an instruction manual within it for parenting, one of the great challenges of our lives? Does the Torah offer us guidance as to how we can raise our kids; how we can help our children mature into happy, well-adjusted human beings?

And let me be clear: Sure, there are probably vignettes here or there in the Five Books of Moses that have some implications for parenting. Maybe Isaac's and Rebecca's relationship with their children can be mined for some insights. Maybe Abraham's talk with Isaac on the way up to Mount Moriah can give us some tips on how parents should or shouldn't speak with their kids. But I'm not asking for a one-off insight here or there. I'm wondering whether the Torah contains anything more comprehensive than that — if not a complete manual, then at least what we might call a quick-start guide.

And the reason I ask is because, to the untrained eye, parenting seems like such an overwhelming endeavor. It blends so many things: driving car pool, arranging the mashed peas on Junior's high chair, strategizing with a high schooler about how to handle a difficult teacher, and the like. Does parenting have some cohesive goal we are trying to achieve and, if so, is there any grand strategy through which we can achieve it? If we *can* isolate some overriding goal, can we break that goal into parts and see how those parts naturally relate to one another? These are the questions I wonder about.

Can the Torah offer us guidance here? If it could, that would be of great service. It would help us wrap our minds around this wonderful but amorphous and bewildering task we call parenting. It would help us understand more clearly what we are doing in the moment, and it might also help us identify when we are getting off track and how we might correct our course.

A Possible Set of Principles

I want to suggest that **Parshat Naso** contains just such a set of guidelines. Within this parsha lies a pithy but surprisingly comprehensive parenting manual. The whole passage is actually only three verses long, but packed into those three verses is the essence of what you need to know to be a good parent.

What *are* those three verses and how do they instruct us?

They are the verses of *birkat kohanim,* the priestly blessing. We first encounter this blessing here in **Parshat Naso**, when God directs Aaron and his sons to bestow this blessing upon the people of Israel. In more recent times, many parents have adopted the custom of borrowing the words of this text to deliver their *own* blessing to their kids, bestowing the hopes of these three verses upon their children each Friday night.

Guidelines for All Parents, Human and Divine

Speaking personally, I find that custom striking and beautiful. It suggests, I think, that this priestly blessing can be seen as a gift of sorts to children: The priests bestow it upon us collectively — for we are, together, children of a Heavenly Parent — and we in turn bestow the same blessing upon our own individual children. But I want to go further and suggest that these three verses that we parents say weekly to our children aren't *just* a blessing. The words convey a certain hope for how God will treat us, His children. And in that hope lies a set of guidelines for us human parents. Through these words, we learn how to treat our kids. We learn how to raise them.

Let's jump in and take a look at the text of the blessing itself, and I'll show you what I'm talking about. Here are the verses:

Numbers 6:22–26

וַיְדַבֵּר יְקֺוָה אֶל מֹשֶׁה לֵּאמֹר:
דַּבֵּר אֶל אַהֲרֹן וְאֶל בָּנָיו לֵאמֹר:
כֹּה תְבָרֲכוּ אֶת־בְּנֵי יִשְׂרָאֵל
אָמוֹר לָהֶם: יְבָרֶכְךָ יְקֺוָה
וְיִשְׁמְרֶךָ: יָאֵר יְקֺוָה פָּנָיו אֵלֶיךָ
וִיחֻנֶּךָּ: יִשָּׂא יְקֺוָה פָּנָיו אֵלֶיךָ
וְיָשֵׂם לְךָ שָׁלוֹם:

And God spoke to Moses, saying: "Speak to Aaron and his sons, saying, 'Thus shall you bless the people of Israel. Say to them: May God bless you and keep you. May God make His face shine on you and be gracious to you. May God lift up His face toward you and give you peace.'"

When we first consider these verses, they might seem like garden-variety biblical poetry — vaguely inspiring, to be sure, but not the kind of passage that contains deep meaning or profound wellsprings of guidance. But looks can be deceiving. Let's try to actually comprehend what these verses might be saying. What, exactly, is their message?

We can begin by noting that the priestly blessing consists of three verses, each seemingly containing a distinct idea. But it's not immediately clear what each of these ideas actually is. Can we paraphrase them in plain English? Can we identify how they actually differ from one another? How, for example, is "blessing and keeping" us different from asking God to "make His face shine" on us? How would each of those be different from the last of the three phrases, where we ask God to "lift up His face" to us?

Also, let's say we *do* succeed in distinguishing the essential ideas of each of the three different verses. We should still wonder: How do these verses relate to each other? Does each aspect of the blessing intuitively progress into the next?

These are the questions I want to focus on with you.

The Meaning of the Word "Blessing"

Let's start with a closer look at the opening of the priestly blessing:

יְבָרֶכְךָ יְקוָה וְיִשְׁמְרֶךָ׃	May God **bless you** and keep you.	Numbers 6:24

First, let's define our terms. The blessing opens with **יְבָרֶכְךָ** (*yevarechecha* — "may God bless you." What exactly does that word "bless" really mean? Sure, it is a nice, spiritual-sounding word. I can close a letter with "Blessings to you," but what does it really mean to say that? Can we actually pin down a meaning for the word "bless"?

Rabbi Chaim of Volozhin, a principal student of the Vilna Gaon, writes about this in his classic work *Nefesh HaChayim*. He argues that the word "blessing" — or in Hebrew, the root **ברך**, *bet-resh-chaf* — doesn't just have vague, spiritual qualities but a very concrete meaning:

אבל האמת כי "ברוך"	However, the truth is that the meaning	*Nefesh HaChayim, Sha'ar* II, 2:2

פירושו לשון תוספת וריבוי, וכענין "קח נא את ברכתי" גו' (בראשית לג:יא), "וברך את לחמך" (שמות כג:כה), "וברך פרי בטנך" וגו' (דברים ז:יג), והרבה כיוצא במקרא. שא"א לפרשם לשון תהלה ושבח, אלא לשון תוספת ורבוי.	of [the word] *baruch*, or "blessed," is an expression of increase and expansion, as [the context suggests] in the verses "Accept, please, my blessing" (Gen. 33:11), and "[God] will bless your food" (Ex. 23:25), and "[God] will bless the fruit of your womb" (Deut. 7:13), and many others similar to these in the Bible. [In all these] it is impossible to translate [the word "blessing" merely] as an attribution of glory and a giving of praise. Rather, [it is] an expression of increase and expansion.

Rabbi Chaim of Volozhin suggests that the word "blessing" conveys the idea of multiplying, of increasing something. So, for example, when the verse in Deuteronomy says

Deuteronomy 7:13

וּבֵרַךְ פְּרִי־בִטְנְךָ וּפְרִי־אַדְמָתֶךָ	He will bless the fruit of your body and the fruit of your land,

it means that God will increase these things. *You will have lots of children; you will have plenty of food coming from crops.* When we ask God to bless something, we are in essence asking Him to increase it. And when we, in turn, say that God is blessed, we mean that we view Him as the source of all flourishing.[1]

Actually, this idea — that *berachah* ברכה, blessing, conveys the idea of increase — emerges, in a way, from the very letters that make up the Hebrew word for "blessing." You may be familiar with the notion of *gematria*, the tradition that each letter of the Hebrew alphabet is associated with a unique numerical value: *alef* (א) with one, *bet* (ב) with two, *gimmel* (ג) with three, and so on. If we do a quick analysis of the numerical value of the of the Hebrew word for "blessing," we'll notice something

1 See *Nefesh HaChayim, Sha'ar* II, 2:2.

remarkable about its letters. The Hebrew root is composed of the letters *bet* (ב), *resh* (ר), and *chaf* (כ):

ח 8	ז 7	ו 6	ה 5	ד 4	ג 3	ב 2	א 1
ע 70	ס 60	נ 50	מ 40	ל 30	כ 20	י 10	ט 9
ת 400			ש 300	ר 200	ק 100	צ 90	פ 80

It's not too hard to discern the pattern that emerges here. The numerical value of *bet* is two; of *resh* is two hundred; of *chaf* is twenty. Each number is a different iteration of the number "two," the essence of growth: Two in the ones column, two in the hundreds, and two in the tens. So this word is *all about twos. Bet-resh-chaf*— blessing — is all about plurality or increase.

At the beginning of the priestly blessing, when we ask God to bless us, we are asking Him to give us the strength to grow, to increase the good we have. And here we arrive at the first great imperative of parenting. The very first, most basic thing a parent does for a child is to seek to "bless" them: to try to multiply their strength, in whatever ways we can. We want to build up a child's physical strength, and to that end, we nourish them. We want to build up their emotional strength, and so we convey affection to them. We want to build up their intellectual strength, so we educate them. We want to build up their moral strength, so we try to help them to discern right from wrong. Eventually, we try to help our child develop economic strength, and so we teach them a trade or profession so they can provide for an eventual family. We seek to bless our children in a kaleidoscope of complementary ways, to help them become the most whole and developed version of themselves possible.

So one fundamental job we have as parents is to help our children grow, to "increase" them in all sorts of ways. But that's not the *only* obligation we have. The need to help children flourish and develop is coupled with another, equally compelling parental obligation, introduced in the very next word of the priestly blessing:

Numbers 6:24

יְבָרֶכְךָ יְקוָה וְיִשְׁמְרֶךָ׃ May God bless you **and keep you**.

Veyishmerecha, from the root שמר, is a plea for God to watch over us, to guard us. To keep us safe. The second fundamental obligation of parents, the one that goes in tandem with "blessing," is the need to watch over our kids, the imperative to ensure their safety and keep them from harm.

We do this in all sorts of ways. We do our best to ward off threats coming their way. We buy cars with airbags; we try to keep our teens away from those who would offer them cigarettes or alcohol; we try to monitor what our youngsters are watching on their screens. And to this end, we give our kids rules to follow: Only cross at the crosswalks. Look both ways. No TV on school nights. Stay away from bars when you're out with your friends.

We sometimes call the sum total of these rules and expectations "setting limits," "enforcing boundaries," or "discipline," depending on your choice of nomenclature. Some of these terms carry a bit of an aftertaste. But when things go right, what makes parental rules acceptable, rather than gratuitous legalities that invite a child's rebellion, is that they are not random. They aren't the product of mere parental whim. They are there because we are genuinely trying to watch over our kids. We are trying to ensure they do not harm others and are not themselves harmed, that they will not degrade themselves physically, emotionally, or spiritually. This is the imperative of *veyishmerecha*.

To some extent, these two goals of parenting lie in tension with one another. To "bless" a child, to seek their growth and their flourishing in this world, is by its nature an expansive endeavor. The desire to foster growth can make limits — either the self-imposed kind or those required by society — seem like an inconvenient barrier to be navigated around, a mere nuisance that gets in the way of a child's ability to develop and express him or herself. Likewise, when parents overemphasize the setting of boundaries, when they devote single-minded attention to reining in potentially problematic behavior, they run the risk of stunting a child's natural curiosity and playfulness, shutting down a kid's ability to make and learn from mistakes.

A parent needs to seek a careful balance between the energies of ***yevarechecha*** and ***veyishmerecha***, blessing their child on the one hand, and watching over them on the other. We must seek to do both at once, even though to do so means we must simultaneously pull in opposite directions.

Two That Are One

To bless and to keep: These two parental imperatives emerge from the first verse of *birkat kohanim*. But as much as it's true that to bless and to keep are in tension with one another, still I'd like to suggest that in reality, there is a deeper unity here, that this first verse of *birkat kohanim* isn't really talking about two imperatives, but two aspects of the *same* imperative. To see how, consider this little thought experiment: When, in our child's life, would you say these two parental imperatives first become operative? When do we first begin to help our kids grow, on the one hand, and keep them from harm, on the other?

I don't think it's coincidental that we start doing these two things at one and the same moment in time. And no, I'm not actually talking about the moment of birth. A parent starts to safeguard a child and help them grow... in the womb.

Yes, we provide safe spaces for our children and seek to help them flourish throughout their lives, but these obligations have their genesis in the seamless and wondrous functioning of the womb. The womb nurtures the developing fetus and physically fosters its growth, and it also, simultaneously, provides a sanctuary of sorts, a safe place in which a child can grow.

So, if these two imperatives of *yevarechecha* and *veyishmerecha* are really two aspects of the same thing — what is that larger category? What would we call it?

I'd argue that there's a single Hebrew word that perfectly captures these two obligations, to bless and to guard: **לרחם, *lerachem*, to be compassionate**.

Many of us tend to think about compassion uncritically, as if it is just a warm, fuzzy-wuzzy feeling. But it actually has two building blocks, two subcategories. One thing compassion leads me to do is to nurture someone, to help them grow, but the other thing compassion leads me to do is to guard them from harm.

And guess what? The Hebrew word for "compassion," *rachamim* — believe it or not — is just another form of the Hebrew word for "womb," *rechem*.

רחם (*rachem*) as a verb	רחם (*rechem*) as a noun
To be compassionate	Womb

The great touchstone for compassion is the womb. The French Jewish literary critic and philosopher Emmanuel Levinas suggests that we humans actually learn the idea of compassion from the womb.[2] Which is to say: Compassion begins in the human being as a natural physical process, as something our bodies automatically do, and then our instincts and eventually our conscious minds pick up the trail from there.

Building on the Foundation of *Rachamim*

The type of womb-like love we call "compassion" lies at the ground floor of parenting. It is the most essential and foundational building block available to us in raising our kids. But it is not the sum total of parenting. We can and must build upon it. There are still two other key aspects of our job as parents, and these, I would argue, find expression in *birkat kohanim*'s next two verses. Let's endeavor to discover what they are.

The second verse in *birkat kohanim* reads:

---

2 In Levinas's thought, compassion is something that we know and understand only through the idea of femininity. Our individual lives begin in the womb, just as human life, writ large, once began with God, whom the Talmud simply calls *Rachmana*, the Merciful One. Levinas writes of *rachamim* and its relation to Godliness:

> *Rakhamim* (Mercy), which the Aramaic term [for God], *Rakhmana*, evokes, goes back to the word *Rekhem*, which means uterus. *Rakhamim* is the relation of the uterus to the *other*, whose gestation takes place within it. *Rakhamim* is maternity itself. God as merciful is God defined by maternity. A feminine element is stirred in the depth of this mercy. ... Perhaps maternity is sensitivity itself, of which so much ill is said among the Nietzscheans. (Emmanuel Levinas, "Damages Due to Fire," in *Nine Talmudic Readings*, trans. Annette Aronowicz [Midland Book Editions, 1994], 183.)

Numbers 6:25

יָאֵר יְקוָה פָּנָיו אֵלֶיךָ וִיחֻנֶּךָּ׃	May God make His face shine on you and **be gracious to you**.

This second part of the priestly blessing introduces us to a close cousin of *rachamim* — a different flavor, as it were, of parental love. The verse describes this kind of love as חן (*chen*, a word that is often translated as "grace").

What exactly is *chen*, this grace-like quality that the *kohanim* ask God to bestow upon us? The Hebrew word *chen* is related to the verb *lechanen* — to give for free; it is also related to the Hebrew word *chinam*, meaning "for free" or "gratuitously." *Chen* — or its English equivalent, grace — is completely undeserved love, what we might call **unconditional love**.

We might not immediately perceive how the love of *chen* is different from the love of *rachamim*. Both seem undeserved. After all, it's not as though a fetus ever did anything to deserve being born, to deserve the womb lavishing care upon it. But still and all, there's a difference. With *rachamim*, I bestow care in order to attain a goal: I'm trying to build you up; I'm trying to foster your growth. The womb bestows its compassion, its nurture and protectiveness, because it perceives potential in the newly conceived zygote and it is trying to nurture that potential. But because *rachamim* is goal-oriented love, it is not truly unconditional.

Chen, on the other hand, is unconditional. It's love that has no goal. It's love because you are my child, and I can't help but smile when I look at you. *Chen* is the kind of love that every father and mother knows when their eyes meet the eyes of their newborn child, and their whole face lights up. The child hasn't done anything to deserve the parent's love and appreciation. They are just being themselves. But that's enough to foster a parent's delight.

This metaphor, by the way — a parent gazing on a child with simple, unmitigated delight — isn't just a random metaphor for *chen*. It actually is the image conjured up by this verse in *birkat kohanim*:

יָאֵר יְקוָה פָּנָיו אֵלֶיךָ וִיחֻנֶּךָּ׃	**May God make His face shine on you** and be gracious to you.

The idea that God would express pleasure, metaphorically, through the "look on His face," so to speak, is described even more vividly by Rashi's commentary on this verse:

Rashi on Numbers 6:25

"יאר פניו" - יראה לך פנים שוחקות, פנים צהובות.

"May He make His face shine" — May [God] show you a smiling countenance, a beaming countenance.

The phrase conjures up divine delight, as if God were looking at us with a beaming smile, with a face that communicates sheer joy.[3] That's the essence of *chen*.

From Where Does *Chen* Emerge?

I suggested earlier that the first stage of parenting, expressed in the first verse in *birkat kohanim*, correlates naturally with a particular moment in a child's development. Fostering a child's growth and keeping them safe is the energy of the womb. If we extend this little thought experiment, we might ask: What about the second verse of *birkat kohanim*? What stage, if any, in a child's development is most obviously ripe for a parent to feel themselves suffused with *chen* toward their child?

Here, I'd argue that the answer is: The next stage after the womb, namely birth. The paradigmatic moment of *chen*, we might conjecture, is right after birth — the moment when the parent holds their new child, looks down upon the infant, meets their eyes, and can't help but smile. That's unconditional love, right there. It is at this moment that *chen* instinctively enters into parents' emotional vocabulary and becomes a feature

3 It is noteworthy that the way Rashi interprets the phrase isn't merely that God should face you, allowing His face to illuminate yours. No, the verse is conveying something much more joyful than this. As Rashi understands it, the phrase יָאֵר יְקוָה פָּנָיו אֵלֶיךָ means "Let God *illuminate* His face [as He gazes] toward you." It is a prayer that God should be so suffused with delight when peering at us that His whole face lights up, so to speak, that His joy becomes obviously apparent.

of how they relate to their child. Hopefully, *chen* continues to flourish as the child grows.

Once we look at the paradigmatic moment of *chen* as the moment of birth, the moment that immediately follows the care bestowed by the womb, we get a hint as to what drives *chen*, what helps it emerge. For we might well ask: If *chen* is really unconditional, does it just emerge spontaneously out of thin air? The answer to that is an emphatic "no." *Chen* does come from somewhere.

If *rachamim* emerges from a focus on the *future*, from the potential that I might nourish in you by virtue of the care I bestow upon you, then *chen* emerges naturally from the past — from the *rachamim* I've *already* invested in you.

Consider the feeling of *chen* that floods a parent in the moments after birth. If we had to take it apart, it might feel something like this: *Here you are, this child of mine. I built you up, I safeguarded you nine months in the womb. Here you finally are, and I can't help but smile.*

What we are beginning to see is that each stage of parenting actually builds on the stage before it. *Rachamim* — nurturing a child and keeping them safe over time — is a real emotional investment in a child and makes *chen* possible. We parents are meant to build on the experience of investing in our child, of bestowing *rachamim* upon them, by introducing a new and powerful kind of love into our relationship with our kids — the particular love of *chen*.

The Irony of *Chen*

The power of *chen*, I would submit, is somewhat ironic in nature. For *chen* — this unconditional love, epitomized by the joyful gaze of a parent toward his or her child — is the greatest nourishment a child's soul can ever get. That's ironic because *chen* is not *intended* to nourish. It isn't intended to do anything at all; it just is. Joy is joy, and that's all that can be said about it. Nevertheless, unconditional love powerfully fuels a child's growth — even more, probably, than love that is carefully calculated to nourish. It's *chen* that a child really lives on. Once you have bestowed *rachamim* — once you've cared for your child, safeguarded them, invested in them, built them up — you are in a position to also feel *chen*. And if and when you do, you add a powerful note of harmony to the care, sustenance, and protection — the *rachamim* — that you continue to provide for your child. Your love is multifaceted now. You are a purveyor of both *rachamim* and *chen*.

The Ties That Bind

Before proceeding to consider the third verse of *birkat kohanim*, let me pause to reconsider a question I first posed to you at the beginning of this essay. I wondered whether, somehow, the Torah might help us wrap our minds around the entirety of parenting, whether it might help us define some overarching activity we engage in when we raise our kids.

I think that by now, having looked at the first two verses of *birkat kohanim*, we are getting a feel for this. The answer to the question of what we are doing when we parent can perhaps be summarized in a single word: love.[4] It is just that the love of a parent comes in different flavors. There is the love of *rachamim*, the love of *chen*, and perhaps there is one more type of love as well, the kind of love expressed in the third and final verse of *birkat kohanim.*

---

4 An intriguing hint that this is so — that the central idea of *birkat kohanim* is love — comes from the liturgy that accompanies *birkat kohanim* in modern times. The custom has developed for the *kohanim* present in the synagogue to actually stand before the congregation at certain times and confer this blessing upon them. But before they do, the *kohanim* actually recite a prefatory blessing acknowledging the privilege and responsibility that lie before them. The words of that blessing are instructive:

אֲשֶׁר קִדְּשָׁנוּ בִּקְדוּשָּׁתוֹ שֶׁל אַהֲרֹן וְצִוָּנוּ לְבָרֵךְ אֶת עַמּוֹ יִשְׂרָאֵל בְּאַהֲבָה.

[Blessed are You, King of the Universe,] who has sanctified us with the holiness of Aaron and commanded us to bless His people, Israel, with love. (*Sotah* 39a–b)

What does that ending phrase, בְּאַהֲבָה, "with love," mean? I suppose one might take it to mean that the *kohanim* should adopt a loving disposition when they bless the congregation assembled before them. And that's certainly possible. But another way to read these words is far more intriguing: that what the *kohanim* are really asking God to confer upon the people ... is *love itself.* That is, God commanded the priests to bless His people with love, by channeling God's love toward them through the words of this blessing.

A Parent's Third Gift

But what might that be? Aren't the first two kinds of love enough? Isn't it enough to bless and keep our children, and also to love them "just because"? What other request could parental love possibly make of us?

It turns out that parents really *can* offer their children a third kind of love, a love that builds upon the first two but is also a more difficult kind of affection to offer. It is described pithily in these final words of *birkat kohanim*:

יִשָּׂא יְקוָה פָּנָיו אֵלֶיךָ וְיָשֵׂם לְךָ שָׁלוֹם׃	**May God lift up His face toward you** and give you **peace**.	Numbers 6:26

The third kind of love is all about granting a child *shalom*, peace. And somehow, the mechanism for doing this is **lifting up your face** toward the child. Let's explore what that could possibly mean.

Jacob And Esau

An important hint comes from the fact that the expression "to lift up one's face" to someone else didn't originate in the book of Numbers, in the words of *birkat kohanim*. The phrase appears all the way back in the book of Genesis, too. As a matter of fact, it may well be that *birkat kohanim* is intentionally quoting that earlier phrase in Genesis, intending the reader to immediately sense the resonance and understand from that, intuitively, what this last kind of love is really all about. Let's take a moment to explore this earlier occurrence in Genesis.

It appears in the story of Jacob and Esau.

Immediately after Jacob deceives his father Isaac and receives the blessing that was meant for Esau, the children's mother, Rebecca, chooses to send Jacob away to her brother Laban. It will be necessary for Jacob to stay away for "just a few days," as she puts it, until Esau's anger abates. But the hope that Esau's anger would dissipate in a short time was just that—a mere hope. The depth and staying power of Esau's rage becomes clear two decades later when Jacob finally leaves the house of Laban, only to hear news that Esau is coming to meet him with four hundred men.

Jacob immediately sends messengers Esau's way, laden with gifts:

Genesis 32:14–15

וַיִּקַּח מִן הַבָּא בְיָדוֹ מִנְחָה לְעֵשָׂו אָחִיו: עִזִּים מָאתַיִם וּתְיָשִׁים עֶשְׂרִים	He took what he had at hand [to create] gifts for Esau, his brother: two hundred she-goats, twenty he-goats.

At first glance, one might see this act of Jacob as a frantic but ultimately insincere attempt to placate his brother by any means possible. But a closer look at the text suggests otherwise. For the blessing that Jacob took from his brother all those years ago had promised him material wealth — and now here he is, giving material wealth to Esau. The blessing had promised that his brother would bow to him — and now, when he finally meets Esau, it is Jacob who bows:

Genesis 33:3

וְהוּא עָבַר לִפְנֵיהֶם, וַיִּשְׁתַּחוּ אַרְצָה שֶׁבַע פְּעָמִים עַד־גִּשְׁתּוֹ עַד־אָחִיו:	He passed before them, and he bowed to the ground seven times until he approached his brother.

Esau at first refuses to take the gifts from Jacob. He has enough wealth, he tells his brother; he really has no need for more. But Jacob insists. And when he does, his words tell why it is so important for him that his brother accept what he is trying to give:

Genesis 33:11

קַח נָא אֶת־**בִּרְכָתִי** אֲשֶׁר הֻבָאת לָךְ	Please, take **my blessing** which was brought to you.

In all sorts of ways, Jacob is trying to symbolically give back the parental blessing he once took from his brother. He is trying to make amends as best he can. And it is in this context that the expression "to lift one's face" toward another is first used in the Torah. It comes when Jacob, getting together the gifts to send to his brother, explains his hope for what might happen when the two finally meet one another:

אֲכַפְּרָה פָנָיו בַּמִּנְחָה הַהֹלֶכֶת לְפָנָי וְאַחֲרֵי־כֵן אֶרְאֶה פָנָיו אוּלַי **יִשָּׂא פָנָי**׃	"Let me find forgiveness [before] his face with the gift that goes before me; afterward I will see his face, [and] perhaps **he will lift up my [own] face**."	Genesis 32:20

Jacob's hope is to reconcile with Esau. And how will that reconciliation express itself? *With a lifting of the face.* The brothers are coming toward one another. Evidently, Jacob's face is downcast (otherwise, why would Esau "lift it up"?). He is evidently ashamed to look his brother in the eye. He wants, more than anything else, to somehow be free of that shame, for his brother to release him of it. And if Esau will only accept Jacob's attempts to make amends — if he will only meet Jacob's gaze — that can be a reality.

In the end, a reconciliation *does* take place. Esau gives Jacob ... **peace**:

וַיָּרָץ עֵשָׂו לִקְרָאתוֹ וַיְחַבְּקֵהוּ וַיִּפֹּל עַל צַוָּארָו וַיִּשָּׁקֵהוּ וַיִּבְכּוּ׃	Esau ran to meet him and embraced him. He flung himself on his neck and kissed him, and they wept.	Genesis 33:4

Two decades earlier, when Jacob had taken the blessing meant for Esau, one brother cried while the other brother ran away from him. Just before Jacob fled from Esau's rage, afraid to confront his brother, the text tells us:

וַיֹּאמֶר עֵשָׂו אֶל אָבִיו, הַבְרָכָה אַחַת הִוא־לְךָ אָבִי? בָּרֲכֵנִי גַם־אָנִי אָבִי! וַיִּשָּׂא עֵשָׂו קֹלוֹ וַיֵּבְךְּ׃	Esau said to his father, "Have you only one blessing, my father? Bless me, me too, my father!" And Esau raised his voice and wept.	Genesis 27:38

But that was then, and this is now. Then, Jacob ran away from his brother; now, Jacob approaches him. Then, only one brother cried. There was a winner and there was a loser. Now, both brothers cry, as the reality of peace between them, so unimaginable for so long, finally washes over them.

Granting Your Child Peace

Birkat kohanim seems to hark back to this moment of reconciliation between two estranged brothers and suggest the hope that God too might "lift His face" toward us, that God too might grant us peace:

Numbers 6:26

יִשָּׂא יְקוָה פָּנָיו אֵלֶיךָ וְיָשֵׂם **לְךָ שָׁלוֹם**:	**May God lift up His face** toward you and give you **peace**.

We human beings aren't perfect. We sin. We occasionally, even regularly, fail to meet the expectations and hopes of our Parent in Heaven. The blessing that the Torah teaches us to ask of God is this: God, when we make choices and those choices are not, perhaps, those You would have wanted us to make, allow us the chance to reconcile with You. Don't keep us in a state of shame forever. Meet our eyes, and in doing so, grant us peace.

In the words of Rashi:

Rashi on Numbers 6:26

"ישא יְקוָה פניו אליך" – יִכְבֹּשׁ כַּעֲסוֹ	[We pray that] He will sublimate his anger.

And so, if *birkat kohanim* really is a parenting manual, if we are to emulate God in how He parents His earthly children, then we too are bidden to do the same. When our children disappoint us, even fail us; when we have words with them — at the end of that discussion, we will have a choice to make. Will we lift our face up to our children? Will we allow our eyes to meet theirs? Will we grant them peace?

Meeting the eyes of our children in circumstances such as this is the third great gift of love we should grant our kids. It conveys the message that even when they choose differently from us, even when they disappoint us, even when they make grievous mistakes that cause us pain — there *is* a way back, and our relationship with them can somehow withstand the ordeal.

I won't keep my eyes averted from you forever. I will meet your eyes as you sit in that room across from me. I will recognize you, a human being who, like me, makes independent choices, even if those choices are not ones I would have made.

Vertical Versus Horizontal

All told, both the second and third verses of *birkat kohanim* seem to speak about a kind of "meeting of eyes" between a parent and child. But the nature of that meeting of the eyes is very different. One is vertical; the other, horizontal. To explain:

At birth — the paradigmatic moment of *chen* — we look at our children from the top down, when we gaze at them in joy. That is a "vertical" gaze. I hold all the cards. I am the only real independent actor; the child is incapable yet of real action. They can do no wrong, quite literally, because they haven't done anything independent in life yet. But all that changes soon enough. When our children become capable of independent choice, they begin to stand before us as a kind of equal. We have to look at them face-to-face, to look at them "horizontally," which creates the question: If their choices leave us feeling displeased, what will we do? Can we, at the end of the day, find a way to accept them, even if we disapprove of the choice? *Can we meet their eyes?*

Birkat kohanim encourages us to figure out how to do that. We are meant to take a cue from God. Forgiveness is possible, and therefore our relationship can and must heal. I have to find a way to raise my face and look you in the eye again. I have to find a way to give you the gift of peace.

The Advent of *Chesed*

In the interest of understanding this third kind of parental love just a little bit better, I want to invite you to join me on a little thought experiment. I suggested earlier that the kinds of love expressed in the first two verses of *birkat kohanim* each had a "name" of sorts that we might give them: *Rachamim* is the Hebrew word for the kind of love described in the first verse, and *chen* for the second. And, although they remain operative on some level throughout the whole of a parent's life with a child, these forms of love naturally each associate themselves with a certain paradigmatic moment in a child's development. We speculated that *rachamim* is the love of the womb and that the paradigmatic moment of *chen* is birth itself, the moment a parent first cradles their newborn child in their arms and gazes upon them with joy.

But we've now added a third kind of parental love to the mix. If such a third flavor of parental love exists, does it too have a name?

I think this third kind of love *does* come with its own name. It is חסד (*chesed*).

In Hebrew, *chesed* — usually translated simply as "kindness" — is a close cousin of *chen* and *rachamim*. A well-known example of their tight relationship is the appearance of all three, one after another, in the famous prayer we know of as Grace After Meals:

בָּרוּךְ אַתָּה יְקוָה אֱלֹקֵינוּ מֶלֶךְ הָעוֹלָם הַזָּן אֶת־הָעוֹלָם כֻּלּוֹ בְּטוּבוֹ בְּחֵן בְּחֶסֶד וּבְרַחֲמִים	Blessed are You, Hashem, our God, King of the Universe, who nourishes the entire world in His goodness — with ***chen***, with ***chesed***, and with ***rachamim***.

In that prayer, we acknowledge that the Almighty, the Parent of all life, provides sustenance for each and every creature on the face of the earth. This care that God provides is described as an amalgam not just of *chen* and *rachamim*, but of *chesed* as well. What, then, is the particular quality of *chesed*? How does it distinguish itself from these other kinds of love, *rachamim* and *chen*?

The distinguishing hallmark of *chesed*, I'd argue, is its "other-directedness." We can discern this meaning by paying careful attention to the way we speak of *chesed* in popular parlance. For instance, many schools require students to devote a number of hours a month to the practice of *chesed,* or community service. Students can visit the sick, help out at a soup kitchen, you name it. But imagine a student who reports to their principal that for their community service hours this month, they babysat their younger sister or helped their mother put away the groceries. The principal isn't likely to be very impressed. Look, it's all well and good for you to help out one of your own, but there's something about the nature of *chesed*, we intuit, that has to do with giving to *someone else*.

Taking that idea into a parenting context, we might say that *chesed* enters the picture of child raising once a child reaches a critical threshold:

once he or she has begun to assert their "otherness," their independence from the parent, even in the smallest of ways.

When might that paradigmatic moment of *chesed* be in child raising? The rabbinic phrase for "the giving of *chesed* to another" provides us with a powerful clue. In Hebrew that would be גמילות חסד (*gemilut chesed*). That first word, from the root גמל, means "to provide" — but it also has another meaning in Hebrew. Consider this auspicious celebration in the lives of Abraham and Sarah, our nation's founding parents:

וַיִּגְדַּל הַיֶּלֶד **וַיִּגָּמַל**, וַיַּעַשׂ אַבְרָהָם מִשְׁתֶּה גָדוֹל בְּיוֹם **הִגָּמֵל** אֶת־יִצְחָק׃	The child grew up **and was weaned**, and Abraham held a great feast on the day that Isaac **was weaned**.	Genesis 21:8

Fascinating. Although *gemilut chesed* colloquially means "providing *chesed*," its more literal meaning might be "the giving of weaned kindness." The moment that a child is weaned is the moment they achieve their first measure of independence from a parent. No longer are they forced to derive their sustenance directly from their parent's body, when their parent chooses to provide it. Now, they look to the world at large for their food. Now, they begin to eat on their own terms. It may seem like only a baby step, but in this very first, little way, the child begins to take on the world on their own.

The giving of *chesed*, kindness, to an inherently independent being, is very different from providing the love of *rachamim*, the nurturing care of the womb, or even the unconditional and overflowing joy of *chen*. This third kind of love comes with a consciousness of, and an attention to, boundaries. This is a balancing act, and it is tricky: I must give what I can, while still respecting the child's budding and developing separateness from me. Indeed, the greatest act of *chesed* might well be fostering the child's separateness: giving them the space and the ability to do things on their own.

As much as this gaining of independence is a transition for the child, it is a transition for the parent, too. *How do I give to someone who is drawing away from me, who doesn't seem to need me as much as before? By giving them more and more tools to be on their own.* If this seems somewhat paradoxical and a little bit sad, you're not off base. There is something bittersweet about this. But to nurture a child's separateness is also, ultimately, to achieve a great triumph. In the end, I achieve the ability to love my child in an entirely new way: Not just top-down, but across. I love my child not just as an extension of me, but as someone who is more powerful, someone who has truly begun to come into him- or herself.

The Strength to Let Go

Birkat kohanim, I would posit, suggests to us that the great test of parental *chesed* comes in moments of crisis: When a child hasn't just gracefully separated from us but has done so more messily — when they've made mistakes along the way, even rebelled against us — what do we do then? *Chesed* in these moments means withstanding the temptation to artificially and indefinitely keep my child attached to me at all costs, using the seductive adhesive of unresolved guilt and shame. It means figuring out a way, after all the words have been said, to meet the eyes of my child in peace.

Cumulative Love

We might ask: *What gives me the strength to do that?* What gives me the strength to accept a child's separateness? What helps give me the strength to claw back my relationship with my child, even after a child's grievous mistake? The answer is: my past interaction with that child. *That's* where I draw the strength from.

And here is where we can see just how cumulative the three phases of parental love really are. If I've invested in that child, if I've given the child *rachamim,* built them up and protected them, if I've bequeathed *chen* to them, looking upon my child as they've grown with delight and unconditional warmth — all these are wellsprings of love that I can later draw from. If I can remember all those treasured moments, I can find the wherewithal, even in subsequent moments of pain, to give them this one last gift: the gift of peace.

It's the greatest and hardest gift a parent can bestow.

Postscript: A Personal Suggestion

I want to end with a short personal suggestion. I mentioned before that many parents have the custom to bestow *birkat kohanim* upon their children each Friday night. I myself try to do so — and this understanding gives me, personally, more of a handle on what I'm saying. It helps make these moments of blessing my children more meaningful to me. If you don't yet bless your children on Friday nights, or any other time regularly, consider doing so. Consider using these precious words of *birkat kohanim* as your prepared text, as it were. Generally speaking, children love the experience. They're so delighted to be blessed by their parents.

And maybe try this: As your child comes over to you, use those few moments before you bless them to think about the three kinds of parental love expressed by *birkat kohanim.* Then ask yourself: *At this moment, which one of these kinds of love does this particular child seem to need from me the most?* Do they need to be built up? Do they need to be guarded and kept from harm? Maybe they need the smile that says I'm just so delighted to spend time with them. Maybe they need to see more *chen* from me. Or maybe ... maybe they need peace from me. Maybe they need me to pick up their chin, to look them in the eye and to tell them that even in the hard times, I can go forward with them in love and respect. Finding a way to love my child with some mysterious but wonderful confluence of all three kinds of love, at least for me, makes the endeavor of parenting my children feel more whole.

Epilogue

The Sabbath and the Priestly Blessing

The Search for a Precedent

IN OUR LAST ESSAY, I suggested to you a theory about *birkat kohanim* — that it acts as a parenting manual, as it were, helping us understand the types of love that we ask God to bestow upon us, and in turn, the types of love that we should bestow upon our own children. But it seems to me that an objection can be raised against this theory, and I'd like to consider that with you.

Here's the objection:

Sure, it's nice to look at *birkat kohanim* as a parenting manual of sorts. It is nice to see this blessing as a request of God that He express three overlapping kinds of parental love to us, and that this, in turn, would serve as some sort of model for how we human beings might parent our own children. But that's all very theoretical. Where, if anywhere, does this model of parenting express itself in the Torah not just in theory, but in actuality? In other words, is there a precedent somewhere in the Torah for God actually *acting* as a parent in the way *birkat kohanim* seems to describe?

Birkat Kohanim and the Birth of All Things

So let's ponder that for a moment. It seems reasonable to believe there *would* be a precedent somewhere. After all, if God really *is* our Parent in Heaven, shouldn't there be some example somewhere of God following His own parenting advice? But where in the Torah would we find it?

The answer might well be: *Right at the moment when humanity and the natural world around us first came into being.* Could that moment — the moment when God first became our "parent," as it were — also be the moment we find the Creator first expressing *birkat kohanim*'s principles of what parenting is all about?

I think it might be. If we read the verses of Creation carefully, I think we will discover not just a precedent for the ideas of *birkat kohanim*, but something else as well — something rather unexpected: how *birkat kohanim* actually helps us resolve some stubborn difficulties in the Torah's account of Creation.

I want to lay out to you three questions concerning the Creation story in Genesis that for a long while have vexed me. Then I want to try to map *birkat kohanim*'s parenting model onto the Creation story. I think doing so may well help us answer those questions, and it may also reveal the "precedent" we've been looking for.

Creation and Division

Here's question number one:

Imagine you were God (don't try this at home). One day you decide to create a universe from scratch. Due to your supernatural creative capacity, you only budget seven meager days for the whole endeavor. So let me ask you: *What would you do during those days?*

Presumably, you'd engage in a frenetic burst of creative activity. You'd make the heavens, complete with the sun, moon, stars, and sky. You'd make the earth, complete with seas. You would bring grasses and trees into being. You'd create all sorts of fish, fowl, and animal life in abundance.

Which, of course, is pretty much what God actually *does* during His own seven days of Creation. God makes lots of things. He seems to fulfill our expectations marvelously. But besides making things, the Master of the Universe also does something else. Over and over again in the verses of Creation, we hear that God *separated* things. Over and over, He took a bunch of elements that were all together and put some over here and others over there:

Genesis 1:4	**וַיַּבְדֵּל** אֱלֹקִים בֵּין הָאוֹר וּבֵין הַחֹשֶׁךְ׃	And God **separated** the light from the darkness.
Genesis 1:6	יְהִי רָקִיעַ בְּתוֹךְ הַמָּיִם וִיהִי **מַבְדִּיל** בֵּין מַיִם לָמָיִם׃	Let there be an expanse in the midst of the water, **that it may separate** water from water.

יְהִי מְאֹרֹת בִּרְקִיעַ הַשָּׁמַיִם **לְהַבְדִּיל** בֵּין הַיּוֹם וּבֵין הַלָּיְלָה	Let there be lights in the expanse of the sky **to separate** day from night.	Genesis 1:14

Why, of all things, does the Torah choose these acts of separation — as the one embellishment to "making things" that the Torah deems important to include in its Creation narrative? Why do we need to hear about all these divisions?[5]

And God Saw That It Was Good

Moving on, here is a second question to consider about the Torah's account of the first six days of existence.

The reader of Genesis chapter 1 will discern a pattern. Throughout the days of Creation, whenever God finishes a particular task, we always seem to get some version of this refrain:

וַיַּרְא אֱלֹקִים כִּי טוֹב	**And God saw that it was good.**

Over and over again, we hear those words: *And God saw that it was good.* We hear them after God created light; after God gathered together the waters in the oceans, allowing dry land to appear; after God created the sun, moon, and stars. God always looks and sees that it is good. What, exactly,

5 To elaborate: Presumably, there are *lots* of things about Creation that the Torah doesn't bother to tell us about. The verses don't specify anything about the biochemical processes that underlie the development of life. The Torah tells us nothing about the thermodynamics that power the sun and the stars. All we hear is that God... made things. And that, in and of itself, isn't problematic. The Torah never represents itself as a science textbook. It just says God made things. If you want to know *how* God made them — well, that's what physics and biochemistry classes are for. And yet, for some reason, the Torah offers this one other bit of detail about Creation other than God actually creating: God *separating* things. Why should this be the one exception? Why gloss over all the rich detail involved in making things to highlight this one other activity of the Creator during the process of Creation?

is the point of that little divine declaration? Why does the Torah have to record that God "saw it was good"?

And here's a part two to that question:

Bear in mind that at a certain point, the little declaration *changes*. When God finishes *everything*, God doesn't look and see that it is good. Instead, we hear this:

Genesis 1:31

וַיַּרְא אֱלֹקִים אֶת־כָּל־אֲשֶׁר עָשָׂה, וְהִנֵּה־**טוֹב מְאֹד**	And God looked at everything that He made, and behold, **it was very good**.

Now, not only is everything good, but it is "very good." What, we might wonder, is the practical difference between "good" and "very good"? Do the angels clap harder in the latter case? Is the point just that God was relieved that He was finally done? What, exactly, does the Torah want the reader to perceive here?

How God Relates to the Sabbath Day

And now for the third question on my list.

God finishes all His labor at the end of six days and rests on the seventh. One might expect that this would be the end of it. But the Almighty doesn't *just* rest on the seventh day. He somehow treats the day itself as special:

Genesis 2:3

וַיְבָרֶךְ אֱלֹקִים אֶת־יוֹם הַשְּׁבִיעִי **וַיְקַדֵּשׁ אֹתוֹ** כִּי בוֹ שָׁבַת מִכָּל־מְלַאכְתּוֹ אֲשֶׁר־בָּרָא אֱלֹקִים לַעֲשׂוֹת:	And God **blessed** the seventh day **and made it holy**, because on it He ceased from all His work that God had created in order to make.

God blesses the day and sanctifies it. Curiously, the Almighty seems to change His relationship to the day itself, if we can wrap our minds around such a notion. But what, really, does it mean to "bless" and "sanctify" a day? How should we understand this?

As unlikely as it may seem, I believe the priestly blessing may offer us some clues in answering all three of these questions. Inasmuch as Creation was the process of God becoming the Parent of all things, *birkat kohanim*, the Torah's little parenting manual, might offer us a path toward solving these three puzzles.

Let's try mapping the priestly blessing onto God's activity in creating the world, and see where it gets us.

The Priestly Blessing as a Lens on Creation

In our analysis of *birkat kohanim* above, you'll recall that we identified several overlapping stages of parental love. The first of these involved two energies that are inherently in tension with one another. In the words of *birkat kohanim*, these were לברך and לשמור, to bless and to keep safe.

The first of these, blessing, is expansive in nature. A parent seeking to bless their child is a parent doing whatever they can to help their offspring grow and flourish.

And if we were to map this drive onto the Creation story, it's not too difficult to see where it would go. This energy of "blessing" manifests itself constantly in the divine workings of the primal six days. It is the essential activity God was involved with. Willing heaven and earth into being, populating the expanse with multitudes, bringing new forms of verdant life into the world — all these are expressions of "blessing."

But as we saw in our analysis of *birkat kohanim*, a good parent doesn't *only* "bless" his or her child. The expansive energy of blessing lives in natural tension with another parental imperative: *to keep one's new creation safe from harm.* When I focus on *keeping safe* what I've brought into the world, I'm not necessarily making it bigger, stronger, and faster. Instead, I am trying to keep it from coming into contact with forces that could impinge on it or, maybe, even destroy it.

We are now in a position, perhaps, to resolve that first question I asked you about Creation — my musing about the need for divine acts of separation. Why does the Torah bother telling us not just what God made, but how God separated things from one another? I would submit that perhaps God was applying the two basic elements of parenting energy that we have been describing. In making and multiplying things, God was bringing "blessing" into the world. And in separating various newly formed elements of Creation from one another, the Almighty was working with a countervailing force: keeping things safe. God was seeking to preserve the integrity of each newly created phenomenon.

For let's consider what Creation would have been like without these basic acts of separation. Try to imagine: What if light and darkness had *not* been irrevocably divided from one another, with each given its separate domain? What if the laws of physics had remained in flux, allowing light and darkness to battle it out for dominance in some chaotic, unpredictable way any time the two found themselves within a stone's throw of each other?

Not a very stable world there, right? All in all, the divisions the Almighty sets up — the divisions between light and darkness, between upper and lower waters, between the seas and dry land — all these give things their own space to be, thereby maintaining the integrity of creation. They create borders that keep things in order. We thus begin to understand why the Torah tells us about these various separations. The *havdalot*, the great divisions that God establishes in the process of Creation, serve to "keep safe" the various forces and phenomena that He's brought into the world. They keep each force or domain from mixing with the others and compromising them.

Rachamim and Judgment in Creation

Earlier, in our analysis of the priestly blessing, I suggested to you that the twin imperatives at the core of the first stage of parental love — to bless and to keep safe — can be summed up in a single Hebrew word: רחמים (*rachamim*), the love of the womb. The womb both nurtures and guards from harm the incipient child within it. But, we suggested, the womb does not do this unconditionally. It lavishes its care *in order to achieve something*, in order to help the child grow into a healthy, functioning human being. If, tragically, the womb deems the embryo not capable of growth, the womb will engineer a miscarriage. This heartbreaking reality emerges from the delicate balance between the nurturing aspect of the womb and its capacity for discernment, even judgment — or in Hebrew, דין (*din*).

Likewise, in Creation, *rachamim* was matched with *din*. God's willingness to bestow blessing and guard — to help newly created things flourish and keep them safe, this lavishing of the Creator's love and care — wasn't entirely unconditional. For in Creation, too, there would come a moment of judgment. It arrived whenever God looked at what He had just created … *and saw that it was good.*

Consider this: Throughout Creation, whenever God pauses to look and evaluate, the response is always, "He saw that it was good." But what if the alternative had been the case? What if God had instead looked and seen that it was bad? What then?

We can't say for sure, but if God had seen that it was bad, one would imagine He would have gotten rid of it. If the phenomenon or species God had just brought forth began to develop in a way that was undesirable, presumably God would have dispensed with it early on and started that aspect of Creation afresh. This helps us understand the meaning of all those declarations of "and God saw that it was good." These were moments of evaluation. It was important for the Creator to evaluate how things were developing at certain, punctuated moments. Bringing things into the world entails a need for regular assessment.

The Mystery of "Very Good"

All of which puts us in a position, I think, to understand more deeply the puzzling pronouncement the text makes at the close of the sixth day of Creation:

וַיַּרְא אֱלֹקִים אֶת־כָּל־אֲשֶׁר עָשָׂה, וְהִנֵּה־**טוֹב מְאֹד**	And God looked at everything that He made, and behold, it was **very good**.	Genesis 1:31

What is the nature of this final pronouncement? Is it a further attempt at evaluation? Well, a further act of judgment would seem irrelevant. After all, every aspect of Creation had already passed muster and thus, by rights, each should remain the continued beneficiary of God's *rachamim*. Each should be allowed to remain in existence. What then is the point of a final evaluative look?

Moreover, even if we were to presume that God, for some unexplained reason, felt the need to evaluate everything one last time, why issue a *new* type of grade? Why declare that everything was *very* good? What's that "very" about?

The Advent of *Chen*

The answer comes, again, from *birkat kohanim*. The priestly blessing teaches that after the love of *rachamim* comes the delight of *chen*. And so it was with God and this newly formed world of His.

God's glance at Creation when He was finally done creating wasn't an *evaluative* act. It was a moment of sheer revelry. Pure delight. At long last, the six days were complete: The work of the divine womb, as it were, was done, and the moment for the world's "birth" had arrived. God had finally brought a completed universe into being, and like any proud parent, so to speak, He was suffused with joy. He gazed upon His newly formed world, and it wasn't just good. It was *very* good. God looked upon His cosmic child, this new universe, with the smiling love of *chen*.

Indeed, if you closely examine the words the Torah uses to describe this final climactic gaze of the Almighty toward the whole of His handiwork, you'll find that the language confirms this interpretation. For the language here differs in a subtle way from the language before, when God looked upon each part that He had just created. It's not just that earlier, each piece was "good" and now it was "very good." Something else is different now, too:

WHAT GOD "SAW" AT THE CLIMAX OF CREATION	**WHAT GOD "SAW" ON THE PRIOR DAYS OF CREATION**
וַיַּרְא אֱלֹקִים אֶת־כָּל־אֲשֶׁר עָשָׂה, **וְהִנֵּה**־טוֹב מְאֹד *And God looked at everything that He made,* ***and behold****, it was very good.*	וַיַּרְא אֱלֹקִים **כִּי** טוֹב And God saw **that it** was good.

Look at the "bridging" word in each pronouncement. When, after each segment of Creation, God looks upon that which He created, the text tells us: וַיַּרְא אֱלֹקִים **כִּי** טוֹב—*And God saw* ***that it*** *was good.* The word כִּי—probably best translated as "that"—suggests that God was looking at what He had made in order to achieve some goal, in order to check that the thing was functioning as it was supposed to.[6] He looked and He saw *that* yes, things were the way they were supposed to be.

But now consider how God looks upon Creation at the end, once He views it as a whole. Gone is the word "that." Instead, God simply "looked at everything that He made" — full stop. There's no ulterior motive for looking, no need to evaluate what was there. God looked ... because God wanted to look. That's it. The next phrase, "**and behold**," suggests almost a sense of surprise or delight or both: *Wow, there it is ... it is very good.* The words suggest the sense of satisfaction of a Creator who is suddenly confronted with the beauty of the newly independent thing before Him. The gaze of the Creator now bespeaks appreciation, not evaluation. It is the gaze of *chen.*

The Coming of Peace

It is not surprising, then, that it is at this very moment that God decides to rest. The Creator is choosing not to let this joy pass in a fleeting moment, to just dissipate. Instead, God would devote an entire day to the remarkable experience of *chen.* To anthropomorphize just a bit: His joy and satisfaction in what was brought forth would be something He could now "spend the day" reveling in.

But the truth is, God's experience of the Sabbath wasn't *just* an experience of *chen.* It was something else also. Merging with God's experience of *chen* was something new, something that corresponds not just to the second of *birkat kohanim*'s parental imperatives, but to its third imperative as well. The Sabbath would be God's way of giving the new world some peace.

With the advent of the first Sabbath came God's active decision to stop creating. And that was a momentous decision. Until now, God's relationship to the universe was that of the insistent developer, the Maker of things, the One who constantly tinkers with Creation to improve it. But now, with the decision to rest, God's relationship with the universe changed. Now God could just sit back, so to speak, and relate to the universe on its own

---

6 In other words, the word "that" in the verse turns the phrase "and God saw" into a colloquial way of saying "God perceived" or "God judged." The bestowal of divine attention on the things being created was purely to evaluate them. God, like any responsible creator, wanted to ensure that He was bringing good things into the world and not bad or defective things.

terms. Could it still be made better? Sure. Could the laws of physics be tweaked further? Perhaps. *But that's not My role anymore.* In renouncing further labor, the Almighty gains the opportunity to relate to creation on its own terms, not just in terms of how it could be improved.

It was as if the universe had been ... weaned. The world had now attained a degree of independence, a degree of welcome detachment from its Creator. The Creator would let it be, would give it ... peace.[7]

God's Sabbath is a watershed moment, a moment when His relationship with the world shifts from that of a parent who is actively shaping a child to that of a parent who appreciates their child for what he or she has finally become.

To Bless and to Keep Safe, Redux

All told, it looks like we've found the model we've been looking for. We've seen how, at the moment when God becomes a parent of sorts — not just to a particular being but to the universe as a whole — His actions seem to evoke those of *birkat kohanim*'s three overlapping stages of love.

1. First, the Master of the Universe "blesses" and "keeps safe" His Creation.
   a. God causes Creation to progressively develop.
   b. And the Almighty simultaneously safeguards Creation by enforcing divisions, keeping certain things separate from other things.
2. Then, as Creation comes to a close, God seems to evoke the particular love of *chen*: He looked — and behold, all was very good.
3. And finally, with the advent of the Sabbath, God bestows a measure of independence to His creation, granting His universe "peace."

Having found in God's process of Creation a version of the three stages of parental love as described in *birkat kohanim,* we might reasonably conclude that the parental dynamic described in *birkat kohanim* has, with the

---

7 This doesn't mean that after Creation is complete, God would have nothing to do with the world anymore. That's like saying a mother has nothing to do with her child after she weans them. But it is time for a new kind of love now. It is time for the love of *chesed* — the love reserved for someone or something that is distinct from you. See our previous essay.

advent of the Sabbath, run its course. And yet, if we look at the language of the very first Sabbath closely, we seem to find that, curiously, this is not the case:

וַיְבָרֶךְ אֱלֹקִים אֶת יוֹם הַשְּׁבִיעִי וַיְקַדֵּשׁ אֹתוֹ	And God blessed the seventh day and made it holy.	Genesis 2:3

Remarkably, the Torah's language here prefigures that of the opening words of *birkat kohanim*:

BIRKAT KOHANIM	**GOD'S EXPERIENCE OF THE FIRST SABBATH**
יְבָרֶכְךָ יְקֹוָה וְיִשְׁמְרֶךָ׃ May God **bless you** and **keep you [safe]** (Num. 6:24)	וַיְבָרֶךְ אֱלֹקִים אֶת־יוֹם הַשְּׁבִיעִי וַיְקַדֵּשׁ אֹתוֹ And God **blessed** the seventh day and **made it holy** (Gen. 2:3)

- The priestly blessing speaks of God blessing us. And the text in Genesis speaks of God blessing *the Sabbath*.
- The priestly blessing speaks of God keeping us safe. And the text in Genesis seems to speak of God keeping *the Sabbath* safe. Indeed, consider what it means to make something *kadosh*, holy. To do this is to separate it from the mundane and to keep the mundane from encroaching upon it. God separated the seventh day from other days to ensure that this day would have its own integrity, separate and apart from the other six days of Creation. It would be special. A day of "non-creation," a day of rest.

So this seems a bit odd, right? We already showed that God implemented the first phase of parenting — "blessing and keeping," so to speak — in the initial six days of Creation. That was followed by the love of *chen* and the giving of peace. So it's over; we are done. Why, then, would a version of *birkat kohanim*'s first verse recur later, on the seventh day? To arrive at the end, at the Sabbath, and to find there echoes of *birkat kohanim*'s first phase, feels like a serious case of textual whiplash.

To Bless and Keep...a Day?

I want to suggest that we can discern the solution to our little conundrum if we focus on exactly what God was "blessing and keeping" in each of these two instances.

Back in the six days of Creation, God was "blessing and keeping" *that which He created.* He was making earth, land, and sea, allowing each to burgeon and develop but also protecting them with divisions, so as to ensure their own individual integrity. In the Sabbath narrative, by contrast, that which God is attending to is not really something He created. As a matter of fact, it is not a "thing" at all. It is a *day*:

Genesis 2:3

וַיְבָרֶךְ אֱלקים אֶת יוֹם הַשְּׁבִיעִי וַיְקַדֵּשׁ אֹתוֹ	And God blessed the seventh day and made it holy.

In a paradoxical way, this day of non-creation, this day that God devoted to resting, to giving His creation a little space from Him — is that day that the Master of the Universe now seeks to "bless and keep." It is that period of rest that the Almighty is seeking to nurture and keep safe.

What are we to make of that?

Parenting Is a Circle, Not a Line

It seems to me that there might be a message here for us humans. If we are indeed to learn about parenting from God, one thing we are intended to glean, perhaps, is the idea that parenting isn't a line. It's a circle. Just when you think you're done, in some paradoxical way you arrive back at the beginning.

At the beginning, when that which we are making is tiny and fragile, we of course seek to multiply it (bless it) and to guard it from harm so that it can flourish. But once the child we are parenting is independent and can stand on their own two feet, and once we respond to that by granting the child some separation from us, some peace — it is at that moment that we come to a point of transition. It is potentially a time of confusion. What do we do next? What does it mean to be a parent now? We might come to believe that our drive to bless and keep must entirely end, that we need to turn off these nurturing energies somehow.

But maybe that isn't the way it works. A parent *always* engages in the twin energies we call "blessing" and "keeping safe." The only question is: What's the target toward which those energies are turned?

When one has finally raised independent children, the energies of parenting come full circle. The parent *returns* to the beginning of the process, to blessing and keeping safe — but the object of those energies changes. This time, what the parents are nurturing with those energies is not the kids *but their own "rest."* They are nurturing their own decision and commitment to pull back.

The Strength to Let Go

Why is it necessary to do this?

Perhaps because letting go is hard to do. It is hard to grant one's creation independence. There is a natural state of sadness, of mourning, that accompanies a parent's choice — perhaps even a divine Parent's choice — not to tinker with their kids anymore, not to actively foster their development. How do I pull this off? How do I — the blesser and keeper of my child — marshal the strength to make that transition?

We learn from God, perhaps, how to do this.

You do what God did with the Sabbath. You take this new moment of separation, the moment that at some level you might fear or shrink away from — and instead, you confront it directly and welcome it. More than that: *You celebrate it.* You pour the energy of blessing and keeping into it. You don't turn your back on the moment of separation as if it is some necessary evil; you don't allow it to be something fleeting that dissipates without even a backward glance. No. You celebrate the moment. You invite all your friends to revel in it with you. You take pictures of it and look back on it and treasure it.

God blessed the Sabbath and kept it safe — and so must you do. You must take your desire to nurture and, paradoxically, turn it inward: *Now you must nurture your own separation from your kid.*

But what does this really mean? It's a nice philosophical idea, perhaps, but how do I do that in real life? Well, here's your strategy: There are moments of independence, of separation from your kids, that are naturally baked into life. Birthdays are just a tiny taste of it; bar and bat mitzvahs; weddings — that's a big one, right there. Take those days, the days you regard with trepidation, the days when you will step away from actively tinkering with your child's life — take their wedding day, for example — and celebrate it. Revel in it like there's no tomorrow. That's how you bless the day. And guard that day, too. Make sure that you don't violate the boundaries of that day and let it slip away and become part of the next ordinary day on the calendar. Consecrate the day and properly guard its perimeter.

The Secrets in Our Parties

Here's a little secret. Why do we celebrate the life cycle moments in our children's lives? Why do we make lavish bar and bat mitzvah celebrations and weddings for our kids? Sure, we are proud. Sure, we want to pamper our kids and throw them a nice party. But there's another reason for these celebrations, too. These celebrations aren't just for the kid. *They are for you.*

There's something about consciously marking off a day of separation (keep it!) and luxuriating in that day (bless it!) that, I would submit, must be part and parcel of granting one's child independence. Instead of dreading the bittersweet moment of separation, we are to look it in the eye and celebrate it. Instead of fighting it, we must choose instead to revel in it. We are to treasure the bittersweetness of giving our child peace. As any chocolate connoisseur knows, it is the complexity of tastes, the mingling of bitter and sweet, that marks true bliss. The holiness of the Sabbath coaxes us toward that sublime appreciation.

BEHA'ALOTECHA

What Is Humility Made Of?

וְהָאִישׁ מֹשֶׁה עָנָו מְאֹד
מִכֹּל הָאָדָם אֲשֶׁר עַל־פְּנֵי
הָאֲדָמָה:

Now, the man Moses was very humble, more than any other person on the face of the earth.

NUMBERS 12:3

BEHA'ALOTECHA

What Is Humility Made Of?

IN PARSHAT BEHA'ALOTECHA, WE get a clue to understanding two abiding mysteries about Moses. Each concerns a way in which the Torah speaks of Moses as standing apart, seemingly, from all other human beings.

Mystery number one: Moses experiences the revelation of God at Sinai in a way that no one else did, or seemingly even could. He is atop the mountain upon which the Master of the Universe descends — while all others were warned that even touching the mountain would be fatal (Ex. 19:12). Apparently, the human body was not made to withstand direct contact with God or divine environs. And yet, Moses successfully encounters God, speaking with the Master of the Universe face-to-face (Num. 12:8). Why? What was different about him?

Whatever the answer to that question is, intriguingly, there is yet another way that Moses stands apart from all other people. This other unique aspect of Moses concerns a character trait of his — a trait he possesses, according to the text of the Torah, in the extreme. The Torah speaks of Moses as having been the most humble of all human beings (Num. 12:3). And yet, here we come to our second mystery: We tend to associate humility with being respectful, perhaps even submissive, meek, or self-effacing. These, at least, are the synonyms your average dictionary gives for "humble." The question is: Does this description fit Moses?

Well, let's look at his record. Over the course of his life, one of the most consistent patterns that emerges in Moses' behavior is his willingness to challenge the powerful in defense of the weak. Indeed, he does so in increasingly intense increments.

First, he challenges ordinary, powerful individuals: the Egyptian taskmaster menacing a Hebrew slave (Ex. 2:12), then, one Hebrew slave who is threatening another (vv. 13–14). After that, he challenges a whole group of people — the Midianite shepherds harassing the daughters of Yitro (v. 17). After that, standing in defense of his people, he confronts Pharaoh himself, the ruler of the mightiest civilization the world had ever known (ibid. 5:1). And that's not all. At some point after all this, Moses challenges the ultimate authority — the Master of the Universe Himself.

In the aftermath of the Golden Calf episode, God stands ready to destroy the entire people and to start over with Moses. But Moses will have none of it. With what can only be described as icy determination, he provides God with a choice:

Exodus 32:31–32

וַיָּשָׁב מֹשֶׁה אֶל־יְקוָה וַיֹּאמַר, אָנָּא חָטָא הָעָם הַזֶּה חֲטָאָה גְדֹלָה וַיַּעֲשׂוּ לָהֶם אֱלֹקֵי זָהָב: וְעַתָּה, אִם־תִּשָּׂא חַטָּאתָם, וְאִם־אַיִן, מְחֵנִי נָא מִסִּפְרְךָ אֲשֶׁר כָּתָבְתָּ:	And Moses went back to God, and he said, "Oh, this people has committed a terrible sin; they have made themselves gods of gold. And now, if You will bear their sin [and forgive them — fine]. But if not, [don't think You can start over with me. I'm not going along with that. If You fail to forgive them, just] erase me from Your book that You have written."

Moses might be described as humble, but doesn't his behavior seem to tell a different story?

Redefining Humility

The case of Moses, I'd like to suggest, forces upon us the notion that the Torah defines humility differently from the way Merriam-Webster does. And in order to see how this is so, I'd like to speculate with you for a moment about a tantalizing possibility:

Maybe the two things that make Moses utterly unique are not two *separate* things at all. We saw earlier that Moses has this uncanny ability to withstand sustained, direct contact with the Divine; his ability to speak to God "face-to-face" is unparalleled. Also, according to the Torah, Moses has another unique quality: He happens to be the most humble man who ever walked the earth. So maybe it wasn't a coincidence that Moses just *happened* to exhibit these two qualities in their extreme form. Maybe these two qualities are really, somehow, two facets of the same thing.

A further indication that this might be so comes from the text of this week's parsha. Because it just so happens that these two unique things about Moses both show up in a single, particular episode in this week's parsha. Let me show you what I mean:

What Is Moses' Humility Doing Here?

Toward the end of **Parshat Beha'alotecha**, Miriam and Aaron speak about their brother, Moses, seemingly behind his back. They complain that he seems to act differently from other prophets. Their words are quoted by the Torah:

הֲרַק אַךְ־בְּמֹשֶׁה דִּבֶּר יְקֹוָה? הֲלֹא גַּם־בָּנוּ דִבֵּר, **וַיִּשְׁמַע יְקֹוָה׃**	"Did God speak only with Moses? Did God not speak with us as well?" **And God heard**.	Numbers 12:2

Now, right after this, the text gets to that point about Moses' humility. It tells us, as an aside to the reader, that:

וְהָאִישׁ מֹשֶׁה עָנָו מְאֹד מִכֹּל הָאָדָם אֲשֶׁר עַל־פְּנֵי הָאֲדָמָה׃	Now, the man Moses was very humble, more than any other person on the face of the earth.	Numbers 12:3

Following this little aside, the text tells us that God goes and calls to Miriam and Aaron, and rebukes them for their words. And in the process of doing so, the text touches on that second point we were talking about: Moses' uniqueness among prophets:

וַיֹּאמֶר, שִׁמְעוּ־נָא דְבָרָי: אִם־יִהְיֶה נְבִיאֲכֶם יְקֹוָה בַּמַּרְאָה אֵלָיו אֶתְוַדָּע; בַּחֲלוֹם אֲדַבֶּר־בּוֹ: לֹא־כֵן עַבְדִּי מֹשֶׁה; בְּכָל־בֵּיתִי נֶאֱמָן הוּא: פֶּה אֶל־פֶּה אֲדַבֶּר־בּוֹ, וּמַרְאֶה וְלֹא בְחִידֹת	And He said, "Hear now My words: If there is a prophet among you, I the Lord will make myself known to him in a vision, and will speak to him in a dream. It is not so with My servant Moses; in all My House he is faithful. Face-to-face will I speak with him, and in a clear vision, and not with riddles."	Numbers 12:6–8

Now, let's analyze these events a little bit, and I want to show you why I think these two aspects of Moses' character might be connected.

Why the Aside?

Let's say I asked you: What was the purpose of that little aside, in the middle of the story we just read, about Moses being the most humble man to walk the earth? Why, exactly, did the Torah feel compelled to pause its retelling of events and provide the reader with this little background information about Moses? Why mention Moses' humility here? Why tell it to us now?

The way I always read the story, I'll confess to you, is that the Torah was explaining to the reader why Moses didn't speak up for himself when Aaron and Miriam were saying disparaging things about him. He didn't feel it was his place. He was a really modest fellow and therefore he didn't say anything in his own defense. So God ended up coming to Moses' aid with a rhetorical broadside against Miriam and Aaron, because Moses was so loath to defend himself.

That *seems* like a reasonable interpretation. But here's the problem with it: Right after Miriam and Moses speak disparagingly about Moses, the text adds a seemingly superfluous couple of words:

Numbers 12:2

הֲרַק אַךְ־בְּמֹשֶׁה דִּבֶּר יְקוָה? הֲלֹא גַּם־בָּנוּ דִבֵּר, **וַיִּשְׁמַע יְקוָה**:

"Did God speak only with Moses? Did God not speak with us as well?" **And God heard**.

Now, why does the text go out of its way to tell us this? God of course sees and hears everything. It therefore seems utterly superfluous for the text to tell us that God overheard what Miriam and Aaron were saying. Unless...

Unless perhaps the text is actually telling us something *else* by way of implication. In other words, it is telling us that *God* heard... but someone else *didn't* hear. And who would that someone else have been? It would have to have been Moses.

In other words, the text is telling us that only the omniscient God was aware of Miriam and Aaron's words. Moses, on the other hand, was unaware of what his sister and brother were saying about him. Miriam and

Aaron weren't criticizing Moses in broad daylight. They were whispering about Moses to *each other*. They were speaking secretly.

So if Moses was really unaware of what they were saying, let's revisit the question I asked you about the need for that little narrative aside. Why does the Torah, smack in the middle of this episode, feel compelled to tell us that Moses was so surpassingly humble? It *can't* be to explain why Moses didn't rise in his own defense. He didn't rise in his own defense because he didn't hear what his siblings were saying about him!

An Underlying Rationale

It must be that the reason the Torah mentions Moses' humility at this point *isn't* to explain to the reader what just happened: why Moses remained silent, why he didn't stand up for himself in the face of criticism from his siblings. Maybe the point is to explain to the reader the *following* event, what was about to happen next in the text. And what happens next is that God declares to Aaron and to Miriam that Moses' kind of prophecy was unique.

In other words, the purpose of the aside is to give you, *the reader*, insight into the engine that drove Moses' unique capacity as a prophet to encounter God "face-to-face." *Why was it* that Moses had this capacity to communicate directly with God in a way that was clear and unencumbered? Why could he survive a direct and unfettered encounter with God when other prophets couldn't? What was so different about Moses?

That engine, the text is telling us, was the quality of humility. Moses was surpassingly humble. The two things that Moses possessed in extreme — an ability to prophesy with unparalleled clarity, and extreme humility — are, in fact, just two sides of the same coin.

The President and His Valet

But now the question is: Why *should* it be that way? Why is it that one's level of prophecy, one's ability to withstand a direct encounter with God, is influenced so profoundly by one's humility, of all things?

Well, it turns out that the Torah might well be trying to explain this very thing to us. Listen to how, in the very next verse, God continues and explains to Miriam and Aaron why Moses' unique ability to prophesy is so different. The Almighty doesn't just say, as a blind fact, that Moses *is* different. He says something *about* where that special quality comes from. That explanation takes the form of an unusual descriptor that God attaches to Moses:

Numbers 12:7

לֹא־כֵן עַבְדִּי מֹשֶׁה; בְּכָל־בֵּיתִי נֶאֱמָן הוּא:	It is not so with My servant Moses; in all of My House he is faithful.

A faithful servant. That's what God calls Moses here. The text seems to tell us that being a "faithful servant" — whatever that means — is the key. It is the essential quality needed to experience the ultimate depths of prophecy. Why? What is "faithful" service all about?

It may be a little abstract to wrap your mind around things like prophecy, direct communication with the Almighty, and being a servant of God. So, might I suggest that we try our hand at a terrestrial analogy?

Imagine an earthly ruler and his servant. At the risk of seeming a bit whimsical, I'll actually refer you to a fictionalized account of a contemporary ruler and his servant — the relationship between the president of the United States and his valet, as characterized on Aaron Sorkin's television series *The West Wing*.

In *The West Wing*, President Bartlett is an imposing figure. Many people with big résumés and even bigger egos are attracted to his orbit. But the one person who gains the *most* direct access to him — the one person on his staff who, quite literally, is trusted in the president's whole house, who can enter the presidential bedroom and wake Martin Sheen up from a nap is not any of those big-résumé people. It's a young man by the name of Charlie.

Charlie has no résumé of note. He's an orphan. His mother was a police officer killed in the line of duty and he stayed home from college to help raise his sister. No Ivy League glamor here. Charlie has no guile and he's not a social climber. For Charlie, working in the White House wasn't a résumé builder. It wasn't about him. He was there to *serve*, faithfully. And it was this that gave him a kind of proximity to the president that no one else could possibly have.

Bottom line: When you are around ultimate power — whether it is the most powerful man on earth, the US president; or whether it is the King of kings in heaven — your own ego can work against you. It can impede your level of access. Sure, a modest share of ego is fine for regular folks. Everyone wants to get ahead in life, right? A smattering of ego is fine for doctors and carpenters and lawyers and bus drivers. But that same, basic sense of ego is somehow dangerous around God. Standing in the presence of the Master of the Universe is too overwhelming an experience for a mortal human being to withstand if there is any part of you that thinks *this is about you.* An encounter with God is survivable only if you are entirely there to serve. Only if you are entirely transparent.

That, really, is the soul of humility: *understanding that, at the end of the day, whoever you are and whatever you achieve — it isn't really about you.* Your contributions don't entitle you to privilege, fame, or honor. On the contrary, you deem it a privilege to be able to serve. The significance of the work that you do isn't the glory that attaches itself to that work, or the congratulations you receive for doing it. The significance of your work *is the work itself.* Recognition is really beside the point.

What Humility Is, and What It Isn't

All of which helps us focus, I think, on what humility is and what it isn't. Humility doesn't mean I'm a pushover. It doesn't mean I can't stand up to power. It doesn't mean I don't recognize my talents or the value of my contributions to the world. In some ways, the very opposite is true. I so deeply recognize the value of my contributions and my own unique ability to make them that I will not let myself be fooled into thinking that those contributions have, as their prime purpose, something much smaller: the aggrandizement of little ol' me. Because my service is of supreme value and I am just the transparent vessel through which it comes into the world.

Nothing Can Survive in the Presence of Nothing

I think we are in a position now to reconsider the mystery I mentioned earlier: Why it is that most mortals would die when encountering the Master of the Universe face-to-face, but, somehow, Moses can encounter God at Sinai and live through that experience. Stop and think about why it is actually so dangerous to encounter God. What is it about this experience that is so challenging to human existence?

We often think of God as such an imposing presence, such a powerful force, that we humans are all but washed away by the force of an encounter with Him. But what if, somehow, the reverse were true? What if the toxicity of an encounter with God comes not from the immensity of God's Presence, but, paradoxically, from the opposite of this: *God's extreme Nothingness*?

To explain: God is the being who lives in a world beyond space and time. You can't see Him or touch Him. He lacks physical substance, even physical dimension. So, ironically, when this most powerful of beings comes into our world, from the standpoint of our human mode of existence, God really shows up as … *nothing at all.* We humans measure presence in terms of the space you take up, and the time you occupy. We speak of inches and feet, meters and kilometers; seconds, hours, and minutes. Paradoxically, while God is the most powerful being we can possibly imagine, by the measures of our time-and-space-bound world, He is also the closest to absolute Nothingness that can possibly be imagined. Kabbalistically, this paradox of God's Presence, beyond space and time, registers as *Ein Sof* (literally "endlessness"), an aspect of what us moderns might call "infinitude."[1]

Extreme Power as an Inverse of Nothingness: Where Else Do We Encounter That?

Now, stay with that thought a minute, and muse with me: Aside from God, do we ever encounter this paradox elsewhere?

The world of modern physics would tell us that there does exist a phenomenon that expresses precisely that paradoxical relationship. It is a black hole. A black hole is both immensely powerful and, from the standpoint of time and space, it is just about as close as you can get to "nothing" in this universe of ours.[2] The extreme nothingness, so to speak, of a black

---

1 Zohar, *Bereshit* 1:15a–16b.

2 A black hole is formed when a mammoth star burns through its helium fuel, and then, pushed by gravity, the shell of the star collapses in on itself. Gravity acts with such intensity that the remaining bulk of the star is condensed into a point in space of near infinite density — a point that physicists aptly call a "singularity."

It is intriguing that when we speak of God, we speak of Him as One. And when scientists speak of black holes, they too, speak of oneness. The "singularity" that is the core of a black hole is tiny from the standpoint of space of time; and yet, that singularity creates a vacuum in surrounding time and space of immense power.

hole consumes literally everything — all matter and energy — in its proximity. Nothing can survive an encounter with a black hole.

The above is obviously only an analogy. But maybe an analogy can be made between the physical aspects of our universe and aspects of its spiritual dimensions. Maybe something like this is true about God. When God, a being devoid of space and time, somehow comes into our world of space and time, the power of His Presence likewise destroys all "somethings" in the vicinity.

What, then, *could* survive in God's Presence?

Perhaps only a similarly extreme version of "nothing." Which accounts, maybe, for why it is that extreme humility is the one quality one must possess to survive a divine encounter. An extremely humble person nullifies their own ego, their own sense of self-importance — and in so doing, they become the "nothing," the completely transparent being, that can withstand the extreme Nothingness of the Divine without injury.

The Power of Humility

The power that comes in the wake of the diminishment of ego should not be underestimated. One sees it, fittingly enough, with Moses himself. In his entire career as leader of the people of Israel, what would you say was Moses' most *powerful* moment? Personally, I'd say it was in the immediate aftermath of the people's worship of the Golden Calf, the moment Moses stood up to the Master of the Universe Himself, when God sought to destroy the people. At that point, God had made an offer to Moses of ultimate aggrandizement: *I will destroy everyone and start over with you.* And Moses turns down the offer.

Not only does he say no, but his actions at that moment have such force that they actually change the direction of history. They change God's plan. God backs down on His threat to destroy everyone. And how does Moses achieve that? Well, listen to his words:

וַיָּשָׁב מֹשֶׁה אֶל־יְקוָֹה וַיֹּאמַר, אָנָּא חָטָא הָעָם הַזֶּה חֲטָאָה גְדֹלָה וַיַּעֲשׂוּ לָהֶם אֱלֹקֵי זָהָב: וְעַתָּה, אִם־תִּשָּׂא חַטָּאתָם, וְאִם־	And Moses went back to God, and he said, "Oh, this people has committed a terrible sin; they have made themselves gods of gold. And now, if You will bear their sin [and forgive them — fine]. But if not, [don't think	Exodus 32:31–32

אַיִן, מְחֵנִי נָא מִסִּפְרְךָ אֲשֶׁר כָּתָבְתָּ:	you can start over with me. I'm not going along with that. If you fail to forgive them, just] erase me from Your book that You have written."

Think about what Moses did here. Ironically, even deliciously, he leveraged his own nothingness. At the moment Moses most fully internalized the truth that it wasn't really about him, at *that moment* he achieved his greatest power. He created a metamorphosis in the direction of the divine plan itself.

God selects Moses because he is the most humble man to have walked the earth. But in doing so, God wasn't selecting a patsy or a yes-man. He was selecting someone who would have the potential for immense power. That power can be described in esoteric terms, the language of infinity, exploding stars, and black holes. But ultimately it is a power that we can all harness, to some extent or another, in our own lives. It is the power that comes from an understanding that *it is not all about me.*

SHELACH

The Spies

וַיֹּצִיאוּ דִּבַּת הָאָרֶץ
אֲשֶׁר תָּרוּ אֹתָהּ אֶל־
בְּנֵי יִשְׂרָאֵל

They brought a disparaging report of the land that they had scouted to the Children of Israel.

NUMBERS 13:32

SHELACH

The Spies

OUR PARSHA TELLS THE calamitous story of the spies. Moses dispatches men to scout out the land of Canaan, the land that God had promised to His people. But when those spies returned and delivered their report, the text relays that the spies spoke badly of the land, that they denigrated it somehow:

וַיֹּצִיאוּ דִּבַּת הָאָרֶץ אֲשֶׁר תָּרוּ אֹתָהּ אֶל בְּנֵי יִשְׂרָאֵל	They brought a disparaging report of the land that they had scouted to the Children of Israel.	Numbers 13:32

When they did this, the entire nation gave way to convulsions of grief, crying that they were doomed to fail in their attempt to conquer the land. In a fever pitch of despair, they talked of appointing a leader to replace Moses and take them back to Egypt. And **Parshat Shelach** goes on to describe God's response to all of this. The Almighty decreed that the people would wander in the wilderness for forty more years, one year for each day that the spies had spent on their mission. During that time, this entire generation of Israelites — all who sought a return to Egypt in the aftermath of the spies' report — would gradually die off. Only their children would enter and inherit the Promised Land.

Some Elephants in the Room

All in all, it is a famous episode. And yet it is also a puzzling episode. Many questions beset a reader seeking to make sense of these events, but two questions, perhaps, stand out as foremost.

First, what exactly did the spies do wrong? The text seems to suggest that their sin lay in the bad reports, the *dibbah*, that they brought back about the land. But that's puzzling, because when Moses sent them, he specifically gave them license to report about all aspects of the land—the good, the bad, and the ugly:

Numbers 13:19

וּמָה הָאָרֶץ אֲשֶׁר־הוּא יֹשֵׁב בָּהּ, הֲטוֹבָה הִוא אִם רָעָה	And tell of the land that the inhabitants dwell in: Is it good or is it bad?

If the spies were encouraged to report back about the land as to whether it was good or bad, how can they be faulted for giving a negative report? What, really, did they do wrong?[1]

That's question number one. And, while we're at it, here's another overriding question about the story: *Why send the spies to begin with?*

Let me elaborate what I mean by this.

According to the text here in the book of Numbers, the idea of sending spies to scout out the land of Canaan seems to come from God Himself:[2]

Numbers 13:1-2

וַיְדַבֵּר יְקוָה אֶל־מֹשֶׁה לֵּאמֹר: שְׁלַח־לְךָ אֲנָשִׁים וְיָתֻרוּ אֶת־אֶרֶץ כְּנַעַן אֲשֶׁר־אֲנִי נֹתֵן לִבְנֵי יִשְׂרָאֵל	God spoke to Moses, saying, "Send for yourself men, and they will scout out the land of Canaan that I am giving to the Children of Israel."

A reasonable reader might ask: Why did God do this? Why instruct the people to send spies to Canaan in the first place? After all, when the time came for the conquest of Canaan, we read in the book of Joshua that God initiated a bevy of divine miracles, from the splitting of the Jordan River to the collapse of Jericho's walls, to engineer that conquest. It was God,

---

1 The *Rishonim* already engage with the question; see, e.g., Ramban on Numbers 13:2.

2 It is true that later, in the book of Deuteronomy (Deut. 1:22–23), when Moses recounts this episode with the benefit of forty years of hindsight, he seems to alter this detail in the narrative. There, in Deuteronomy, Moses appears to lay the blame for sending the spies on himself, and leaves out mention of God instructing him to send these people to Canaan. Nevertheless, the text in Numbers is quite clear that the instructions to send the spies came from God; which leads us to the question: Why?

primarily, who made the conquest happen. So were spies really necessary? Did God need them to reconnoiter the land and pave the way for its conquest? That seems doubtful in the extreme. Just look at God's prior track record: The Master of the Universe had managed to pull off each of the ten plagues without the help of any human advance team that scouted the Egyptians for potential weaknesses. God had likewise managed to split the Sea of Reeds without any military engineers sounding out the depth of the waters or assessing the direction of the prevailing winds. God, omniscient and omnipotent, quite obviously has no need for such human assistance. So why command the people to send scouts? It seems like a total waste of time.

Now, we are not the first to consider this question, and a number of possible solutions have been proffered by the classical commentaries. Our Sages propose that God suggested to the people that they could send spies if they wanted to.[3] Others, like Ramban, have suggested that maybe God wanted the people to conquer the land in as normal a way as possible.[4] In this line of thinking, since it is a normal thing for people to send scouts for reconnaissance purposes before engaging in any military conflict, that's the way God told the Israelites to act, even if the ultimate victory over the Canaanites would be engineered by the Almighty.

I would like to suggest that another solution to both of these "elephants in the room" can be discerned if we attune ourselves to a series of remarkable hints given obliquely by the text itself. Seen in their totality, these amount to a series of breadcrumbs that lead us straight to an earlier story in the Torah, a story the text seems to regard as a kind of "sister narrative" to that of the spies. By setting up these links, the Torah seems to be asking the reader to read the two stories in tandem with one another, indeed, to see each as a kind of commentary on the other. It is almost as if one story acts as an interpretive lens through which to see the other. And while that analogy may sound esoteric to you, I think that's just because we're talking about it in the abstract here. Once you actually see the links in question and start to ponder, along with me, what they might mean, I think you'll understand what I'm talking about. So, without any further ado, let's get started.

---

3 Sotah 34b.

4 Ramban, Numbers 13:2.

Part I: The Resonances: Bad Reports

Take a moment, if you would, to scan the story of the spies. Read its verses, and as you do, play a little game. Ask yourself: *Where have I heard all this before?*

As you read more and more of the story of the spies, a suspicion may start to sneak up on you: I *have* heard all this before. It all sounds a lot like another famous biblical story, way back in the book of Genesis.

To see what I mean, let's consider some of the language the text employs in the story of the spies. For example, in the text describing what, exactly, the spies did wrong when they returned with their report about the land, we read:

Numbers 13:32

וַיֹּצִיאוּ דִּבַּת הָאָרֶץ אֲשֶׁר תָּרוּ אֹתָהּ אֶל־בְּנֵי יִשְׂרָאֵל

They brought a disparaging report of the land that they had scouted to the Children of Israel.

So the spies denigrated the land somehow. Exactly why, what, and how is beyond our concern right now. For the time being, let's just focus on the language. Look at the Hebrew word for those disparaging reports:

דִּבַּת הָאָרֶץ
Dibbah of the land

The text employs the very unusual term דִּבָּה, ***dibbah***. What, exactly, does it mean? It is a rare word in biblical literature, so it is hard to translate. Naturally, one looks for parallel cases of the word to try to piece together what it might mean — but there aren't many parallels. The word appears in only one other context in the entire Five Books of Moses, way back in the book of Genesis.

In a moment, I'll reveal to you where that is. But before I do, just imagine that you're a linguistic researcher; you're reading the story of the spies and you're trying to figure out what *dibbah* means. Your quest brings you to that other story in the book of Genesis, the only other time the term appears. And there you are, sitting at your desk, with one copy of the *Chumash* open to the book of Numbers, and the other open to Genesis. You're looking at the word *dibbah* in both these contexts, and suddenly you realize that's not the only connection between the two stories. There's more.

You look back, for example, at the moment the scouts return from the land of Canaan, and issue their report to Moses, Aaron, and the whole community of Israel:

וַיָּשִׁיבוּ אֹתָם דָּבָר And they brought back word to them. Numbers 13:26

But that phrase, וַיָּשִׁיבוּ אֹתָם דָּבָר, is also rare. Your eyes glance over at the other copy of the *Chumash*, the one open to that other story in Genesis that talked about *dibbah* — and wouldn't you know it? That same phrase about "bringing back word" appears there, too. On a lark, you pull a concordance off your shelf to check — and lo and behold, you find that these are the only two times that phrase appears in the entire Five Books of Moses.

And as you do a little more digging around, you discover that the resonances between the texts don't stop with the two you've just discovered. There's even more.

Consider the following turn of phrase:

שְׁלַח־לְךָ אֲנָשִׁים Send for yourself men. Numbers 13:2

That was the phrase God, our Heavenly Father, used when He instructed Moses to send the spies on their mission to check out Canaan. But it turns out there's actually *another* biblical story in which a father sends a child on a mission to go check something out. And in that other story, the father uses almost exactly the same expression. In the story of the spies, God said "שְׁלַח־לְךָ"; in the other story, the father told the child:, "לְכָה וְאֶשְׁלָחֲךָ, Come, and I will send you." You glance over at your copy of Genesis, open already to that other story. And there it is: That phrase לְכָה וְאֶשְׁלָחֲךָ is staring back at you, right next to דבה and "bringing back word."

You then notice a fourth echo. It turns out that, in rabbinic literature, this entire saga of the spies here in the book of Numbers gets known as the story of the מְרַגְּלִים, *meraglim*. That's the Hebrew word for "spies" that the Sages of the Talmud adopt. But the Rabbis didn't come up with that word out of thin air. Because although *meraglim* is a very rare word in the Bible, it *does* appear in the Five Books of Moses. It appears a grand total of once. Where is its lone occurrence? In that same, other story back in Genesis. That same other story that includes דִּבָּה, that same other story that includes a version of וַיָּשִׁיבוּ אֹתָם דָּבָר, that same other story that includes a version of שְׁלַח־לְךָ. That *same other story* also speaks of spies, and it calls them *meraglim*.

So…what is that other story?

Joseph and His Family

I'm glad you asked. It's the story of Joseph and his brothers.

Of course, on the face of it, the stories seem very different. In one case, a child is victimized by sibling rivalry and sold as a slave to Egypt. In another, a generation seems to lose confidence in their ability to prevail against their enemies and they begin to rebel against God. But still, the textual echoes between the two stories seem unmistakable. Let's see how the parallels play out.

The eerie foreshadow of the spies begins right at the start of the Joseph story. The first thing we hear about Joseph is:

Genesis 37:2	Joseph brought ***dibbah*** [disparaging reports] about his brothers to their father.	וַיָּבֵא יוֹסֵף אֶת־דִּבָּתָם רָעָה אֶל־אֲבִיהֶם׃

That, you'll remember, is the very same phrase that the text uses later to characterize the way the spies disparaged the land. But now, keep reading the Joseph story. The tensions between Joseph and his brothers rise and, eventually, after Joseph keeps on having these dreams that seem to portend his ruling over the family—their father chooses to send Joseph on a mission. He tells him:

לְכָה וְאֶשְׁלָחֲךָ אֲלֵיהֶם "Come, and **I will send you** to them." Genesis 37:13

Sounds a lot like what God will ultimately say to Moses centuries later, when *he* sends men on a mission:

שְׁלַח-לְךָ אֲנָשִׁים "**Send for yourself** men." Numbers 13:2

So we go back and continue reading the story of Joseph. We learn that Jacob asks Joseph to go check on his brothers and report back to him:

וַהֲשִׁבֵנִי דָּבָר "**And bring back word to me**." Genesis 37:14

Well, that's the third echo we talked about above. The spies, too, come back with a report:

וַיָּשִׁיבוּ אֹתָם דָּבָר **And they brought back word** to them. Numbers 13:26

Then, long after Joseph is cast into a pit, Joseph's brothers come to Egypt. They are desperately seeking grain in order to survive during a famine, and that's when they encounter Joseph. But by now, Joseph has become the grand vizier of Egypt, and when they stand before their brother, they don't recognize him. Joseph, on the other hand, recognizes *them* — and he responds to their request for grain with an angry accusation:

מְרַגְּלִים אַתֶּם "You are **spies**!" Genesis 42:9

"You are *meraglim*," Joseph says. *Spies*. That word Joseph uses to characterize his brothers is the very same word the Sages ultimately use to characterize the scouts sent by Moses here in **Parshat Shelach**. Welcome to our fourth echo.[5]

THE JOSEPH STORY	THE STORY OF THE SPIES
Bad Reports	
וַיָּבֵא יוֹסֵף אֶת־דִּבָּתָם רָעָה אֶל־אֲבִיהֶם׃ And Joseph brought **disparaging reports** of them [his brothers] to their father. (Gen. 37:2)	וַיֹּצִיאוּ דִּבַּת הָאָרֶץ אֲשֶׁר תָּרוּ אֹתָהּ And they brought a **disparaging report** of the land that they had scouted. (Num. 13:32)
Bring Back Word	
וַיֹּאמֶר לוֹ, לֶךְ־נָא רְאֵה... וַהֲשִׁבֵנִי דָּבָר And he said to him, "Go, please, and check on ... **and bring back word to me**." (Gen. 37:14)	וַיָּשִׁיבוּ אֹתָם דָּבָר וְאֶת־כָּל־הָעֵדָה **And they brought back word to them**, and the whole community. (Num. 13:26)
Send for Yourself	
לְכָה וְאֶשְׁלָחֲךָ אֲלֵיהֶם "Come, and **I will send you** to them." (Gen. 37:13)	שְׁלַח־לְךָ אֲנָשִׁים וְיָתֻרוּ אֶת־אֶרֶץ כְּנַעַן "**Send for yourself** men to scout the land of Canaan." (Num. 13:2)

5 See, for instance, Malbim on Genesis 42:9, who picks up on this parallel and compares and contrasts the two types of spies.

Meraglim	
וַיֹּאמֶר אֲלֵהֶם, **מְרַגְּלִים** אַתֶּם לִרְאוֹת אֶת־עֶרְוַת הָאָרֶץ בָּאתֶם: And [Joseph] said to them, "You are **spies**! You have come to see the land in its nakedness." (Gen. 42:9)	The Sages of the Talmud speak of the spies as *meraglim*.

The resonances don't seem like isolated coincidences.[6] But what should we make of them? What are they trying to teach us?

Spying in the Family

In general, when the Torah offers an extensive series of parallels between stories, what it is really saying to us, I think, is that each story is meant to shed light on the other. How? Well, the parallels themselves are clues. They don't just *establish* connections; they help us understand what those connections *mean*. It is as if the text is saying: *Here, dear reader, are a whole bunch of data points that will help you understand how one story relates to the other.*

In the pages that follow, we are going to go through some of those data points together and try to discern what they are telling us. As we do that, a new picture of each story will begin to emerge: first of the Joseph story, then of the story of the spies. And, as our view of each story gets somewhat reshaped, we may well find that some of the nagging difficulties in each story will begin to melt away and new understandings of these two stories will emerge.

So let's get started. We will revisit our first parallel and see where that takes us.

---

6 For the reader who is less than fully persuaded that these parallels are intentional and not the product of mere happenstance, I would invite them to consider whether still other parallels exist between the two stories which reinforce the general sense that we are looking at parallel narratives here. As for me, I have included a list of a good many other parallels that I've found as an addendum to this essay; see below.

Dibbah

Dibbah: It is the word that describes the disparaging reports that the spies bring back about the land — and it's also the word that describes the reports Joseph would bring back about his brothers to his father:

Genesis 37:2

וַיָּבֵא יוֹסֵף אֶת־דִּבָּתָם רָעָה אֶל־אֲבִיהֶם׃	Joseph brought *dibbah* [disparaging reports] of them [his brothers] to their father.

So let's ponder that and, as we do, we can play a little game I like to call "Cast of Characters." When two biblical stories seem to be connected, we can ask: Who, exactly, in story A is the counterpart of whom in story B? In our case, we can ask: If, in Genesis, Joseph is bringing back *dibbah* to his father, who is his parallel in the book of Numbers?

Well, who brings back *dibbah* there? The answer is: The spies do.

It seems that Joseph was acting as … a spy.

That might not seem like much of a revelation, but it is. It sheds new light on Joseph's actions, early on in the story. Because imagine that you're unaware of these parallels with the story of the spies, and you just open up chapter 37 back in the book of Genesis and start reading . You might have just said to yourself: *So here's Joseph; he brings those bad reports back about his brothers to Dad. I guess he was just saying something not so nice about them.* Not a huge deal, right? But now, the picture seems a little darker. The text seems to position Joseph as doing something more deliberate; he was actually "spying" on his own brothers. And that is troubling. Because spying connotes probing and reporting back on the weaknesses of an enemy. Is the text implying, then, that Joseph was treating his brothers as if they were an enemy?

A Mission…to Spy?

As if that weren't surprising enough, our little game of Cast of Characters has more surprises in store for us. For a bit later in the Joseph story, as tensions rise between his children, Jacob chooses to send Joseph on a mission to check on his brothers:

לְכָה וְאֶשְׁלָחֲךָ אֲלֵיהֶם... וַהֲשִׁבֵנִי דָּבָר	"Come, and **I will send you** to them... **and return word to me.**"	Genesis 37:13–14

But those words spoken by Jacob reappear in the story of the spies: Moses, acting at God's behest, sends the spies with these words:

שְׁלַח־לְךָ אֲנָשִׁים וְיָתֻרוּ אֶת־אֶרֶץ כְּנַעַן	"**Send for yourself** men to scout the land of Canaan."	Numbers 13:2

And when the spies come back with their reports, we have this:

וַיָּשִׁיבוּ אֹתָם דָּבָר וְאֶת־כָּל־הָעֵדָה	**And they returned word to them**, and the whole community.	Numbers 13:26

So let's apply our little Cast of Characters game to Jacob. In Numbers, Father-in-Heaven deliberately chose to send some spies. In Genesis, then, when Jacob, an earthly father, chose to send Joseph to check on his brothers, was he deliberately choosing to send a spy, too?

What a troubling conclusion. At the height of a crisis in the family, with tensions between the brothers at a fever pitch—*was Jacob actually sending Joseph to spy on his brothers?* Why in the world would he do that? How could that possibly have seemed like a good idea?

It seems so strange.

Part II: Joseph's Mission

There is, perhaps, a way of making sense of these startling conclusions, and it comes to us via Rabbi Samson Raphael Hirsch, the great nineteenth-century biblical commentator. Let me introduce to you a view of Jacob's actions that Hirsch would like us to consider.[7]

The casual reader of the Joseph story might well adopt a view of Jacob, Joseph's father, as somewhat benighted. One might see him, perhaps, as a bit out of touch, maybe a little naive, when he sent Joseph on that mission to his brothers. One supposes, maybe, that Jacob didn't quite seem to realize that the tensions between Joseph and his brothers were already at a crisis point. But the text seems to suggest otherwise — that father was well aware of the jealousy in the family when he sent Joseph on that mission. In the words of the verse:

Genesis 37:11	וַיְקַנְאוּ־בוֹ אֶחָיו, וְאָבִיו שָׁמַר אֶת־הַדָּבָר:	The brothers were jealous of him, and his father kept the matter in mind.

While the language is somewhat ambiguous, it does seem to suggest that Jacob was aware of the jealousy and was trying to keep a lid on the situation. All of which intensifies the question we asked earlier: If the brothers were resentful of Joseph's *dibbah*, why in the world would Jacob, at this delicate moment, proactively send Joseph on a mission to do the very thing the brothers were so angry about? Why send him to spy yet again?

The answer, maybe, is that there's a way to spy within the family that's problematic, and there's a way that's healing and wonderful. Hirsch suggests that Jacob was aiming for the latter when he sent Joseph on his mission. And in doing so, Jacob was choosing a sophisticated, if risky, course of action. Rather than opposing Joseph's problematic actions outright, Jacob was trying to take what Joseph was doing and redirect it. It is as if Jacob was saying to his son:

---

7 Rabbi Samson Raphael Hirsch on Genesis 37:13.

Look, this thing you've been doing with your brothers — spying, observing them carefully, being curious about their actions, bringing back reports about them — that in itself isn't problematic. What's problematic is *how* you've been doing it. Don't look at your brothers as if they were a foe, as if there was some weakness in them that could be exploited, if you could only uncover it. Instead, spy — use your powers of observation and your curiosity — in a way that seeks to heal and make things better. Use these qualities in a way that actually promotes peace and welfare within the family.

Once we open our minds to such a possibility, we might be in a position to understand a quirk of language that shows up in Jacob's instructions to Joseph when he asks him to check in on his brothers. Jacob tells Joseph:

לֶךְ־נָא רְאֵה אֶת־**שְׁלוֹם** אַחֶיךָ וְאֶת־**שְׁלוֹם** הַצֹּאן	"Go, please, and check on the **peace** of your brothers and the **peace** of the sheep."	Genesis 37:14

We are no strangers to the word *shalom* in the story. For right before this, we heard that tensions between Joseph and the brothers were so bad that:

וְלֹא יָכְלוּ דַּבְּרוֹ **לְשָׁלֹם**׃	And [the brothers] couldn't [even] speak in **peace** with [Joseph].	Genesis 37:4

Maybe Jacob's singling out of *shalom* twice in his instructions to Joseph, wasn't coincidental. Indeed, maybe it is precisely the missing and elusive "peace" between Joseph and his brothers that Jacob sends Joseph to seek out. And that's really Rabbi Hirsch's point. Rabbi Hirsch argues that Jacob dispatched Joseph on a challenging, peacemaking mission: Could Joseph take the brothers he spoke רַע (*ra*), badly about and transcend that, seeking their peace instead? "Go and check on them," Jacob was saying, "and use your powers of observation to promote harmony among you and your siblings rather than anger and division."

How? By inquiring after their welfare. You know, when we first greet people, we find that it is polite to ask them how they are. Such a question is usually a formality. But it doesn't have to be. Indeed, the reason it is polite to ask others how they are doing is probably a relic of the fact that, in some way, such a question *can* be among the deepest gifts we give another person. For one can ask this question in a way that is intimate, that suggests a desire to really connect with someone. Just that question, "How are you?" — coupled with a willingness to hear a real, unfiltered response and to accept that response without judgment — that *itself* is a way of promoting peace.

And it is here that we come to the difference between Joseph's prior acts of spying — where he brought *dibbah* that was *ra*, bad, back to his father — and this new mission to go look in on his brothers and seek their "peace." I don't think it is coincidental that the Hebrew root שלם (*shin-lamed-mem*) doesn't *only* mean peace and welfare; it can also mean wholeness — *shalem*. Seeking someone's wholeness is worlds apart from bringing back bad reports about them. It is even worlds apart from bringing back *good* reports about them. Good and bad are judgmental words. Evaluating if something is good or bad often entails breaking that which you are looking at into parts and then passing judgments on one or more of those parts, isolating it from the rest of what you see. That's what you do if you want to exploit a weakness in a foe. But then there's the kind of "spying" — the kind of looking in on someone — that you do for those you love or care about. And that is all about seeing the other as a whole, and becoming attuned to how that "whole" is doing, and how, perhaps, you could help it flourish even more.[8]

Perhaps the directive to go seek the *shalom* of your brothers was a directive to stop finding aspects of your brothers that are bad, and instead to accept the whole of who they are, as you seek to offer them your care.

It's an idealistic mission. It's a tall order and it goes horribly wrong. Joseph's responds to his father's request that he go meet his brothers and seek their peace with a simple, solitary, word:

---

8 Indeed, when you seek out someone's wholeness, it doesn't mean you *ignore* the bad parts of what you see. It means you see those unsavory parts of the other as part of an indivisible whole -- and that changes everything. The truth of each of us is that we are a whole human being, and we can't really be broken down into parts that we can label good and bad.

הִנֵּנִי׃ "Here I am!"

Genesis 37:13

The term connotes readiness. I am ready to do what you ask.

So far so good. It seems that Joseph is on board with the peacemaking mission. All that needs to happen now is for Joseph to get to the brothers and sincerely approach them in fraternal companionship. Hopefully, the brothers will then get their first, refreshing, look at the "new" Joseph, and soon enough, everything should be coming up roses. Familial bliss will once again return to the family of Jacob.

But that's not what happens. Instead, when the brothers see him coming, they plot to kill him. So what went wrong?

The tragedy of the situation, I would submit, comes to us in three poignant words.

וַיִּרְאוּ אֹתוֹ מֵרָחֹק, וּבְטֶרֶם יִקְרַב אֲלֵיהֶם, וַיִּתְנַכְּלוּ אֹתוֹ לַהֲמִיתוֹ׃ וַיֹּאמְרוּ אִישׁ אֶל־אָחִיו, הִנֵּה בַּעַל הַחֲלֹמוֹת הַלָּזֶה בָּא׃

And they saw him from afar; and before [Joseph] drew near to them, they [had begun to] plot to kill him. And they said, one man to his brother, "Here comes that dreamer!"

Genesis 37:18–19

The brothers never gave him a chance. They saw him coming from afar, and when they did, they immediately jumped to a conclusion about who he was, and what he was after. *He was the dreamer.* He was probably coming to fulfill those dreams, the ones that had them bowing to him.

They came to their conclusion when Joseph was still at a distance from them, before Joseph even drew near them, before he even had a chance to say a word to them. In a certain kind of way, the brothers *too* were spying—because what, after all, does one call it when you view something from afar and draw conclusions about it? That's intelligence gathering. Except the brothers were in this case doing an exceptionally poor job of it. They committed what, for a spy, is a cardinal sin. They allowed their preconceived beliefs to drive them into making a snap judgment about what they saw. They didn't take the time to *really* look.

The brothers only saw Joseph from afar. What if they had allowed him to draw close before coming to conclusions? The reader is left to wonder:

What would they have seen then? They might have seen the whole of Joseph, in all his complexity, instead of a little slice of him easily identified as good or bad. Sure, he would have still been the one with the dreams. But if they had been good observers of data, they would have noticed that there was something different about Joseph this time. Here was a brother who seemed to genuinely be seeking their welfare. He didn't seem to have the attitude that so irked them in the past. He didn't seem to want to lord himself over them. The reader wonders: Would the story have ended differently if they had allowed themselves to see that?

Joseph's Accusation

It's not for nothing, then, that, many years later, when Joseph finally encounters his brothers again — when he recognizes *them* but they do not recognize *him* — that he accuses them, of all things, of being spies. We noted before that this choice of accusation seemed random, almost inexplicable. These very brothers kidnapped him and sold him off as a slave. Joseph couldn't come up with anything better than spying to accuse them of?

Except, maybe that's how Joseph sees it. In his eyes, they really *were* spies. The last time he encountered them, they were doing exactly what spies do: watching his behavior and drawing conclusions about him. Only they were flawed versions of spies, just as Joseph himself had once been a flawed spy. They saw only what they let themselves see. They allowed preconceived notions to irreparably prejudice their perceptions of him.

Looking back, then, on the events leading up to Joseph's sale, one detects a catastrophic series of failures, all of which revolve around a version of the same thing. First, Joseph spies on his brothers. His father seemingly recognizes this as a problem and seeks to rectify it. But that mission fails. Why? Because when the brothers catch sight of Joseph approaching from afar, *they* become the ones to assume the role of spies. It's almost as if spying within the family is a kind of primal scourge that haunts Jacob's family.

And the effect of that scourge? It is momentous. It catalyzes the first great exile of the incipient nation of Israel. For when the brothers see Joseph approach and tell each other "here comes that dreamer," it is then that they cast him into a pit, and shortly after that, Joseph is sold as a slave and loaded onto a caravan bound for Egypt. He becomes the first Hebrew slave in Egypt, and he won't be the last. Soon, the entirety of Jacob's family will be engulfed in the tragedy that becomes Egyptian slavery.

Getting Back to That Elephant in the Room

All of this, I think, puts us in a position to reassess the story of the spies in the book of Numbers. In particular, it may help us answer that basic question that almost every reader of the story finds themselves wondering about — that elephant-in-the-room question we began this essay with, namely: *Why did God choose to have Israel send the spies at all?*

The answer might have something to do with the historical arc of tragedy that we've just charted. This issue of spying in the family of Israel, spying gone wrong, never really got fixed. It became the pernicious flaw that ultimately led to our departure from Canaan and exile into Egypt. And if that's the case... well, wouldn't it stand to reason that when Israel finally exits Egypt to make her way back to the land of Canaan, that somehow, she would need to deal with this issue of spying in the family? We, as a nation, would need to come to some resolution of this issue that had plagued us so and led to our exile in the first place.

And so perhaps God ordained that Israel would have one more chance to redeem her difficult past. Which may explain one of the crucial parallels we saw between the story of Joseph and the story of the spies:

SEND FOR YOURSELF	
לְכָה **וְאֶשְׁלָחֲךָ** אֲלֵיהֶם	**שְׁלַח־לְךָ** אֲנָשִׁים וְיָתֻרוּ אֶת־אֶרֶץ כְּנָעַן
"Come, and **I will send you** to them." (Gen. 37:13)	"**Send for yourself** men to scout the land of Canaan." (Num. 13:2)

In these texts, God's language mirrors Jacob's directive to send Joseph to his brothers. In each story, perhaps, a father is sending a child to spy — for redemptive purposes. They are trying to create a chance for children to right a terrible wrong. To learn how to use their powers of observation and curiosity in ways that heal rather than in ways that harm.

What I'm suggesting here is that the mission Jacob sent Joseph on may well match up with the mission God sent the spies on. Just as Jacob was apparently trying to redeem a previous, ruinous act of spying gone wrong, maybe the divine motive for sending spies was something similar: to redeem previous acts of spying gone wrong. Which acts are we talking about? Why, the unresolved spying in the Joseph story, of course! That, after all, is how we got to Egypt in the first place!

When a Question Is Its Own Answer

Now, at this point, I can imagine you perhaps scratching your head and thinking that something doesn't quite add up. You might say to yourself:

Look, I grant you that the Torah seems to compare, on some level, Jacob's action in sending Joseph to spy on the brothers with God's action in sending the spies to scout the Promised Land. But, at some point, the analogy seems to break down. Because how could God's directive to Israel to send spies to scout the land possibly redeem the sins of spying in the family that led to our exile in Egypt? The scouts in Numbers were spying on *land*; they weren't spying on *family*!

That's a really good question. But maybe the question is itself the answer. Yes, of *course* the scouts were spying on land. But who says the Promised Land isn't a kind of family?

Is Land a Thing or a Being?

You know, the Torah looks at land a little differently than us moderns do. We tend to look at land as a thing, an object, something you can exploit and live off of. It is a precious resource, to be sure, but in the end, nothing more than a resource. Land is a thing. The Torah, though, doesn't really see land that way. It looks at land as a *being*. We are commanded, for example, not to work the land every seventh year:

Leviticus 25:2 — וְשָׁבְתָה הָאָרֶץ שַׁבָּת לַיקֹוָק׃ — The land shall observe a sabbath of God.

It isn't merely that we humans need to take a rest from working the land. It is that the land *itself* needs to experience rest. The land, at some level, is being treated as if it is capable of experience. It is a being of sorts, even if it is not sentient in the way that you and I think of sentience.

But if land is a being, it isn't any old being; it is a being we have a terribly important relationship with. Consider what land really *is*, and what our relationship to it is. We *come* from the land. God formed the original man, Adam, according to the Torah, from the earth itself. The earth is one of our parents, one of our creators. Indeed, in creating man, God famously declared:

נַעֲשֶׂה אָדָם Let us make man.

Genesis 1:26

The classical commentators all struggle to identify who God was talking to when He said "let us." Was it the angels? Was God talking to Himself, using the "royal We"? Ramban's response, though, is that *God was talking to the land.* God was saying, in effect: *Hey, land — let us, you and Me, make man. I'll contribute the soul, you contribute the body. And we'll get a human being out of our collaboration!* [9]

Throughout human history, this intuition that land is somehow our collective parent has nagged at our collective consciousness. Consider, for example, the tug of nationalism, how people relate to their land, their country, as not just their home but ... the *motherland,* or the *fatherland.* At some level, we really *do* intuit that land is part of the family. A really *important* part of our family. For at some deep level, not only do we come from land, but, like a true parent, land continues to provide for us even after our inception. Land gives you what you need to eat. Land gives you shelter. Land takes care of you in all the ways your parents take care of you.

Mind Your Manners

What, then, was our Heavenly Parent doing when He instructed us to send scouts to spy out the land? Well, God — one of the parents of our nation – was bringing us to meet another long-lost "parent" of ours: our homeland, as it were — the land of Canaan. It is the home we used to be in, before the sale of Joseph sent us careening down into slavery in Egypt. Now, centuries after that terrible debacle, we are poised to go back into that land. But what's the right way to approach that precious land from which we had been estranged for so long? *Are you just going to go into the land as if it were a thing, eat its fruit, and go and exploit it?*

---

9 See Ramban on Genesis 1:26.

No. You're not going to do that. You're going to send an advance party to get to know the land. You're going to do what you do whenever you first meet someone special you haven't seen in a long time. You're going to ask: *How do you do?* You're going to do what Jacob once sent Joseph to do: You're going to inquire about the welfare, the *shalom*, of your family.

It's only right.

The Grapes of Omaha Beach

And it was doubly important to do so, because these family members — the people of Israel on the one hand, and the Promised Land on the other — had had some tensions between them as of late.[10] The people of Israel, at various points on their journey, had pined for Egypt. Indeed, just before the story of the spies, the people had complained that they'd had enough of manna, this wondrous food from heaven; they remember the fleshpots of Egypt — why couldn't they have some of *that* food (see Num. 11:4–6)?[11] This fantastical glorification of Egypt — what did that amount to if not an implicit dissociation from their true homeland? And so, the Almighty wanted this generation to meet her, the land; to see how she was doing, to get a sense of her.

One might object to this theory on grounds that the mission of the spies seemed to have military significance. The scouts were supposed to report on the strength of the cities and the inhabitants of the land. But a closer look at their mission reveals other themes that aren't really consistent with a military reconnaissance mission. For example, the spies are told:

---

10 Just as there were tensions between Joseph and his brothers just before Jacob dispatched Joseph to look in on them, so too were there tensions between Israel and the land just before God asked them to send the scouts.

11 See also, for example, Exodus 16:3:

וַיֹּאמְרוּ אֲלֵהֶם בְּנֵי יִשְׂרָאֵל, מִי יִתֵּן מוּתֵנוּ בְיַד יְקוָה בְּאֶרֶץ מִצְרַיִם, בְּשִׁבְתֵּנוּ עַל סִיר הַבָּשָׂר, בְּאָכְלֵנוּ לֶחֶם לָשֹׂבַע

And the Children of Israel said to them, "Would that we had died at the hand of God in the land of Egypt, while we sat by the meat pot, while we ate our fill of bread!"

וּמָה הָאָרֶץ, הַשְּׁמֵנָה הִוא אִם רָזָה, הֲיֵשׁ בָּהּ עֵץ אִם אַיִן וְהִתְחַזַּקְתֶּם וּלְקַחְתֶּם מִפְּרִי הָאָרֶץ

And [see] what the land is, whether it is fat or lean, whether there are trees therein or not. Strengthen yourselves, and bring from the fruit of the land.

Numbers 13:20

Now, why instruct the scouts to bring back fruit from the land of Canaan, of all things? Imagine it is May 1944, just weeks before D-Day. A force of scouts parachutes onto Omaha Beach, climbs up the cliffs, and enters the hedgerows of the local vineyards. And what do they do there? Why, they gather some grapes to bring back with them to England, just so everyone can see how delicious and sweet they are. That would be madness, right? So why did Moses, presumably relaying instructions from God, include these directives in the spies' mission?

The answer would seem to be: The mission of the spies was not exclusively military in nature. God, our Heavenly Father, wanted the people to reach out to the land, as Jacob once wanted Joseph to reach out to *his* family members. God wanted us to establish family ties with the land, to see the land as something that would care for them, just as they would be pledged to care for her. The first step in doing that would be to go and "meet" the land, observing it carefully — and attuning themselves both to its potential gifts and to its needs. If we were to be caretakers of this sacred family member, we would have to see what Jacob once sent Joseph to see — the *shalom* of the other family member — its *wholeness*, as it were. How is it doing? How does it nurture the inhabitants of the land? Are they strong, or are they weak? Is the land fertile, or parched? There are aspects of a strategic inquiry here, but it is also something more: *What's the totality of the land like?*

The larger point of such a mission is to create connection. Say the spies come back with reports that the land seems parched. *Well, if it needs water, you'd have to make plans to water it. You'd have to take care of it. That's what family does for family.* You have to first see the whole of it, and then you can both appreciate it, and see what you can do to be of assistance. After all, what, in the end, *wouldn't* you do for another precious member of your family? Your parent is parched and thirsty and you won't pour them a drink? In the words of the early "Hovevei Zion, Lovers of Zion" in the nineteenth century: *Kach bonim et ha'aretz;* this is how you build the land! It is a cry that is both loving and tenacious. You are there to serve, to do what you can to take care of the land that you love. You drain the swamps of the Hula Valley, if that's what you have to do. Is it fun to battle the mosquitoes? No. But if the land was neglected, you do what you have to do to make it lush and fertile again. You take care of it.

How Did the Spies Fail?

Maybe the spies were on a peace mission, as it were. Maybe, in the long arc of history, it was a chance to redeem the scourge that brought us down to Egypt in the first place. But if so, that mission went awry. Tragically, as happened when an earthly father, Jacob, sent Joseph to check on the welfare of his brothers, when Father in Heaven later sent His children to check in on a "family member," things went terribly wrong once again.

What, exactly, went wrong? *Dibbah* went wrong — a version of the same thing that went wrong the first time. You'll recall that the Torah first used this word to characterize the disparaging reports Joseph brought back about his brothers and then uses the very same, unusual word to characterize the disparaging reports the spies brought back about the land:

Numbers 13:32

וַיֹּצִיאוּ **דִּבַּת** הָאָרֶץ אֲשֶׁר תָּרוּ אֹתָהּ אֶל־בְּנֵי יִשְׂרָאֵל לֵאמֹר, הָאָרֶץ אֲשֶׁר עָבַרְנוּ בָהּ לָתוּר אֹתָהּ אֶרֶץ אֹכֶלֶת יוֹשְׁבֶיהָ הִוא

And they brought a disparaging report (***dibbah***) of the land that they had scouted to the Children of Israel, saying, "The land through which we have gone to scout, is a land that devours its inhabitants."

Dibbah was the poison, the second time as well as the first.

One might be tempted to translate *dibbah* merely as a bad report: a description, by a spy, of what he or she is looking at, which skews toward the negative, be it disappointing, daunting, or cautionary. But *dibbah* actually seems to be something more nuanced than that. After all, the spies had said a number of disappointing and daunting things about the land — and the Torah did not castigate *those* reports as *dibbah*. For instance:

אֶפֶס כִּי־עַז הָעָם הַיֹּשֵׁב בָּאָרֶץ, וְהֶעָרִים בְּצֻרוֹת גְּדֹלֹת מְאֹד, וְגַם־יְלִדֵי הָעֲנָק רָאִינוּ שָׁם:

"Nevertheless, the people who live in the land are brazen, and the cities are walled and very great, and moreover, we saw the children of giants there."

Numbers 13:28

Those are sobering words, even deflating. They might well scare the people into thinking they can't successfully prevail against the Canaanites. But still, this is not *dibbah*. Apparently, this is OK. After all, Moses asked the spies to report back about both the good and the bad — so he can't blame them for saying some bad or intimidating things. And, in line with this, the Torah doesn't, at this point, accuse the spies of speaking *dibbah*. That comes only a few lines later, when the spies say this:

וַיֹּצִיאוּ דִּבַּת הָאָרֶץ אֲשֶׁר תָּרוּ אֹתָהּ אֶל־בְּנֵי יִשְׂרָאֵל לֵאמֹר, הָאָרֶץ אֲשֶׁר עָבַרְנוּ בָהּ לָתוּר אֹתָהּ **אֶרֶץ אֹכֶלֶת יוֹשְׁבֶיהָ הִוא**

And they brought a disparaging report (*dibbah*) of the land that they had scouted to the Children of Israel, saying, "The land through which we have gone to scout **is a land that devours its inhabitants**."

Numbers 13:32

What was wrong with saying that it is a land that devours its inhabitants? It's not that these are negative words. It is more than that. There is something bitter, even contemptuous, about how these words come together. *Dibbah,* I would suggest, isn't necessarily false. It is, rather, a choice to focus on only a partial truth, and then to render a verdict on something as if this partial truth were the whole. *Dibbah* renders a scornful verdict on an entire thing based upon an exaggerated, narrow perception of a certain, small, aspect of it.

This is a subtle point and it is worth taking a moment to ponder it just a bit.

A Pernicious Indicator

Marital therapist John Gottman has been known to make an audacious claim: That if he watches a couple interact with one another for fifteen minutes, he can make a fairly accurate prediction as to whether they will still be married in another five years.[12] What does he look for in that fifteen-minute conversation? One thing above all others: signs of scorn or contempt.

An attitude of contempt or scorn, Gottman argues, is one of the most corrosive forces that can possibly emerge within a relationship. It doesn't even need to come across overtly. It can be non-verbal, in something as simple as an eye roll.

What is so pernicious about contempt?

Contempt has the effect of breaking someone apart into component pieces, where each is less than the sum of its parts. Your partner: In reality, he or she is a complex human being, with delightful and difficult potentiality all bundled into one. But contempt breaks apart that gift of who they are. It first isolates the flaws in your partner and then, because there is no context for that flaw anymore — this is all who they are to you now — it exaggerates those flaws. Scorn so exaggerates the importance of the flaw it focuses on that it crowds out almost everything else from the field of our perception. Thus, scorn destroys our ability to see others as complex wholes.

A Supercharged Bargain

Let's think about the spies' *dibbah*, their particular accusation about the land, in terms of this model.

It is an intriguing accusation, to say that the land "devours its inhabitants." To some extent, the spies must have been right. Because, to some extent, *all* land devours its inhabitants. We don't like to dwell on it much, but the fact is: We all die. And when we do, our bodies go back to the earth, from where we once came. Is that *bad*? Not really. It's the way the gift of land works. It's a *whole* gift. It comes with a bargain. *You nourish us with your fruits when we are alive, and after we are no longer, our flesh goes back to you and we, in turn, nourish you, the earth.* That's the bargain.

---

12 See A. S. Gurman, J. L. Lebow, and D. K. Snyder, eds., *Clinical Handbook of Couple Therapy* (Guilford, 2022), 129–57.

The Land of Israel contains the same bargain, but in a more concentrated way. For this is not just any old land; it is God's land. On the one hand, the land has an uncommon capacity to nourish its inhabitants. The fortified cities that the spies observe, and the physical stature of its inhabitants are evidence of that power.[13] But, being God's land, it has its unique sensitivities as well. It not only nourishes its inhabitants in a special way, but it is also, perhaps, uniquely attuned to their moral character. The land is likewise uniquely offended by abominable behavior. Indeed, the Torah elsewhere warns Israel to adhere to an upright standard of morality while in the land —

וְלֹא־תָקִיא הָאָרֶץ אֶתְכֶם	so that the land will not vomit you out,	Leviticus 18:28

suggesting that the land simply can't tolerate elevated levels of corruption.

So if that's true, maybe the land, on some level, really *could* devour you. And maybe, like the spies reported, there really were "children of giants" there — people of power and stature. But all this is simply evidence of how the land could and should nourish its inhabitants; it can make them grow strong, indeed.

Somehow, the spies sensed something of this immense, but also foreboding, power of God's land. But instead of communicating the truth of the land as a whole — *here is a land that lives in the shadow of the Divine, and which has the gifts and challenges one might expect would come along with that* — they spoke scornfully about a splintered-out quality of the land. That had the effect of eclipsing everything else, and, in effect, rendering a distorted verdict on the land. *That* was the crime of those words, "a land that devours its inhabitants."

---

13 Indeed, Moses told the spies to "strengthen yourselves" and bring back the fruits (Num. 13:20). It seems like a strange thing to say: How much strength does one have to have to bring back fruits? But one way to interpret the command is that Moses was bidding the spies to *become* strong by taking the fruits; i.e., partake of some of the fruits and taste thereby their unique capacity to enrich your being. These weren't just any fruits. These were the fruits of God's special land.

The Ultimate "Unresolved" Story

The story of the spies really is the ultimate "unresolved" story. Spying within the family seems to have haunted the family of Israel going all the way back to the inception of the original twelve tribes. It seems that Jacob had attempted to redeem that flaw. Centuries later, God even seems to have attempted to redeem it. But alas, it seems like this flaw somehow continues to haunt us.

And when I say "us," I don't just mean "us" in some vague, communal way. I mean "us" in a very direct, personal way, too. Somehow, when we, as individuals, look at members of our own families, when we observe them and draw conclusions about them, when we size them up, we engage in a very tricky dance. On the one hand, we should see the truth about our loved ones in an unvarnished way. But there's a bargain that love asks of us. It asks us to see context. To see those we love as a whole person, not a collection of fragmented parts.

This is a lesson that I, personally, learned the hard way. I remember talking with my wife once during our courtship. After we had been going out for a while, I initiated a conversation with her about our relationship. I was young, naive, and there I was, having this cringe-worthy discussion with her. I seemed to be trying to break apart her personality and analyze her qualities out loud. The whole thing is really quite embarrassing to look back upon, to be perfectly honest. This went on for a few minutes until she mercifully put an end to the conversation. With a little dollop of good humor and a healthy dose of self-confidence, she said to me: "Look, David, you can't really take me apart into little puzzle pieces like that. I'm a whole person."

And she was right. At the time, we moved on to talk about other things; the moment, happily, was over, and that was the end of it. But over the years, I've seen more and more how right she was about this. I think one of the things we *all* want most deeply, in love, is to be taken by another as a whole person. It is a hope we should seek to fulfill for those we love. It's a hope we want others to fulfill for us.

In some mysterious way, we are who we are because of all parts of ourselves, even the ones that seem less savory when viewed in isolation. Not to see this is to misinterpret someone. And, well, to misinterpret someone you meet in the street and never see again is a small tragedy. But to misinterpret your family, those you should love — that's a big tragedy. In love, we need to attune ourselves to the reality that those we are looking upon are unified beings. We don't really get the option of taking only the parts we think we want.

Reconciling ourselves to that truth, I believe, is what turning our back on *dibbah* is all about.

Addendum

Further Connections Between the Story of the Spies and Joseph and His Brothers

ABOVE, WE NOTED SEVERAL connections between the story of the spies and the story of Joseph. On the face of it, the existence of the parallels seemed significant and purposeful; not the kind of stuff that is the product of mere coincidence. And yet, a reasonable person could, perhaps, dispute this claim, and argue that the parallels are mere happenstance. To establish that a real pattern of correspondence exists here, one might wonder whether the pattern continues. That is, as we continue to peruse each story, does the sense of *déjà vu* between them continue? Are there even more parallels between them?

I would suggest that the answer to that question is a resounding "yes." In point after point after point, the echoes just don't stop. To try to demonstrate that for you, I've appended a further listing of those connections, as best as I can discern them, below.

The Rest of the Picture

To begin to see the rest of the parallels, let's pick up where we left off in the story of the spies. Moses sends the spies on their mission. But ask this: Where, exactly, did he send the spies from? And where, exactly, did they go, once they were sent?

Well, the first part of that is easy. We know that Israel was in the wilderness, the *midbar.*

וַיַּעֲלוּ וַיָּתֻרוּ אֶת־הָאָרֶץ מִמִּדְבַּר־צִן עַד־רְחֹב לְבֹא חֲמָת׃	They went up and scouted the land, from the **Wilderness** of Zin to Rechov at Levo-Chamat.	Numbers 13:21

They were traveling from the wilderness, and according to the text, here was their first destination:

וַיָּבֹא עַד־חֶבְרוֹן	And he arrived at **Chevron**.	Numbers 13:22

Now turn back to the Joseph story. Joseph was **sent** by his father to check on his brothers. Let's ask the same question: Where was he sent from, and at what destination did he arrive?

The text tells us:

וַיִּשְׁלָחֵהוּ מֵעֵמֶק חֶבְרוֹן	And he sent him from the valley of **Chevron**.	Genesis 37:14

And where, in the end, did Joseph travel to? Unbeknownst to him, he would be traveling to a pit. A pit located … in the wilderness, of all places:

אֶל־הַבּוֹר הַזֶּה אֲשֶׁר בַּמִּדְבָּר	"[Let's cast him] into this pit that's in the **wilderness**."	Genesis 37:22

Chevron to wilderness. Wilderness to Chevron. A perfect inverse.

A Land That Devours Its Inhabitants

Let's move on. When the spies speak disparagingly about the land, they describe their destination, the land of Canaan, as:

Numbers 13:32	אֶרֶץ אֹכֶלֶת יוֹשְׁבֶיהָ	a land that **devours its inhabitants**

Now think of Joseph and *his* destination on that ill-fated trip that his father sent him on. Does "a land that devours its inhabitants" remind you of anything relevant to where Joseph actually ended up? Here is the text describing what the brothers said to one another as they saw Joseph approaching them:

Genesis 37:20	וְעַתָּה לְכוּ וְנַהַרְגֵהוּ וְנַשְׁלִכֵהוּ בְּאַחַד הַבֹּרוֹת	"And now, come, let us kill him **and cast [his body] into one of these pits**."

Had this plan been carried out, and Joseph had found himself deep in a pit, wouldn't that have amounted to the land devouring one of its inhabitants?

And consider what happened just a little after the spies came back with their report about the land devouring its inhabitants. The report sends the entire congregation into panic and they ended up saying this:

Numbers 14:4	וַיֹּאמְרוּ אִישׁ אֶל־אָחִיו, נִתְּנָה רֹאשׁ וְנָשׁוּבָה מִצְרָיְמָה:	And they said, one man to his brother, "Let's appoint a leader **and return to Egypt**."

Now, turn back to the Joseph story. What happens there, at the corresponding moment? That is, what happens after the brothers cast Joseph into the pit, leaving him to be "devoured" by the earth? They sit down to eat lunch and notice a caravan of Ishmaelites in the distance. And where is it headed?

הוֹלְכִים לְהוֹרִיד מִצְרָיְמָה׃	They were headed **to [take cargo] down to Egypt.**	Genesis 37:25

In both stories, land devouring its inhabitants gets ominously followed by... a potential journey to slavery in Egypt.

Torn Clothes

As if this weren't enough, the connections continue. You see them if you continue reading each story in tandem. First, the spies: Let's pick up from the moment the people come up with this great idea, to have a new leader take us back to Egypt. What happens next? Well, Joshua and Caleb, two spies who opposed the general sentiment of their compatriots, respond with searing grief at the catastrophe unfolding around them:

וִיהוֹשֻׁעַ בִּן־נוּן וְכָלֵב בֶּן־יְפֻנֶּה... **קָרְעוּ בִּגְדֵיהֶם׃**	And Joshua son of Nun and Caleb son of Jephuneh...they **tore their clothes**.	Numbers 14:6

And in the Joseph story? Well, *after* the brothers plotted to have a brother devoured by the earth, *after* the caravan of Ishmaelites showed up heading down to Egypt, *after* all of that, Reuben — one of the brothers who, like Caleb in the story of the spies, also opposed the general sentiment of his compatriots — comes back to the pit, sees that Joseph isn't in it, and...

וַיִּקְרַע אֶת־בְּגָדָיו׃	**And he tore his clothes**.	Genesis 37:29

And finally, here's one last one for you:

In the story of the spies, after Caleb and Joshua tear their clothes, and once the people hear the decree from God that an entire generation will be lost — that this generation will be doomed to wander in the desert for forty years — they mourn:

Numbers 14:39	וַיִּתְאַבְּלוּ הָעָם מְאֹד׃ The people **mourned greatly**.

Notice that the text doesn't *just* say that the people mourned; it emphasizes that they mourned in an extreme fashion. Now ask yourself: Does anybody in the Joseph story mourn in a similarly extreme fashion?

Why yes, they do. For *after* the brothers plot to have somebody devoured in the land, *after* the caravan going down to Egypt, *after* Reuben goes and rips his clothes, Joseph's father, Jacob, finds himself confronted with the bloody coat of his lost son. And when that happens, he reacts by talking about ... extreme mourning:

Genesis 37:35	וַיֹּאמֶר, כִּי־אֵרֵד אֶל־בְּנִי אָבֵל שְׁאֹלָה And he said, "**I will go down to Sheol mourning my son**."

Jacob intuits that no matter how long he lives, he will never be consoled for the loss of his son. In normal circumstances, mourning lessens with time. But not for Jacob. He will mourn forever.

THE JOSEPH STORY	STORY OF THE SPIES
Bad Reports	
וַיָּבֵא יוֹסֵף אֶת־דִּבָּתָם רָעָה אֶל־אֲבִיהֶם׃ And Joseph brought **disparaging reports** of them [the brothers] to their father. (Gen. 37:2)	וַיֹּצִיאוּ דִּבַּת הָאָרֶץ אֲשֶׁר תָּרוּ אֹתָהּ And they brought **a disparaging report** of the land that they had scouted. (Num. 13:32)

<table>
<tr><th colspan="2">Bring Back Word</th></tr>
<tr>
<td>וַיֹּאמֶר לוֹ לֶךְ־נָא רְאֵה אֶת־שְׁלוֹם אַחֶיךָ וְאֶת־שְׁלוֹם הַצֹּאן וַהֲשִׁבֵנִי דָּבָר

And he said to him, “Go, please, and check on … and return word to me.”
(Gen. 37:14)</td>
<td>וַיָּשִׁיבוּ אֹתָם דָּבָר וְאֶת־כָּל־הָעֵדָה

And they returned word to them, and the whole community.
(Num. 13:26)</td>
</tr>
<tr><th colspan="2">Send for Yourself</th></tr>
<tr>
<td>לְכָה וְאֶשְׁלָחֲךָ אֲלֵיהֶם

Come, and I will send you to them.
(Gen 37:13)</td>
<td>שְׁלַח־לְךָ אֲנָשִׁים וְיָתֻרוּ אֶת־אֶרֶץ כְּנַעַן

Send for yourself men to scout the land of Canaan.
(Num. 13:2)</td>
</tr>
<tr><th colspan="2">Meraglim</th></tr>
<tr>
<td>וַיֹּאמֶר אֲלֵהֶם, מְרַגְּלִים אַתֶּם! לִרְאוֹת אֶת־עֶרְוַת הָאָרֶץ בָּאתֶם:

And [Joseph] said to them, “You are spies! You have come to see the land in its nakedness.”
(Gen. 42:9)</td>
<td>The rabbis of the Talmud speak of the spies as מְרַגְּלִים.</td>
</tr>
<tr><th colspan="2">Chevron/Desert</th></tr>
<tr>
<td>וַיִּשְׁלָחֵהוּ מֵעֵמֶק חֶבְרוֹן

And he sent him from the valley of Chevron.
(Gen. 37:14)</td>
<td>וַיַּעֲלוּ וַיָּתֻרוּ אֶת־הָאָרֶץ מִמִּדְבַּר־צִן עַד־רְחֹב לְבֹא חֲמָת:

They went up and scouted the land, from the Wilderness of Zin to Rechov at Levo-Chamat:
(Num. 13:21)</td>
</tr>
</table>

Genesis	Numbers
הַשְׁלִיכוּ אֹתוֹ אֶל־הַבּוֹר הַזֶּה אֲשֶׁר **בַּמִּדְבָּר** "Cast him into this pit that's in the **wilderness**." (Gen. 37:22)	וַיַּעֲלוּ בַנֶּגֶב וַיָּבֹא **עַד־חֶבְרוֹן** They went up into the Negev and he arrived at **Chevron**. (Num. 13:22)
Land That Devours Its Inhabitants	
וְעַתָּה, לְכוּ וְנַהַרְגֵהוּ **וְנַשְׁלִכֵהוּ בְּאַחַד הַבֹּרוֹת** "And now, come, let us kill him **and cast [his body] into one of these pits**." (Gen. 37:20)	אֶרֶץ **אֹכֶלֶת יוֹשְׁבֶיהָ** הִוא It is a land **that devours its inhabitants**. (Num. 13:32)
A Descent into Slavery in Egypt	
וְהִנֵּה אֹרְחַת יִשְׁמְעֵאלִים בָּאָה מִגִּלְעָד, וּגְמַלֵּיהֶם נֹשְׂאִים נְכֹאת וּצְרִי וָלֹט, הוֹלְכִים **לְהוֹרִיד מִצְרָיְמָה**: And behold, a caravan of Ishmaelites was coming from Gilead, their camels bearing gum, balm, and ladanum, headed to take [the cargo] down **to Egypt**. (Gen. 37:25)	וַיֹּאמְרוּ אִישׁ אֶל־אָחִיו, נִתְּנָה רֹאשׁ **וְנָשׁוּבָה מִצְרָיְמָה** And they said, one man to his brother, "Let's appoint a leader and return **to Egypt**." (Num. 14:4)

The Tearing of Clothes	
וַיָּשׁב רְאוּבֵן אֶל־הַבּוֹר וְהִנֵּה אֵין־יוֹסֵף בַּבּוֹר **וַיִּקְרַע אֶת־בְּגָדָיו׃** When Reuben returned to the pit and saw that Joseph was not in the pit, he **tore his clothes**. (Gen. 37:29)	וִיהוֹשֻׁעַ בִּן־נוּן וְכָלֵב בֶּן־יְפֻנֶּה מִן־הַתָּרִים אֶת־הָאָרֶץ **קָרְעוּ בִּגְדֵיהֶם׃** And Joshua son of Nun and Caleb son of Jephuneh, of those who had scouted the land, **tore their clothes**. (Num. 14:6)
Extreme Mourning	
וַיֹּאמֶר, **כִּי־אֵרֵד אֶל־בְּנִי אָבֵל שְׁאֹלָה** And he said, "**I will go down to my grave mourning my son.**" (Gen. 37:35)	**וַיִּתְאַבְּלוּ** הָעָם **מְאֹד׃** The people **mourned greatly**. (Num. 14:39)

The parallels are profuse enough, relentless enough, that it seems we can be pretty confident that we've seen something *real* here, that our imaginations haven't tricked us into seeing something that's not really there. In the essay above, we've sought to interpret some of the implications of these parallels. You, dear reader, are invited to continue that quest on your own to perhaps unearth other secrets that may be buried here.

KORACH

Korach, Aaron, and the Angel of Death

וְהָיָה הָאִישׁ אֲשֶׁר אֶבְחַר
בּוֹ, מַטֵּהוּ יִפְרָח

It will happen that the man whom I shall choose, his rod will flower.

NUMBERS 17:20

Korach, Aaron, and the Angel of Death

PARSHAT KORACH TELLS OF a brazen rebellion launched by Korach against the leaders of the people, Moses and Aaron:

וַיִּקָּהֲלוּ עַל מֹשֶׁה וְעַל אַהֲרֹן, וַיֹּאמְרוּ אֲלֵהֶם, רַב־לָכֶם, כִּי כָל הָעֵדָה כֻּלָּם קְדֹשִׁים וּבְתוֹכָם יְקֹוָה, וּמַדּוּעַ תִּתְנַשְּׂאוּ עַל קְהַל יְקֹוָה:	They assembled against Moses and against Aaron, and said to them, "You have gone too far, since all the congregation, all of them, are holy and God is among them; why then lift yourselves up above the assembly of God?"	Numbers 16:3

In response to the uprising, Moses tells Korach and his band of mutineers that God Himself will settle the dispute between them. And indeed, God does: The earth opens up to swallow the rebels alive. And afterward, something equally dramatic happens. Two hundred and fifty people, a faction of Korach's uprising, had gathered together to offer the incense that typically Aaron the high priest would offer. It was a bid to do away with the office of Aaron and the notion of the high priesthood itself; a bid to actualize Korach's argument that "all the congregation, all of them, are holy," and thus challenge the entire institution of leadership. But that bid is conclusively refuted. A fire comes from before God and consumes them all.

One would have thought that these miracles would have been enough to settle the matter. But they are not. Consider what happens the following day:

Numbers 17:6

וַיִּלֹּנוּ כָּל עֲדַת בְּנֵי יִשְׂרָאֵל מִמָּחֳרָת עַל־מֹשֶׁה וְעַל־אַהֲרֹן, לֵאמֹר, אַתֶּם הֲמִתֶּם אֶת־עַם יְקֹוָק

But on the following day, all the congregation of the Children of Israel murmured against Moses and against Aaron, saying, "You have killed the people of God!"

The people accuse Moses of illegitimately engineering the death of "the people of God." This seems inexplicable. How could they still be skeptical? How could they continue Korach's rebellion by persisting in doubting the legitimacy of Moses and Aaron? One wonders what the people were waiting for. Had I been there at the time, I think I'd have been very impressed with that great earth-swallowing event. If I had had any doubts as to whether Aaron was indeed meant to be the true high priest, I think that first miracle would have gone a long way toward settling the question for me. And if that were not enough, God's flames wiping out the next set of naysayers definitely would have done it for me. But the people do not see it that way.

Were they waiting for some even more incredible, *more* impressive miracle? Maybe a tidal wave in the middle of the desert or something like that? In the end, no such greater miracle materializes. Instead, a *smaller* one does. God tells the princes of the people to take twelve staffs, one for each of their fathers' houses, and every man's name should be written on his rod. Aaron, too, should take a staff for himself, and they are all to be laid before God. And...

Numbers 17:20

וְהָיָה הָאִישׁ אֲשֶׁר אֶבְחַר־בּוֹ, מַטֵּהוּ יִפְרָח

It will happen that the man whom I shall choose, his rod will flower.

So this is the last, final test meant to demonstrate that Aaron is the chosen Kohen to lead the people: a test of staffs. And indeed, the staff of Aaron wins out:

Numbers 17:23

וַיְהִי מִמָּחֳרָת, וַיָּבֹא מֹשֶׁה אֶל־
אֹהֶל הָעֵדוּת, וְהִנֵּה פָּרַח מַטֵּה־
אַהֲרֹן לְבֵית לֵוִי, וַיֹּצֵא פֶרַח
וַיָּצֵץ צִיץ וַיִּגְמֹל שְׁקֵדִים׃

It happened on the next day, that Moses went into the tent of the testimony; and behold, the rod of Aaron for the house of Levi had flowered, and put forth buds, and produced blossoms, and bore ripe almonds.

It is this last, gentle miracle that seems to finally persuade the people that God has, in fact, chosen Aaron.

And one has to wonder why. It is hard to make the case that the flowering of Aaron's staff is a more definitive divine test than the fire that consumed 250 rebels against Aaron's priesthood or the earth opening up to swallow Korach's minions. Why, then, does this "small" miracle carry the day?

The *Terumah* Connection

To understand this, we need to look at some events that immediately precede this miracle with Aaron's staff.

I mentioned earlier that after the earth swallowed up Korach and the fire devoured the 250 bringers of incense, the people were still grumbling. They accused Moses of illegitimately engineering these deaths. Well, let's go back to that moment and look at precisely what happened. The text tells us that the people's unwillingness to conclusively give up on Korach's vision does not sit well with God. The Almighty tells Moses and Aaron the following:

Numbers 17:10

הֵרֹמּוּ מִתּוֹךְ הָעֵדָה הַזֹּאת
וַאֲכַלֶּה אֹתָם כְּרָגַע

Raise yourselves up from among this congregation, and I will destroy them in a moment!

How do Moses and Aaron respond? Tellingly, they don't do what God says.

Numbers 17:10

וַיִּפְּלוּ עַל־פְּנֵיהֶם׃

And [Moses and Aaron] fell on their faces.

Interesting, right? God said, lift yourselves up, and they go and do the exact opposite. They cast themselves down. And if you watch carefully, you'll see this is actually the beginning of a pattern.

Let's continue and we'll see how that's so.

Right after Moses and Aaron fall upon their faces, Moses understands that God's threat has begun to become a reality: A plague has begun to radiate out into the people. Everyone's lives are at risk. And somehow, Moses not only knows that a plague had begun to affect the people, but he also knows exactly how to stop it. He tells his brother Aaron to run and act, that there's not a moment to lose:

Numbers 17:11

וַיֹּאמֶר מֹשֶׁה אֶל־אַהֲרֹן, קַח אֶת הַמַּחְתָּה, וְתֶן־עָלֶיהָ אֵשׁ מֵעַל הַמִּזְבֵּחַ, וְשִׂים קְטֹרֶת, וְהוֹלֵךְ מְהֵרָה אֶל־הָעֵדָה וְכַפֵּר עֲלֵיהֶם כִּי־יָצָא הַקֶּצֶף מִלִּפְנֵי יְקוָה; הֵחֵל הַנָּגֶף׃

Moses said to Aaron, "Take your fire pan, and put fire from off the altar in it, and lay incense on it, and carry it quickly to the congregation, and make atonement for them. For wrath has gone out from God; the plague has begun."

As the plague rolls through the congregation, killing everyone in its path, Aaron takes the incense with him out into the people, as Moses instructed. He finds the edge of the advancing, concentric circle of death that the plague has created — and stands there, quite literally perched between the living and the dead. Somehow, miraculously, this is precisely what is called for. The plague stops. So Moses and Aaron throwing themselves down on their faces instead of rising up as per God's instructions is just the first taste of what's to come. This little act of "disobedience" becomes emblematic of Moses' and Aaron's entire approach to how they are going to deal with both God and Israel in this moment of profound crisis. God had started a plague and had asked Moses and Aaron to remove themselves from the people so that divine destruction could ensue, unimpeded by their presence among the people. But they weren't going to go along with that. They weren't going to stand by and allow the destruction to come. They were going to oppose it.

Aaron and the Angel of Death

At this point, it seems reasonable to wonder: If the omnipotent Master of the Universe was intent on carrying out His threat, what hope could mere mortals have in frustrating those designs?[1] And it is seemingly with this question in mind that the Sages offer us a mysterious tale.

They tell us a story about the precise moment that Aaron stood between the living and the dead and stopped the plague. At that moment, the Sages tell us, Aaron met an angelic being; none other than ... the Angel of Death:

אחז את המלאך והעמידו על כרחו. אמר לו, "הנח לי לעשות שליחותי." אמר לו "משה צוני לעכב על ידך." אמר לו, "אני שלוחו של מקום, ואתה שלוחו של משה." אמר לו, "אין משה אומר כלום מלבו, אלא מפי הגבורה. ואם אין אתה מאמין, הרי הקב"ה ומשה אל פתח אהל מועד; בא עמי ושאל." וזהו שנאמר, "וישב אהרן אל משה" (במדבר יז:טו).

He (Aaron) seized the Angel of Death and stopped him by force. The angel said to him, "Let me be so that I can carry out my mission!" He (Aaron) answered him, "Moses directed me to prevent you." To this, the angel replied, "[Your directive from Moses is irrelevant. After all,] I am the messenger of the Omnipresent God, while you are but the messenger of [a mortal human being,] Moses!" To this, Aaron retorted, "Moses does not say anything on his own, but only at the instruction of the Almighty. And if you do not believe me — look, the Holy One, blessed be He, and Moses are [both] at the entrance of the Tent of Meeting. I invite you to come with me, and you can ask them [both]!" [And that's what happened. Aaron and the Angel of Death both came back to Moses.] And this is the meaning of what is stated, "And Aaron returned to Moses" (Numbers 17:15) [i.e., he returned together with the Angel of Death, and only then, did the plague stop].

Rashi on Numbers 17:13, paraphrasing Midrash Tanchuma, Tetzaveh 15

1 One discerns here echoes of the Golden Calf story, where God also threatened to destroy the people, and Moses interceded. We'll speak more about the resonance of this story with the Golden Calf below.

What underlies the Midrash, I think, is the Sages' understanding that Aaron — and Moses, for that matter — noticed something significant about God's command. They noticed an implication lurking within it.

Here, once again, is what God told Moses and Aaron, just before the onset of the plague:

Numbers 17:10

הֵרֹמּוּ מִתּוֹךְ הָעֵדָה הַזֹּאת וַאֲכַלֶּה אֹתָם כְּרָגַע

"Raise yourselves up from among this congregation, and I will destroy them in a moment!"

That command, to raise yourself up, seems odd. Is God incapable of destroying the people unless Moses and Aaron walk a few steps away? Couldn't the Almighty have designed a little force field around Moses and Aaron to protect them while He did away with everyone else? What's the significance of telling Moses and Aaron to "raise themselves up."

I'd like to suggest that the command is important not so much for what it says but for what it implies. If the Almighty tells you to "*Lift yourselves up* and I will destroy them!" — that opens up in your mind an intriguing possibility: *What if I don't lift myself up?* What happens then?

A Precedent

There was a precedent for such a surreptitious implication in God's words. It happened another time in which God had considered destroying the Jewish People. Indeed, there God also used that very same, fearsome verb to convey the threat of destruction — the Hebrew root verb *kaf-lamed-heh*. I'm thinking of the story of the Golden Calf.

Back then, the people had been dancing around an idol of their own making, while Moses had been on top of a mountain, communing with God. And God had said this to him:

Exodus 32:7–10

לֶךְ־רֵד, כִּי שִׁחֵת עַמְּךָ אֲשֶׁר הֶעֱלֵיתָ מֵאֶרֶץ מִצְרָיִם:... וְעַתָּה, הַנִּיחָה לִּי וְיִחַר־אַפִּי

Go down now, because your people, that you brought up out of Egypt, they have corrupted themselves.... And now, let

בָּהֶם וַאֲכַלֵּם, וְאֶעֱשֶׂה אוֹתְךָ לְגוֹי גָּדוֹל:	Me be, and My anger will burn against them and I will destroy them, and I will make you into a great nation.

As Rashi points out there, Moses understood that God had created an implicit opening with His words. "Let Me be … and I will destroy them" creates the question: *What if I don't leave You alone?* It sounds like if I don't leave You alone, maybe You won't destroy them. So that's precisely what happens. Moses chooses *not* to leave God alone; *not* to descend the mountain as God had told him to do.[2] Instead, Moses stays at the top of the mountain, *with* God — mustering any possible argument that might forestall God's threatened action.

Something like that seems to be going on here, in **Parshat Korach**, as well. If God says: Lift yourselves up and I will destroy them — there is an implication here. *You don't have to go along with Me,* God is saying. More: God is *inviting* Moses and Aaron *not* to go along with him.

So Moses and Aaron *do* listen to God. But they listen not just to His overt message but to His covert message, too.

The Angel of Death Doesn't Have a Monopoly on Truth

I'd like to suggest that this distinction between overt and covert messages helps explain the meaning of the cryptic story the Sages tell us about Aaron and his debate with the Angel of Death. I wonder if covert messages from God are actually something that only we humans — and not angels — have the capacity to discern. These subtleties of divine communication; what God is saying by *not* saying something — this kind of thing gets lost on an angel.

Why? Because an angel, when it comes right down to it, is just a messenger.[3] A messenger translates divine words into action, in as straightforward a way as possible. Once God declares an intent to destroy the people

2 Cf. Ramban there.

3 In fact, the word for "angel" in Hebrew — *malach* — literally just means "messenger."

in the aftermath of Korach's rebellion — well, if you're the Angel of Death, the case is closed: It's your job to take that intent and make something of it.

But the Angel of Death doesn't have a monopoly on truth. It takes a human being — a person, with his or her own sense of self, creativity, free will; his or her own sense of pluck — to actually hear something else in God's words, and take action on that basis. That action may be risky, but it is also heroic. Moses and Aaron took that action, betting — correctly, as it turns out — that they had put their finger on a deeper, more subtle layer of divine intent.

What Is Leadership Made Of?

I would like to go a bit further, and suggest that this quality of Moses and Aaron — this willingness to challenge God, or at least, to listen for the covert undertones of divine compassion, even in moments of deepest crisis — was, more than anything else, what made them fit to be the true leaders of the people.

Consider Moses, for example. If I asked you: Why did God choose Moses, of all people, to lead the Israelites out of Egypt? You might protest that you could not possibly know the answer to that question. It is given nowhere, explicitly, in the text of the Torah. But it *is* given implicitly. I speculated about this in the Exodus volume of these *Parsha Companions*,[4] and I'd like to remind you of that argument here. It had to do with the selection of stories the Torah chooses to relate to us about Moses, in the leadup to the story of the Burning Bush. He sees an enslaved Israelite being beaten by an Egyptian overseer, and he intercedes. Next, he witnesses another altercation — this time, between two Israelites. Again, he intercedes to save the victim. And finally, he does it again: He stands with Yitro's daughters against a gang of shepherds harassing them.

What is the common denominator in all these episodes? *Moses consistently puts himself at risk to save others who are in danger.* Factor out everything else, and it is this that remains. It doesn't matter who the potential victim is, Israelite or gentile. It doesn't matter who the aggressor is, Israelite or a gentile. He always intercedes to save those in peril, no matter how powerful the aggressor. He never remains a mere bystander.

---

4 See *Exodus: A Parsha Companion*, **Parshat Ki Tisa**, "Moses' Benevolent Chutzpah."

And then, immediately after we hear about all these stories, we hear that God appears to Moses at the Burning Bush and selects him, against his own vigorous objections, to lead Israel out of slavery. I would submit that the juxtaposition here is not a coincidence. In telling us these stories first, the Torah isn't just entertaining us. It is telling us why he was chosen: Moses is willing to go against any aggressor, no matter how powerful, to save someone in danger.

A Refusal to Stand By

Why would *that* particular quality be so important for Israel's leader to possess? The answer might have something to do with the Golden Calf. I would argue that perhaps this is the moment Moses was chosen for. It is the moment in which Israel's continued existence is called into question, when the nation faces the justified anger of the most powerful being of all: the Master of the Universe.

As he did in all those previous episodes, Moses refused to remain a bystander. He took God's command to stand aside and heard in it ... something else: *The possibility that he could disobey the command, and destruction might not come.*

Indeed, the root of all those prior experiences of Moses — standing, with compassion, against those who are threatened — took place, arguably, when Moses was just an infant. Pharaoh's daughter stood against her own father, when she saved Moses at the shore of the Nile. Perhaps Moses drew on that experience to arrive at what seemed to him a self-evident truth: Compassion was not just a quirk of his own personality, but a deep reflection of his Maker. *Even when you couldn't see it, God was compassionate, too.* He *had* to be.

Ultimately, that perception of God is vindicated when, a bit later in the story of the Golden Calf's aftermath, Moses seeks to understand God's innermost nature. And God reveals to Moses that, despite His great overt anger toward the people, still, the deepest essence of the Divine ... remained love and compassion, not hate or vengeance:

וַיַּעֲבֹר יְקֹוָק עַל־פָּנָיו, וַיִּקְרָא, יְקֹוָק יְקֹוָק קֵל רַחוּם וְחַנּוּן	God passed before him, and proclaimed, "Hashem, Hashem, a merciful and	Exodus 34:6–7

אֶרֶךְ אַפַּיִם וְרַב־חֶסֶד וֶאֱמֶת: נֹצֵר חֶסֶד לָאֲלָפִים; נֹשֵׂא עָוֹן וָפֶשַׁע וְחַטָּאָה	gracious God, slow to anger, abundant in steadfast kindness, who keeps kindness to the thousandth generation, who forgives iniquity, crime, and sin."

The God who decreed destruction against Israel — *overtly* — is the same God who, *covertly,* chose a Moses who, one day, could be counted on to challenge the Divine and to reveal that there was more to God than anger, even in the darkest of times.

This is the God that Moses knew; the God who, even at the most treacherous and desperate of times, remembered His people and forgave them, choosing not to destroy them. And the same God who gave Moses the opportunity once to save His people at the Golden Calf would ultimately do so again, in the days of Korach.

Aaron's Flowering Staff

This time, Aaron would partner with his brother. I would argue that Aaron's willingness to challenge God along with Moses is what gives *him* the right to lead, too. It is what makes him the rightful high priest.

To see that, let's return to the moment Aaron and Moses both fall on their faces, and Aaron runs out to stop the plague, standing between the living and the dead. I asked you earlier: When the earth opened its gaping maw to devour Korach's followers, when the fire erupted from the Mishkan to devour the 250 rebels who had offered incense — why wasn't all that enough to quell the rebellion? It isn't every day that miracles of this magnitude occur. They would seem to constitute a pretty definitive statement of divine intent. Why wasn't that the end of the Korach story? Why, instead, does a lesser miracle carry the day — the softer, gentler, miracle of the flowering of Aaron's staff? Why is that the thing that quells the rebellion once and for all?

Evidently, the magnitude of the miracle isn't the issue in **Parshat Korach**; it is the particular *quality* of the miracle that makes it special. And what quality is that?

Well, recall that Aaron had stood ... *between the living and the dead* to stop the plague. And in the miracle that immediately ensues, Aaron's staff—just a piece of dead wood, really—it suddenly becomes *alive*. Do you see the pattern? Death and life with the people; death and life with the staff.

God had decreed death upon the entirety of the people. But Aaron wouldn't accept the reality of that decree. The people were as good as dead in God's way of seeing things, and Aaron stood against that vision. Because of Aaron, those whom God decreed were to be given up for dead, would in fact live.

In reality, Aaron had tuned into a covert aspect of divine intent. *The dead didn't have to be dead;—they really could be alive, if someone like Aaron would just stand up for them.* Thus, in the miracle of the flowering staff, all God was doing was symbolically demonstrating this very truth about Aaron: There would be a staff, a piece of dead wood—or more precisely, a piece of wood that in "God's book" is dead—but suddenly, once Aaron's name is written on the staff; once the dead wood becomes associated with Aaron—it is revealed to be very much alive and flourishing.

The same God who had decreed death for them could allow them to live, if Aaron could find the covert implication in God's words that would allow for this truth to manifest. If Aaron would stand up for this understanding, it would become so.

This is what made Aaron and Moses fit to lead. That's what the people recognized when they finally abandoned their rebellion against Aaron and Moses. Yes, Aaron was the rightful high priest. They accepted this not because the power of a divine miracle had intimidated them into standing down. They accepted it because, with their own eyes, they had now seen it to be true. To resist Aaron's leadership, at this point, would simply be silly.

Aaron's willingness to stand with the people, even as they rebelled against him; to discern in the divine will the covert and undying sparks of compassion for the very people who were rebelling against God and who were simultaneously rebelling against *him*—these are the qualities that would be needed to truly be a high priest; to connect God and man, even when the possibility of connection between them would seem all but impossible to maintain.

Terumah and the Aftermath of Korach's Rebellion

And so, perhaps, it is no coincidence that, immediately after the story of Aaron's actions to staunch the plague, the Torah gives us the laws of *terumah* — the various gifts that Aaron and his children, all generations of future priests, are entitled to receive from the people within the embrace of their care:

Bamidbar 18:8

וַיְדַבֵּר יְקוָה אֶל־אַהֲרֹן, וַאֲנִי,
הִנֵּה נָתַתִּי לְךָ אֶת־מִשְׁמֶרֶת
תְּרוּמֹתָי, לְכָל קָדְשֵׁי בְנֵי־
יִשְׂרָאֵל, לְךָ נְתַתִּים לְמָשְׁחָה,
וּלְבָנֶיךָ, לְחָק עוֹלָם:

God spoke to Aaron, "I, behold, I have given you the care of **My *terumah***, from all the holy things of the Children of Israel; to you have I given them by reason of the anointing, and to your sons, as a portion forever."

The name for all of these gifts? Why, of course, they would be called *terumah* — literally a "lifting up."

The man who refused to *lift himself up* from among the people; who placed himself firmly within them, even as they rebelled against his authority to represent them before God — it is only fitting that the people would, in gratitude, gift to him and his children items that *they* would "*lift up*." For indeed, it was Aaron's insistence on being part of the people — even in their darkest moment, even when God had ostensibly told him not to — that gave him the real authority to lead them.

CHUKAT

Water from the Rock

וַיֹּאמֶר יְקֹוָה אֶל־מֹשֶׁה
וְאֶל־אַהֲרֹן, יַעַן לֹא־
הֶאֱמַנְתֶּם בִּי לְהַקְדִּישֵׁנִי
לְעֵינֵי בְּנֵי יִשְׂרָאֵל לָכֵן לֹא
תָבִיאוּ אֶת־הַקָּהָל הַזֶּה
אֶל־הָאָרֶץ אֲשֶׁר־נָתַתִּי
לָהֶם׃

God said to Moses and Aaron, “Because you didn’t trust in Me, to sanctify Me in the eyes of the Children of Israel, therefore you shall not bring this assembly into the land which I have given them.”

NUMBERS 20:12

CHUKAT

Water from the Rock

PARSHAT CHUKAT TELLS THE story of one of the most puzzling events in the entire Torah, an event that contains an almost painful mismatch of crime and response: Moses hits a rock instead of speaking to it, and as a result, he is barred by God from leading the people into the land of Canaan, the obvious culmination of his life's quest.

It seems so strange. Here is Moses, arguably God's favorite person. He takes the people out of Egypt with signs and wonders and splits the Sea of Reeds. He goes up to Mount Sinai, accepts the tablets from God, and teaches Torah to the entire people. And beyond all this, in the aftermath of the Golden Calf, he quite literally puts his life on the line to save the people. Those are (just some of) the good things he's done. And the bad things? *He hit a rock.*

In response to that one bad error, God denies Moses the one thing he seems to want most of all — the chance to lead the people into the land.

It just seems inscrutable. How are we to possibly understand such a punishment? What's the big deal with hitting the rock? And while we're at it: For Moses' part, why didn't he just follow what God said to do? Was he *trying* to be insubordinate by hitting the rock? Can we know anything of Moses' motivation in making the choice that denied him entrance into the land?

In this essay, I'd like to try to understand this very difficult story.[1]

---

1 I will say at the outset that this is no easy task. I intend to treat this issue, actually, in two separate essays in this book — the one you are reading right now, here in **Parshat Chukat**, and another essay later in this book, in **Parshat Pinchas** (where God directs Moses to ascend *Har Ha'Avarim*, the mountain on which he is destined to die). Each of these essays will attack the question I've outlined above from a somewhat different, but (I hope) complementary, angle. This essay will focus more on the larger meaning of the apparently trivial sin of striking, rather than speaking to, the rock that would give its water. The essay in **Parshat Pinchas** will focus on the reader's gnawing suspicion that, even after explaining the larger meaning

Part 1: A Crisis of…Faith?

The episode of Moses hitting the rock takes place forty years after he first led the people of Israel into the desert. The generation of the spies has finally died off, and the nation is poised to enter the Promised Land, the long-delayed culmination of their wanderings in the wilderness. But the people find themselves facing a crisis: There is no water for them to drink. And God instructs Moses and Aaron to solve the problem by speaking to a rock:

Numbers 20:8	קַח אֶת־הַמַּטֶּה וְהַקְהֵל אֶת־הָעֵדָה, אַתָּה וְאַהֲרֹן אָחִיךָ, וְדִבַּרְתֶּם אֶל־הַסֶּלַע לְעֵינֵיהֶם וְנָתַן מֵימָיו.	Take the staff, and assemble the congregation, you and Aaron your brother, and speak to the rock before their eyes, that it will give forth its water.

Moses famously disobeys. He chooses to address the people rather than the rock, accusing them of being rebellious; and then, he strikes the rock that he was supposed to speak to with words:

Numbers 20:11	וַיָּרֶם מֹשֶׁה אֶת־יָדוֹ וַיַּךְ אֶת־הַסֶּלַע בְּמַטֵּהוּ פַּעֲמָיִם, וַיֵּצְאוּ מַיִם רַבִּים	Moses lifted up his hand, and struck the rock with his staff twice, and water came forth abundantly.

In the end, water *does* flow from the rock, and the thirst of the people is sated. But Moses, and for that matter, Aaron too, will bear a heavy price:

Numbers 20:12	וַיֹּאמֶר יְקוָה אֶל־מֹשֶׁה וְאֶל־אַהֲרֹן, יַעַן לֹא־הֶאֱמַנְתֶּם בִּי	God said to Moses and Aaron, "Because you didn't trust in Me, to sanctify Me

---

of the sin of hitting the rock, there seems no escaping the conclusion that God's decree just feels unfair.

לְהַקְדִּישֵׁנִי לְעֵינֵי בְּנֵי יִשְׂרָאֵל, לָכֵן לֹא תָבִיאוּ אֶת־הַקָּהָל הַזֶּה אֶל־הָאָרֶץ אֲשֶׁר־נָתַתִּי לָהֶם:	in the eyes of the Children of Israel, therefore you shall not bring this assembly into the land which I have given them."

So, that's the general background here. We're going to try to make some headway in dealing with the overarching question I raised above — *what's the big deal about hitting a rock?* — but in order to do that, I'd like to raise a number of other, smaller questions that I think the story is *also* inviting us to ask. By getting our minds around some of these, we should be able to get the evidence and context we need in order to ultimately see the story in a new light.

OK, are you still with me? Let's try some of these other, smaller questions on for size:

What Does Lack of Faith Have to Do with It?

Let's talk about the nature of the misdeed. What, exactly, was wrong with hitting the rock? The text, interestingly, is very explicit about that. God tells Moses and Aaron that they have been guilty of having a lack of faith:

יַעַן לֹא־הֶאֱמַנְתֶּם בִּי לְהַקְדִּישֵׁנִי לְעֵינֵי בְּנֵי יִשְׂרָאֵל	Because you didn't trust in Me, to sanctify Me in the eyes of the Children of Israel.	Numbers 20:12

But it is worth asking: How, exactly, does hitting the rock, rather than speaking to it, demonstrate a lack of faith? Had God accused Moses of something else — say, not following directions precisely enough — then sure, I can see how Moses would be guilty of *that*. But lack of faith? It is hard to understand why getting a miracle to happen through a different modality — by hitting a rock instead of speaking to it — shows anything that might remotely be called a lack of faith.

An Easier Indictment

Moreover, if lack of faith was *really* going to be the shortcoming that seals the deal for Moses, that which makes him unfit, in God's eyes, to enter the Land of Israel — God could have called him out for this offense much earlier on in his career as leader. Consider, for example, something that occurred forty years prior to this incident with Moses and the rock, an event recounted earlier in the book of Numbers, in **Parshat Beha'alotecha**. The people are craving meat, and Moses has none to give them. God tells him not to worry; by evening time, they will have the meat they desire. They will have meat for a whole month, until it comes out of their noses, the Master of the Universe promises. But Moses, upon hearing that, turns to God and says this:

Numbers 11:21-22

שֵׁשׁ־מֵאוֹת אֶלֶף רַגְלִי הָעָם אֲשֶׁר אָנֹכִי בְּקִרְבּוֹ, וְאַתָּה אָמַרְתָּ בָּשָׂר אֶתֵּן לָהֶם וְאָכְלוּ חֹדֶשׁ יָמִים: הֲצֹאן וּבָקָר יִשָּׁחֵט לָהֶם וּמָצָא לָהֶם? אִם אֶת־כָּל־דְּגֵי הַיָּם יֵאָסֵף לָהֶם וּמָצָא לָהֶם:

The people among whom I am are six hundred thousand men on foot, and You say, "I will give them meat, that they may eat a whole month"? Will whole flocks and herds be slaughtered for them, and put in front of them? Will all the fish of the sea be gathered for them, and put in front of them?

Moses raised the obvious logistical issues with feeding hundreds of thousands of people meat for a sustained period of time in the middle of a wilderness. And here was God's response:

Numbers 11:23

וַיֹּאמֶר יְקוָה אֶל־מֹשֶׁה, הֲיַד יְקוָה תִּקְצָר? עַתָּה תִרְאֶה הֲיִקְרְךָ דְבָרִי אִם־לֹא:

God said to Moses, "Has God's hand [suddenly] grown short? Now you will see whether My word will happen to you or not!"

Now, God doesn't angrily go and accuse Moses of having a lack of faith, and He doesn't bar Moses from leading the people into Canaan. No.

Instead, the Almighty gently asks Moses to remember that he is speaking to the Master of the Universe.

How do we understand God's forbearance here? That's easy: Seemingly, the Almighty has a certain tolerance for people — even men as great as Moses — momentarily losing sight of the fact that they are speaking to the Master of the Universe. God basically gave Moses a pass on that oversight here. But for some reason, in the story of Moses and the rock, no pass is given. God gets angry with Moses for having a lack of faith, when it seems hard to even figure out why faith was an issue at all. God's choice of moments to become angry with Moses over faith seems strange, indeed.[2]

The Role of the Staff

And finally, let's pose one more question about this strange story. This question has to do with what might easily be dismissed as a simple prop. I want to ask you about the role of the staff in our little episode.

Moses hits the rock with a staff. But one might wonder: If Moses really and truly *wasn't* supposed to hit the rock with that staff, if the whole point of the miracle was supposed to be that Moses would *speak* to the rock but not *strike* it, then why does the Almighty give him this instruction about how to approach the rock:

קַח אֶת־הַמַּטֶּה וְהַקְהֵל אֶת־הָעֵדָה, אַתָּה וְאַהֲרֹן אָחִיךָ, וְדִבַּרְתֶּם אֶל־הַסֶּלַע לְעֵינֵיהֶם וְנָתַן מֵימָיו	**Take the staff**, and assemble the congregation, you and Aaron your brother, and speak to the rock before their eyes, that it will give forth its water.	Numbers 20:8

What's the logic in telling Moses to take his staff along with him, if he's not going to be doing anything with it? And it gets worse than that. Because the text goes out of its way to tell us that, when Moses *did* pick up that staff — he was doing exactly as God commanded him to:

2 Rashi raises this issue in his commentary on Numbers 20:12. His answer is that the episode involving Moses questioning God's ability to provide meat occurred in private, whereas in **Parshat Chukat**, God instructed Moses to publicly speak to the rock in front of the entire congregation. Hence, the latter was considered a graver sin.

Numbers 20:9

וַיִּקַּח מֹשֶׁה אֶת־הַמַּטֶּה מִלִּפְנֵי יְקוָה **כַּאֲשֶׁר צִוָּהוּ**׃	And Moses took the staff from before God, **just as He commanded him**.

So, just to keep this straight, even though when Moses *hits* the rock with the staff, he's doing so in contravention of God's command, the text wants us to know that when he first *took* the staff, he was doing exactly the right thing. He was following God's command. It seems like this staff has an important role. But how could a staff that you are supposed to merely take, and not *do* anything with, be so important?

One Staff—or Two?

I want to suggest to you that this mystery about the staff will help us begin to penetrate some of the deeper layers of this story. And in order to unravel the mystery, we need to confront a simple but beguiling question: Exactly *whose* staff was it that Moses used to hit the rock?

Perhaps you think I'm being faintly ridiculous in asking this question. *Who cares whose staff it was; it is just a staff!* But bear with me for a minute and consider that question seriously: *Whose staff was it that Moses used to hit the rock?*

Most of us would assume it was Moses' staff. And at first glance, the text seems to bear this out:

Numbers 20:11

וַיָּרֶם מֹשֶׁה אֶת־יָדוֹ וַיַּךְ אֶת־הַסֶּלַע **בְּמַטֵּהוּ** פַּעֲמָיִם	Moses lifted up his hand, and struck the rock **with his staff** twice.

His staff. So we'd be justified in assuming that it was Moses' own staff. But there's a little problem with that supposition. Just look at where Moses took the staff *from*, in the verse cited above:

וַיִּקַּח מֹשֶׁה **אֶת־הַמַּטֶּה מִלִּפְנֵי יְקוָה** כַּאֲשֶׁר צִוָּהוּ׃

And Moses took **the staff from before God**, just as He commanded him.

The staff that Moses took was the staff that had been resting "before God," which is to say, in the Tabernacle, in the Holy of Holies. But here's the thing. There is only one staff that fits this particular description, and it isn't Moses' staff. It is the staff belonging to his brother, Aaron.

Numbers 17:25–26

וַיֹּאמֶר יְקוָה אֶל־מֹשֶׁה, הָשֵׁב אֶת־מַטֵּה אַהֲרֹן לִפְנֵי הָעֵדוּת לְמִשְׁמֶרֶת לְאוֹת לִבְנֵי־מֶרִי... וַיַּעַשׂ מֹשֶׁה כַּאֲשֶׁר צִוָּה יְקוָה אֹתוֹ; כֵּן עָשָׂה:	God said to Moses, "Put back the staff of Aaron before the [Ark] of Testimony; there it shall be kept as a sign against those who would rebel..." And Moses did as God commanded him; so he did.

That verse appears just a couple of chapters ago, back at the end of **Parshat Korach**. And if you follow the story there, you'll know why Aaron's staff was meant to be kept "before God" — because it played a pivotal role in quelling the greatest rebellion amongst the people in all their wanderings in the desert: the revolt engineered by Korach. That revolt had finally been quieted when Aaron's staff miraculously sprouted and flowered, after which God commanded that the staff should remain in the Tabernacle for all time, as a kind of sign to those who would, in the future, rebel.

Now, remember: We are told all this at the end of **Parshat Korach**. **Parshat Chukat**, where we encounter our story about Moses, the rock, and the staff — that's the very next parsha. So when we hear God commanding Moses to take the staff, and (a) we are told that he took it "from before God," and (b) we realize that, in **Parshat Chukat**, we have a little rebellion going on — the people are fed up with being stuck in the wilderness and are complaining bitterly about the lack of fruit trees and the lack of water[3] — well, the reader can put two and two together and figure out:

---

3 Indeed, the text emphasizes the sense of rebellion here:

Numbers 20:3–5

וַיָּרֶב הָעָם עִם־מֹשֶׁה וַיֹּאמְרוּ לֵאמֹר, וְלוּ גָוַעְנוּ בִּגְוַע אַחֵינוּ לִפְנֵי יְקוָה: וְלָמָה הֲבֵאתֶם אֶת־קְהַל יְקוָה אֶל הַמִּדְבָּר הַזֶּה לָמוּת שָׁם אֲנַחְנוּ וּבְעִירֵנוּ: וְלָמָה הֶעֱלִיתֻנוּ מִמִּצְרַיִם לְהָבִיא אֹתָנוּ אֶל־הַמָּקוֹם הָרָע הַזֶּה, לֹא מְקוֹם זֶרַע וּתְאֵנָה וְגֶפֶן וְרִמּוֹן, וּמַיִם אַיִן לִשְׁתּוֹת:	The people argued with Moses, and spoke, saying, "We wish that we had died when our brothers died before God! Why have you brought the assembly of God into this wilderness, that we should die there, we and our animals? Why have you made us to come up out of Egypt, to bring us in to this evil place? It is no place of seed, or of figs, or of vines, or of pomegranates; there is not even any water to drink!".

Oh, I get it, God was instructing Moses to take Aaron's staff, the staff that was designed to deal with precisely this type of situation.

This is especially true because the text tells us that Aaron's staff had been designated by God as an **אוֹת לִבְנֵי־מֶרִי**, *a sign meant for rebels*, and that exact same language is used now, in Chukat, to tell us about the people: Just before Moses hits the rock with the staff, Moses addresses the people, saying,

Numbers 20:10

שִׁמְעוּ־נָא **הַמֹּרִים**! הֲמִן־הַסֶּלַע הַזֶּה נוֹצִיא לָכֶם מָיִם:	Hear now, **you rebels**; shall we bring forth water for you from this rock?

Clearly, then, *that* staff — Aaron's staff — was the one Moses was meant to take with him as he went to speak to the rock. And yet, although Moses was instructed to take Aaron's staff along with him, and although the text tells us he *did* take that staff, just as he was commanded — still, at the last moment, something changed.

Strange as it sounds, Moses seems to have made a last-minute staff switch:

Numbers 20:11

וַיָּרֶם מֹשֶׁה אֶת־יָדוֹ וַיַּךְ אֶת־הַסֶּלַע **בְּמַטֵּהוּ** פַּעֲמָיִם, וַיֵּצְאוּ מַיִם רַבִּים	Moses lifted up his hand, and struck the rock **with his staff** twice, and water came forth abundantly.

Instead of simply approaching the rock and speaking to it while holding Aaron's staff, Moses puts Aaron's staff down, takes up his own, and strikes the rock. A surreptitious staff switch.[4]

---

4 Rav David Zvi Hoffman makes this same textual observation (published in a note to his commentary on Ex. 11:10), that the verses indicate that the staff that Moses took was Aaron's staff that had been placed "before God." However, instead of saying there was a staff switch, he uses this interpretation to support the translation of *matehu* as "the staff in his hand" rather than "his staff."

So What Was the Plan?

Why did Moses switch staffs at the last minute? It is hard to know. In our previous essay, on **Parshat Korach**, we spent some time reflecting on Aaron's staff and why, exactly, it might have served as a "sign against those who would rebel." We suggested that there was something soothing about Aaron's staff, something that could quell rebellion by gently removing the underlying basis for it, rather than trying to tamp rebellion down through threats of violence or other such incentives. Dealing with the people's rebellion *that* way seems to have been God's plan, and it stands to reason that there was something about speaking to that rock, rather than striking it, that was consistent with this plan. Somehow, Moses chose a different path when he struck the rock.

These are the general outlines of a theory, but admittedly, the picture is still quite hazy and undefined, to say the least. Versions of the basic questions we started with are still around: *Sure, maybe Aaron's staff pointed to a unique way to quell a rebellion — but still, what exactly is achieved by speaking to a rock instead of hitting it? After all, it's just a rock! And why would Moses be so insistent on hitting that rock? Why not just do what God asked?*

To achieve more clarity here, we need to gather a bit more evidence. And that evidence, dear reader, just happens to be ours for the taking. For there's a startling fact that we have until now overlooked: In **Parshat Chukat**, when Moses struck the rock to get water from it — that's not the first time he ever did such a thing. He did it once before, forty years ago. And when he struck the rock back then, he did so… *at God's behest.*

The First Time Moses Struck a Rock

It was just after the people had crossed the Sea of Reeds and seen the Egyptian army smashed before their eyes. Right after that, a new crisis faced the people. They were in the wilderness; how were they going to get water? The people responded by complaining bitterly. They hurled accusations at Moses, telling him that he was wrong to ever take them out of Egypt, where life was better than this (Ex. 17:3).

So, just to take stock, people back then were thirsty. *Just like now.* The people back then had been rebellious. *Just like now.* But something happened then that was very different from now. Back then, God said this to Moses:

Exodus 17:5–6

וּמַטְּךָ אֲשֶׁר הִכִּיתָ בּוֹ אֶת־הַיְאֹר, קַח בְּיָדְךָ וְהָלָכְתָּ... וְהִכִּיתָ בַצּוּר, וְיָצְאוּ מִמֶּנּוּ מַיִם, וְשָׁתָה הָעָם. וַיַּעַשׂ כֵּן מֹשֶׁה לְעֵינֵי זִקְנֵי יִשְׂרָאֵל:

"And your staff with which you struck the [Nile] river, take in your hand and go...and you shall strike the rock, and waters will go forth from it, and the nation will drink." And Moses did so before the eyes of the elders of Israel.

So the mystery deepens. Forty years before all this, in the midst of a water crisis, God had actually commanded Moses to *strike* a rock to get water from it. Moreover, which staff did God tell Moses to use to do this? His *own* staff, of course:

וּמַטְּךָ אֲשֶׁר הִכִּיתָ בּוֹ אֶת־הַיְאֹר, קַח בְּיָדְךָ וְהָלָכְתָּ:

And **your staff** with which you struck the [Nile] river, take in your hand and go.

But for some reason, forty years later, in **Parshat Chukat**, when the people found themselves facing a similar water crisis — at that moment, there was a new set of divine instructions. You weren't supposed to hit the rock anymore. You were supposed to speak to it. And you weren't supposed to approach it with your own staff. You were supposed to take Aaron's staff with you instead.

Now, the second time around, Moses didn't follow instructions. That much we know. And we know that he paid dearly for that. But it makes one wonder: If, forty years prior, hitting rocks with your own staff was a perfectly legitimate way to get water from a rock — what, exactly, changed *now*, forty years later? And furthermore: Granted, Moses didn't follow the new instructions, but still, why was it *so* terrible for Moses to reenact a divine command that was solidly rooted in his past? And why would that be called a lack of faith?

The answers will come, I think, if we shift our focus away from the hitting-the-rock story in **Parshat Chukat**, and rewind forty years to look more carefully at the *first* hitting-the-rock story, back in the book of Exodus. We need to figure out why, back then, God commanded Moses to get water from a rock by striking it. . Only once we understand *that* will we be able to discern why, forty years later, as the events of the past began to replay themselves, it was so important to seek a different approach.

Part II: The Shattered Rock at Chorev

So here we are, forty years back in time. I ask you to forget, for the moment, everything that's preoccupied us about that later story in *Chukat*, the hitting-the-rock episode that augurs Moses' untimely death. For the time being, we need to be fully focused on the event that started it all, back in the book of Exodus, just after the Splitting of the Sea. I'll lay out the verses for you. As you read them, take a moment to let them sit with you … and see if any questions come and introduce themselves to your curious mind:

Exodus 17:1–7

וַיִּסְעוּ כָּל־עֲדַת בְּנֵי־יִשְׂרָאֵל
מִמִּדְבַּר־סִין לְמַסְעֵיהֶם עַל־
פִּי יְקֹוָה, וַיַּחֲנוּ בִּרְפִידִים,
וְאֵין מַיִם לִשְׁתֹּת הָעָם: וַיָּרֶב
הָעָם עִם־מֹשֶׁה, וַיֹּאמְרוּ,
תְּנוּ־לָנוּ מַיִם וְנִשְׁתֶּה!
וַיֹּאמֶר לָהֶם מֹשֶׁה, מַה־
תְּרִיבוּן עִמָּדִי? מַה־תְּנַסּוּן
אֶת־יְקֹוָה: וַיִּצְמָא שָׁם הָעָם
לַמַּיִם, וַיָּלֶן הָעָם עַל־מֹשֶׁה
וַיֹּאמֶר, לָמָּה זֶּה הֶעֱלִיתָנוּ
מִמִּצְרַיִם לְהָמִית אֹתִי
וְאֶת־בָּנַי וְאֶת־מִקְנַי בַּצָּמָא:
וַיִּצְעַק מֹשֶׁה אֶל־יְקֹוָה
לֵאמֹר, מָה אֶעֱשֶׂה לָעָם
הַזֶּה? עוֹד מְעַט וּסְקָלֻנִי:
וַיֹּאמֶר יְקֹוָה אֶל־מֹשֶׁה, עֲבֹר
לִפְנֵי הָעָם וְקַח אִתְּךָ מִזִּקְנֵי
יִשְׂרָאֵל וּמַטְּךָ אֲשֶׁר הִכִּיתָ בּוֹ
אֶת־הַיְאֹר קַח בְּיָדְךָ וְהָלָכְתָּ:
הִנְנִי עֹמֵד לְפָנֶיךָ שָּׁם עַל־
הַצּוּר בְּחֹרֵב, וְהִכִּיתָ בַצּוּר
וְיָצְאוּ מִמֶּנּוּ מַיִם וְשָׁתָה
הָעָם. וַיַּעַשׂ כֵּן מֹשֶׁה לְעֵינֵי

And the entire congregation of the Children of Israel traveled from the Wilderness of Sin, in their journeys, at the directive of God, and they camped at Refidim. There was no water for the people to drink, and the people quarreled with Moses, and they said, "Give us water and we will drink!" And Moses said to them, "Why do you quarrel with me? Why do you test God?" The people thirsted there for water, and they grumbled against Moses and said, "Why have you brought us up from Egypt, to kill me and my children and my livestock with thirst?" Moses cried out to God, saying, "What shall I do for this people? A little more and they will stone me!" And God said to Moses, "Pass before the people, and take with you from the elders of Israel; and the staff with which you struck the river, take in your hand and go. Behold, I [will] stand before you there, upon the rock at Chorev; and you shall strike the rock, and waters will go forth from it, and the nation will drink." And Moses did so before the eyes

זִקְנֵי יִשְׂרָאֵל׃ וַיִּקְרָא שֵׁם
הַמָּקוֹם מַסָּה וּמְרִיבָה, עַל־
רִיב בְּנֵי יִשְׂרָאֵל וְעַל נַסֹּתָם
אֶת־יְקוָה, לֵאמֹר, הֲיֵשׁ יְקוָה
בְּקִרְבֵּנוּ אִם־אָיִן׃

of the elders of Israel. He named the place Masah and Merivah, because of the quarrel of the Children of Israel and because of their testing of God, saying, "Is God among us or not?"

Well, let's compare notes. Did anything puzzle you about this little episode?

Here are a few things that struck me, if you'll pardon the pun.

Why Not a Rain Dance?

First, consider God's command to Moses to strike the rock. Maybe, as you read the verse that describes this command, it didn't seem all that out of the ordinary. But that's probably just because you've read the story before, so you're no longer surprised by it. Imagine you were reading this episode for the very first time. That command, I bet, would elicit your curiosity. Because look, God is an all-powerful being, and He would have had many and varied ways of effecting a water-producing miracle. God could have asked Moses to wave his arms in front of the rock, to look skyward and start a rain dance, to gaze at a cactus and smile. You name it, God could have chosen it. Why, of all things, to strike the rock?

And yes, it could be that there's no particular meaning in it, that God just chose any old symbolic action out of the proverbial hat, and could just as easily have chosen any other. But maybe not. Maybe there's something special about striking the rock. Would we have any way to discover what, if anything, the meaning of that specific act might be?

Geo-Locating God

And here's another curiosity: a verse that makes a big deal about God's location, of all things:

Exodus 17:6

הִנְנִי עֹמֵד לְפָנֶיךָ שָׁם

Behold, I [will] stand before you there,

עַל־הַצּוּר	upon the rock.

It just seems odd. Ask yourself: When reading about any other biblical miracle, did you ever find the Torah directing your attention to where God was *located* when the miracle took place? Like, when the manna fell from the sky — did the text bother mentioning to you where God was standing when that happened? When God split the sea, did the text tell us that God was standing right there the whole time? Of course, we hear nothing like that in either miracle. We hear nothing like that in almost any other miracle that I can think of. It is a peculiar thing for the text to harp on God situating Himself on that rock. Why does the text bother to tell us this strange detail?

Where, Exactly, Was the Rock?

And one more question, while we're at it. Not only does the Almighty geo-locate Himself relative to the rock, but He also geo-locates the rock, relative to where the people are standing. And what God tells us about the location of the rock is astounding, indeed:

Exodus 17:6

הִנְנִי עֹמֵד לְפָנֶיךָ שָּׁם עַל־הַצּוּר **בְּחֹרֵב**	Behold, I [will] stand before you there, upon the rock **at Chorev**.

God tells Moses that the rock that will give its water … is to be found at Chorev. Now, it's easy to read the verse quickly and simply ignore this little, inconvenient geo-marker. But inconvenient, it certainly is. Because … *the people weren't actually at Chorev at the time.*

We know this because the Torah goes out of its way to tell us exactly where the whole story of the people, Moses, and the rock took place. It happened at a site in the wilderness known as Refidim:

Exodus 17:1–3

וַיִּסְעוּ כָּל־עֲדַת בְּנֵי־יִשְׂרָאֵל מִמִּדְבַּר־סִין לְמַסְעֵיהֶם עַל־פִּי	And the entire congregation of the Children of Israel traveled from the

יְקוָה, **וַיַּחֲנוּ בִּרְפִידִים**, וְאֵין מַיִם לִשְׁתֹּת הָעָם:...וַיִּצְמָא שָׁם הָעָם לַמַּיִם	Wilderness of Sin, in their journeys at the directive of God, **and they camped at Refidim**. There was no water for the people to drink...and the people thirsted there for water.

Refidim? That most definitely was *not* the same place as Chorev. The Torah hammers that home to the reader when it tells us, a few chapters later, that the people *left* Refidim, journeyed for a while, and *then* came to the Sinai Desert — and it was there that they encountered the mountain known as Sinai:

Exodus 19:1–2

בַּחֹדֶשׁ הַשְּׁלִישִׁי לְצֵאת בְּנֵי־יִשְׂרָאֵל מֵאֶרֶץ מִצְרָיִם, בַּיּוֹם הַזֶּה בָּאוּ מִדְבַּר סִינָי: **וַיִּסְעוּ מֵרְפִידִים וַיָּבֹאוּ מִדְבַּר סִינַי**, וַיַּחֲנוּ בַּמִּדְבָּר, וַיִּחַן־שָׁם יִשְׂרָאֵל נֶגֶד הָהָר:	In the third month of the Children of Israel's going forth from the land of Egypt, on that day, they came to the Wilderness of Sinai. **They traveled from Refidim and came to the Wilderness of Sinai** and camped in the wilderness; Israel camped there in front of the mountain.

Sinai, of course, is another name for Mount Chorev.[5] The bottom line: Once you do the math, it becomes clear that Chorev must have been *kilometers* away from Refidim. Far enough that the entire people had to break camp in one place, journey to another place, and then encamp there. So

5 The Torah sometimes calls the mountain at which the Revelation took place by the name of Mount Sinai, and other times, it calls it Chorev. See, for example, Deuteronomy 1:6, where Moses speaks of the moment the people finally left Mount Sinai, where they had received the Torah: "יְקוָה אֱלֹקֵינוּ דִּבֶּר אֵלֵינוּ בְּחֹרֵב לֵאמֹר רַב־לָכֶם שֶׁבֶת בָּהָר הַזֶּה, Hashem our God spoke to us at Chorev, saying, 'You have stayed long enough at this mountain.'"

how, exactly, was Moses supposed to go ahead and strike a rock that wasn't even remotely in his proximity?[6]

I'll be honest with you: I don't have an answer to that question. Where, exactly, that rock was, and how Moses could possibly reach it, seems utterly mysterious to me. Perhaps that was to be part of the miracle of striking the rock: Moses reaching out to something utterly beyond his reach and miraculously reaching it anyway.[7] I don't know. But what I *do* know is that the Torah wants us, the reader, to relate to the rock that Moses hit as being situated not in Refidim but at Chorev. And that strikes me as *very* interesting. Because that one little detail — the statement that, in the Exodus story, the rock Moses hit was situated at Chorev — that sets up a breathtaking story arc for this humble, battered rock of ours. It seems to suggest that there is an easily overlooked, but important, next chapter in its story. Because, as it turns out, this rock that Moses hit at Chorev is called by a special name, a *tzur*. This is a very unusual word for rock. So much so that *tzur* is used to describe a particular rock only one other time

---

6 Malbim suggests that Moses needed to travel personally to Chorev from Refidim to go and bring the rock back to the people — but such an interpretation seems difficult to force into the text. The sense of the text is that Moses, standing right where he was standing, was commanded to strike a rock at Chorev, and was moments away from doing so.

7 It is almost as if Moses, in the act of taking that staff and preparing to strike the rock, is advancing to a time and place he and the rest of the people are *about to be at* in a few days from now. How one could possibly explain that seems impossible without resorting to a miracle. But then again, the whole story here is miraculous: Getting water from a rock is a miracle, and the place where the rock is ostensibly located — Chorev — is where the greatest miracle in the history of humankind is about to take place. *God is going to reveal Himself here.* The Master of the Universe, a being who unquestionably lives beyond time and space, is going to come into our world, a world of time and space — right here, right now, on top of a mountain known as Chorev.

To engage in a bit of wild speculation: Perhaps as the people get closer to Chorev — as they approach the *site* at which God's revelation will take place, and as they approach the *time* at which that revelation will happen — maybe all bets are off when it comes to time and space. Time and space as we know it start to bend in unforeseen ways when the Master of the Universe is on His way into our world.

ever in the Torah.[8] And if you look at that one other lonely time we ever encounter a *tzur*, you'll notice something astonishing.

Make sure you're sitting down for this.

That *tzur* just happened to be in Chorev, too.

A Close Encounter with the Divine

Later in the book of Exodus, in the aftermath of the sin of the Golden Calf, Moses finds himself bargaining with God to save the people of Israel from destruction. As those negotiations play out, Moses ascends Mount Sinai, otherwise known as Mount Chorev, and seeks a direct encounter with the Divine. In response, God tells him this:

Exodus 33:20–23

וַיֹּאמֶר, לֹא תוּכַל לִרְאֹת אֶת־פָּנָי, כִּי לֹא־יִרְאַנִי הָאָדָם וָחָי: וַיֹּאמֶר יְקוָה, הִנֵּה מָקוֹם אִתִּי וְנִצַּבְתָּ עַל־**הַצּוּר**: וְהָיָה בַּעֲבֹר כְּבֹדִי וְשַׂמְתִּיךָ בְּנִקְרַת **הַצּוּר** וְשַׂכֹּתִי כַפִּי עָלֶיךָ עַד־עָבְרִי: וַהֲסִרֹתִי אֶת־כַּפִּי וְרָאִיתָ אֶת־אֲחֹרָי, וּפָנַי לֹא יֵרָאוּ:

He said, "You won't be able to see My face, because man cannot see Me and live." But God said, "Behold, there is a place with Me; you shall stand on **the rock**, and when My glory passes, I will place you in the cleft of **[that] rock**, and I will screen you with My palm until I pass. When I remove My palm, you shall see my back; but My face shall not be seen."

Well, there it is. There's the *tzur* at Chorev, one more time.

How mysterious! Is our mind playing tricks on us … or does the Torah want us to relate to these two *tzurs* as if they were one and the same rock?[9]

---

8 As we shall see later, the word *tzur* is used quite often metaphorically — see **Parshat Ha'azinu** — but is only very rarely used to denote an actual, particular rock.

9 Or, perhaps a bit more conservatively: Whether or not they *actually* were one and the same, is the Torah in effect asking the reader to treat the two *as if* they were one and the same?

Ibn Ezra (on Ex. 33:22) seems to align with the theory that these two rocks are one and the same. Indeed, Ibn Ezra goes even further, and seems to suggest that,

The answer to that, I'd suggest, is a resounding "yes." Because it's not just that this boulder that shields Moses during his divine encounter is called by the unusual name *tzur*, like the rock that Moses hit; and it's not just that its peculiar location was at Chorev, just like the *tzur* that Moses hit. It's *everything* about the *tzur*. The whole story of Moses' divine encounter in Exodus 33 carries memories of the Moses-hitting-the-rock episode in chapter 17. Consider, for example, precisely where God situates Moses the second time the *tzur* makes its appearance:

וְשַׂמְתִּיךָ בְּנִקְרַת הַצּוּר
"I will place you in the cleft of [that] rock."

Hmm, so the *tzur* had a cleft in it, did it? It had some sort of gash in its walls which Moses could step into. *I wonder how that gash got there*?

Sure. Go ahead and ask the question: How *did* that gash get there?

Yes, dear reader, you know the answer: *It's because Moses struck the tzur with his staff the first time he encountered it.* The gash in the rock, we are being invited to consider, is the lasting legacy of the violence committed against it when Moses struck it with his staff.

Indeed, Rashi implicitly asks us to consider as much when he comments that the staff used by Moses to originally strike the *tzur* was made of especially hard material. Hard enough, he writes ... *to shatter a rock*:

Rashi on Exodus 17:6, from Mekhilta DeRabbi Yishmael 17:6:2

"וְהִכִּיתָ בַצּוּר" - "עַל הַצּוּר" לֹא נֶאֱמַר, אֶלָּא "בַּצּוּר" - מִכָּאן שֶׁהַמַּטֶּה הָיָה שֶׁל מִין דָּבָר חָזָק, וּשְׁמוֹ סַנְפִּירִינוֹן, וְהַצּוּר נִבְקַע מִפָּנָיו.

"And you shall strike the rock"—It does not say "you shall smite על הצור," *upon* the surface of the rock, but בצור, right *into* the rock. From this it follows that the staff must have been composed of a kind of hard material, the name of which is sapphire, and the rock was split by it.

---

in each case, the word *tzur* refers to a cliff face that was part of the mountain of Sinai itself (see also Ibn Ezra on Ex. 17:6).

Trading Places

To add to the intrigue, consider another element of this second story involving our trusty *tzur* at Chorev. Note where God chooses to situate Himself, relative to Moses, as the encounter between the Master of the Universe and Moses plays out:

וַיֹּאמֶר יְקוָה, הִנֵּה מָקוֹם אִתִּי וְנִצַּבְתָּ עַל־הַצּוּר:	God said, "Behold, there is a place with Me; **you shall stand on the rock.**"	Exodus 33:21
וַיַּעֲבֹר יְקוָה עַל פָּנָיו	**And [then] God passed** before him.	Exodus 34:6

One second; that sounds familiar, right? Because the first time we met the *tzur*, back when the people were encamped in Refidim — then, too, we had a situation where someone "stood on the rock" and someone else "passed before" that someone. God had told Moses that He, the Almighty, would be **standing on the rock**, and Moses was **to pass before Him** and then strike the rock.

Evidently, then, now — in the second story — God seems to be telling Moses that they will have to trade places. *You, Moses, are going to be the one to stand on the rock, and I, God, am going to be the one to pass before you.*

All in all, it seems pretty clear that the text is asking the reader to see the story of Moses in the cleft of the *tzur* (in the aftermath of the Golden Calf) as a continuation of the story of Moses hitting the *tzur* at Refidim and getting water from it. It also seems pretty clear that the second story involves some sort of reversal that brings the first story full circle:

- The first time around, God would "stand" on the rock (whatever that means); and the second time around, it would be Moses who would stand in that position.
- The first time around, Moses would pass before God; the second time around, it would be God who would pass before Moses.
- The first time around, Moses would strike the rock (and, according to Rashi, shatter its outer wall); the second time around, Moses would stand in the very cleft in the rock that he himself had created.

The Secret of the *Tzur*

What secret is this story of the *tzur* still hiding from us? Why the reversal in roles? And why, when Moses sought a direct and personal encounter with God, did the Almighty bring Moses back to the shattered *tzur* and ask him to stand inside it?

It turns out that the Torah gives us the answer to these questions. But the answer doesn't appear in the story of Refidim, when Moses struck the *tzur*. Nor does it appear in the aftermath of the Golden Calf, when Moses stood in the cleft of the rock whose surface he had shattered. The answer doesn't even come in the book of Numbers, when Moses once again strikes a rock (this time, contravening God's command). The answer comes at the very end of the Torah, in a mysterious song that God would reveal to Moses just before his death.

On the cusp of entering the Land of Israel, God would reveal what has become known as the song of *Ha'azinu* (Deut. 32) to Moses, and to the entire people — and in it, He would speak once more about the *tzur*. In that song, God would retell, in the form of poetry, some of the history of Israel's early wanderings after its grand Exodus. It relates how God cared for the people in those early days in the wilderness; how the Almighty gave them manna to eat, and water to drink from the rock, from the *tzur*.

I believe that if we listen carefully to this song, we will learn something remarkable about the *tzur*: that it had a mysterious, hidden identity. This mysterious, hidden nature of the *tzur* will help us understand everything else: Why, in the first story, God would tell Moses that the Almighty Himself would be standing on the rock when it would give of its water; why, in the second story, after the Golden Calf, God would want Moses to trade places with Him at the *tzur*; and why, forty years later, in **Parshat Chukat**, Moses' choice to strike the rock rather than speak to it was a moment of such terrible gravity, with such far-reaching implications.

Let's take a look at that song.

Part III:
The Song of Ha'azinu:
The Story of Israel's Birth

Ha'azinu starts its narrative from the moment Israel found itself in the wilderness, newly released from Egyptian slavery. Yes, the people of Israel had existed prior to that. But they existed as a family. That was really their identity throughout the book of Genesis, up until the moment they descended, seventy people in all, into the land of Egypt for what became centuries of enslavement. It was when they emerged from Egyptian slavery, hundreds of thousands strong and newly independent, that they could first lay claim to being a nation.

At that moment, they were free but alone, and vulnerable in a barren wasteland. And that's where *Ha'azinu* picks up the tale. There, in the wilderness, the God who was responsible for delivering them from their oppressor gently nurtured them and protected them from the dangers that were all around them:

Deuteronomy 32:10

יִמְצָאֵהוּ בְּאֶרֶץ מִדְבָּר וּבְתֹהוּ
יְלֵל יְשִׁמֹן; יְסֹבְבֶנְהוּ יְבוֹנְנֵהוּ
יִצְּרֶנְהוּ כְּאִישׁוֹן עֵינוֹ:

He found him in a desert land, in the waste of a howling wilderness. He surrounded him, built him up, sheltered him like the pupil of His eye.[10]

---

10 The words here are eerily reminiscent of Creation. Take the verse I just cited:

יִמְצָאֵהוּ בְּאֶרֶץ מִדְבָּר וּבְתֹהוּ יְלֵל יְשִׁמֹן; יְסֹבְבֶנְהוּ יְבוֹנְנֵהוּ יִצְּרֶנְהוּ כְּאִישׁוֹן עֵינוֹ:

He found him in a desert **land**, in the **waste** of a howling wilderness. He surrounded him, built him up.

If you listen carefully, you'll hear echoes of one of the first verses of the Creation story, the verse that signals the very beginning of a new, fledgling universe:

Genesis 1:2

וְהָאָרֶץ הָיְתָה תֹהוּ וָבֹהוּ

and the **earth** was **formless** and **void**.

The fledgling nation, just released from Egypt, was like a newborn. And it was up to God, the nation's Creator, to care for it and provide for its every need. Chief among those was its need for food. And water:

Deuteronomy 32:13

יַרְכִּבֵהוּ עַל־[בָּמֳתֵי] (במותי) אָרֶץ וַיֹּאכַל תְּנוּבֹת שָׂדָי וַיֵּנִקֵהוּ דְבַשׁ מִסֶּלַע וְשֶׁמֶן מֵחַלְמִישׁ צוּר׃	He made him ride on the high places of the earth, and [Israel] ate the produce of My fields. And [God] suckled him with honey from the rock, and oil from the flinty *tzur*.

Honey and oil. Perhaps that is how the water must have seemed to the desperate, thirsting people. It was the most prized and delightful substance they could possibly imagine, as rich and precious as honey or oil, whose every drop is to be savored. But beyond just the sweetness or richness of the life-giving liquid, consider the remarkable, poetic verb that *Ha'azinu* uses to describe how God provided this water to them:

וַיֵּנִקֵהוּ דְבַשׁ מִסֶּלַע וְשֶׁמֶן מֵחַלְמִישׁ **צוּר**׃

[God] **suckled him** with honey from the rock, and oil from the flinty ***tzur***.

God as Mother-in-the-Sky

That Hebrew word וַיֵּנִקֵהוּ is quite a metaphor: *God suckled us through that rock.* The verse portrays the incipient nation as if we were the Almighty's nursing infant. And, when you get right down to thinking about it, there is a certain logic to that: Newly released from Egypt, we had just been born. And everyone knows that a parent's job doesn't end with birth. Far from it. Once a little baby is born, its mother must provide it with food and drink, and she needs to do so consistently and reliably. She needs to nurse the child.

That, the song of *Ha'azinu* tells us, is precisely what God set out to do. But God isn't a human being possessed of a physical body. So how would

---

This echo, and others in the immediately following verses, give the impression that what God was doing in Genesis, He was doing again in Exodus — or at least, He was doing a version of it: *a new creation was coming into being.* This time, it was not a universe that God was birthing, but a nation.

the Master of the Universe "nurse" us? The answer is: God would co-opt nature to do His bidding. The *tzur*, this mighty boulder in the desert, a bone-dry, rock-hard symbol of power and might — the *least* likely source imaginable for the life-giving liquid we so desperately sought — this *tzur* would be co-opted by the Almighty, as if it were... a divine breast, the softest, most generous giver of life imaginable.

Ha'azinu's Surprise Beginning

It is because of this, perhaps, that the song of *Ha'azinu* begins its poetic retelling of Israel's history with a brief prologue that speaks not of Israel, but of God. The chief point of that prologue seems to be to give God a moniker. The prologue calls God, of all things, "the *Tzur*":

Deuteronomy 32:4

The Rock; His work is perfect, for all His ways are justice. A faithful God, without blemish; righteous and just is He.	**הַצּוּר**, תָּמִים פָּעֳלוֹ, כִּי כָל־דְּרָכָיו מִשְׁפָּט. קֵל אֱמוּנָה וְאֵין עָוֶל; צַדִּיק וְיָשָׁר הוּא:

Nicknames are usually cute, but not that big of a deal. Why does *Ha'azinu* take its new name for God so seriously? Over and over again in the song (and nowhere else in the Torah), *Ha'azinu* will return to its moniker for the Divine, calling God "the *Tzur.*" It seems that referring to God as the *Tzur* is *Ha'azinu*'s way of speaking of God not just as our Father in Heaven, but as our Mother-in-the-Sky as well. Someone who is faithfully there for you.[11]

---

11 A newly born child, even before it opens its eyes and can see, experiences its mother through the act of nursing. Israel, too, would be unable to see its transcendent Creator, and yet, God would suckle her through the *tzur*.

To speculate a bit further: The shock of watching a barren, stone-cold rock, the least likely thing in the world to provide for you, suddenly give forth torrents of lifesaving water, is not all that different, probably, from the radical surprise, delight, and joy an infant experiences when she first receives milk from her mother. It must seem like a miracle to her. Here is this helpless infant. She has no independent means of feeding herself, of slaking her thirst. In her hour of need, as she lies there crying, the whole world must seem like a barren wilderness to her young eyes. And yet, mother redeems this for her, with the surprising gift of sustenance

Faithfulness: Where Love Is First Born

Coming back to the story in the book of Exodus where the people were first introduced to the rock that gave of its waters, we can finally understand why God told Moses that He — the invisible Master of the Universe — would be "standing," so to speak, on that rock. Yes, generally, it is not important where God is. God is everywhere and nowhere at the same time. But not now. The people needed to *relate to* that rock as if it were God's chosen vehicle to take care of them, as if it were an extension of a divine being that has no natural body. Humans would need to imbibe life-sustaining liquid directly from their Creator. There had to be a physical medium for doing that. That medium would be the *tzur*. If God is akin to the nation's mother, the rock is the breast of the Divine, the extension of Mother-in-the-Sky, who faithfully nourishes her young.[12]

The critical word here, by the way, is "faithfully." It isn't enough for mom to provide milk to her infant sporadically. She has to do this consistently if the child is to survive. And when she does, the infant gets something of immense value from her, above and beyond its mere survival. The child gets a lesson in faithfulness. The child learns, gradually, that mom can be *counted on*. That mom will *always* be there for her child. The child who consistently experiences her thirst being eased by her mother learns to trust her. And in that trust, love is first born.

---

from her own body. *Who would have thought?* The infant learns that mother has ways of caring for her that defy her understanding. And so it was meant to be for Israel in the wilderness. The rock would teach that Mother-in-the-Sky could be counted on to take care of you. Delightfully and wondrously, She would provide, even if all seemed hopeless.

12 This may seem strange, as most of us are used to relating to God as "our Father in Heaven." But if God is our Creator, and God is One, it would be strange if the Almighty *didn't* express feminine aspects as well. Indeed, there is a strong tradition in Jewish thought of relating to this feminine side of God (see, for example, Zohar 3:97a, where the Divine Presence is portrayed as a nurturing mother). One of the passages in the text that seems to emphasize this is *Ha'azinu*'s portrayal of God as a nursing mother.

Part IV: The Unfolding Story of the Tzur: Three Crucial Moments

What I'd like to do now is take this understanding that *Ha'azinu* has given us, and use it to recreate the unfolding story of the *tzur*. That story will have three main chapters, as it were; three crucial moments of interactions with a rock that would have profound implications for the relationship between God, Moses, and the people of Israel. We've looked at each of these episodes already, but we now possess the framework that will help us understand them. I want to take you through these three events and explore the through-lines that connect them. They are:

1. Moses' and the people's initial encounter with the *tzur* in Refidim;
2. Moses and the *tzur* in the aftermath of the Golden Calf;
3. Forty years later, Moses is told to speak to the rock, but strikes it instead.[13]

Let's start from the very beginning (a very nice place to start, as Julie Andrews might say), with the nation's first encounter with the *tzur*.

MOMENT 1: REFIDIM

Ha'azinu helps us understand just how pivotal a moment that first encounter was meant to be. It was designed to foster a transition in how the nation understood their God. Because in the wilderness, before we encountered the *tzur*, God had shown up as our savior, but in a more archetypically masculine kind of way. God had majestically parted the sea and had destroyed the Egyptian armies in its converging waves. And look how Israel responded, in the Song of the Sea:

---

13 Technically, the Torah uses the word *sela*, rather than *tzur*, to refer to the rock in **Parshat Chukat** — the one that Moses struck when he had been told to speak to it. The Sages, however, make the argument that this was the same rock as the *tzur* that Moses struck forty years earlier, back in the book of Exodus (see, for example, Rashi on Num. 20:2; 20:10).

Exodus 15:2–3

עָזִּי וְזִמְרָת יָהּ; וַיְהִי־לִי
לִישׁוּעָה.... יְקֺוָה אִישׁ מִלְחָמָה;
יְקֺוָה שְׁמוֹ:

God is my might and my song; He was for me a salvation.... God is a man of war; God is His name.

Pharaoh's chariots and archers had conspired to hem us in, but God, the ultimate man of war, saved us from that threat. That's how Israel perceived God as they surveyed the ruins of Pharaoh's chariots on the shores of the sea. But God as the ultimate warrior... that conception of God is too narrow an understanding to suffice for Israel in the long haul. Just days after the nation emerged from the sea, they were confronted by a new kind of water crisis. This time, we would be threatened not by too much water but by too little. We traveled by the hundreds of thousands through the desert, and for three days, we didn't find any water. Our enemy now was thirst. How would God as man of war save us from *that*?

Eventually, the people came upon an oasis, and their hopes rose. But then it became clear that the waters they were so overjoyed to see were in fact bitter. All seemed lost. And the question that confronted the people was this: Yes, God was powerful. He was undoubtedly a man of war. But was He more than that, too? Was there perhaps a more tender, "feminine" side to this God? Could God also nurture us when we didn't know how to provide for ourselves?

The answer to that began to reveal itself in stages. First, God miraculously sweetened those bitter waters. The immediate crisis was over, but soon the people would be thirsty again. God, though, helped His people a second time: He led them to another oasis, to the wellsprings of Eilim:

Exodus 15:27

וַיָּבֹאוּ אֵילִמָה, וְשָׁם שְׁתֵּים
עֶשְׂרֵה עֵינֹת מַיִם וְשִׁבְעִים
תְּמָרִים, וַיַּחֲנוּ־שָׁם עַל־הַמָּיִם:

They came to Eilim—and there, there were twelve springs of water and seventy palm trees. They camped there by the water.

A Culmination of Care

With these two water crises and successful resolutions, God was establishing a track record. He had begun to show that He wasn't just the great celestial Warrior who could defeat the armies of Pharaoh; He was also caring and attentive, and would nurture the people. He would be there for them. The Almighty was there for the people at Marah; He was there for them at Eilim. Whenever they thirsted, God found a way to provide drink for them, even in the barren and parched desert.

All of which sets the stage for the third time the people thirsted, the moment they found themselves in Refidim, standing before the *tzur*.

This time, God would show, definitively, that He would *always* be there for them. In a way, the *tzur* would institutionalize divine care. This rock would be there, from God, to suckle the people time and time again, offering its sweet waters whenever they would get thirsty:

Deuteronomy 32:13

וַיֵּנִקֵהוּ דְבַשׁ מִסֶּלַע וְשֶׁמֶן מֵחַלְמִישׁ צוּר:	**[God] suckled him** with honey from the rock, and oil from the flinty *tzur*.

The *tzur*, this veritable "breast of the Divine," would make tangible the truth that God could be counted on. Our Heavenly Mother's care would be there for us whenever needed. A baby learns over time that he doesn't need to wonder whether he will thirst to death; mom will be there for him when he needs her. And the *tzur* would show this newborn people something similar. It would show that God was faithful. In the words of *Ha'azinu*:

Deuteronomy 32:4

הַצּוּר, תָּמִים פָּעֳלוֹ...קֵל אֱמוּנָה וְאֵין עָוֶל	The Rock; His work is perfect...a faithful God, without blemish.

All told, the advent of the *tzur* was designed to create a radical transition. Until now, every few days there was another water crisis. That was natural enough; after all, they were in the desert, so what else would you expect? But after Refidim, when the people encountered the *tzur*, the rock that

God told Moses to hit — the fact is, they never experienced another water crisis again for the next forty years. Why was that? Evidently, despite traveling through parched and hostile terrain, they possessed a reliable source of water from there on in. According to the Rabbis of the Midrash, the *tzur* is the vehicle that engineered that change. The Rabbis argued that once the *tzur* began to give of its water, it never stopped. The people took the *tzur* with them; it became a traveling wellspring and ceased to give of its water only once Miriam died, as recorded in **Parshat Chukat**. Indeed, because of this, the Sages called the *tzur* the Well of Miriam.[14]

Crisis at the *Tzur*

The revelation of the *tzur* at Refidim was supposed to change everything. Except that just then, something went awry. Yes, the rock would indeed provide faithfully and reliably over time. But *how* it would come to do so didn't go according to plan.

By the time the people approached Refidim and were confronted with a lack of water for the third time, their complaints escalated into outright panic. Moses tried to reason with them. He begged the people to restrain their aggressive tone, but his entreaties fell on deaf ears:

---

14 See Bamidbar Rabbah 1:2, and Rabbeinu Bachya on Exodus 17:6. Miriam, the woman who stood by baby Moses when he thirsted in that pitiful basket by the Nile's reeds; Miriam, who suggested to the daughter of Pharaoh that she could help find a nurse to suckle the crying child; Miriam, who delivered him to the "nurse" who was none other than the child's true mother — it would be *she* who, in the eyes of the Rabbis, would become the namesake of the *tzur*. If the purpose of the *tzur* was to help the nation recognize its true mother — its Mother in Heaven — Miriam would be the perfect earthly avatar for that quest.

It seems possible that it is Moses' destiny to do for the newly born nation what Miriam once did for him as an individual: bring the nation-child to the *tzur* who could slake its thirst, when secretly, the *tzur* was just an extension of the nation's true, celestial, unseen Mother. (See also our essay on **Parshat Beshalach**, "What Does It Mean to Have Faith?" in *Exodus: a Parsha Companion* [Jerusalem: Maggid Books, 2020], 63–74, for a closer look at the persona of Miriam, and how events in the Exodus mirrored her individual interactions with Moses and the daughter of Pharaoh).

Exodus 17:2–3

וַיֹּאמֶר לָהֶם מֹשֶׁה, מַה־תְּרִיבוּן
עִמָּדִי? מַה־תְּנַסּוּן אֶת יְקוָה:...
וַיָּלֶן הָעָם עַל־מֹשֶׁה וַיֹּאמֶר,
לָמָּה זֶּה הֶעֱלִיתָנוּ מִמִּצְרַיִם
לְהָמִית אֹתִי וְאֶת־בָּנַי וְאֶת־
מִקְנַי בַּצָּמָא:

Moses said to them, "Why do you fight with me? Why are you testing God?"... and the people grumbled against Moses and said [with one voice], "Why have you brought us up from Egypt, to kill me and my children and my livestock with thirst?"[15]

And then, the situation started to careen out of control:

Exodus 17:4

וַיִּצְעַק מֹשֶׁה אֶל־יְקוָה לֵאמֹר,
מָה אֶעֱשֶׂה לָעָם הַזֶּה? עוֹד
מְעַט **וּסְקָלֻנִי**:

Moses cried out to God, saying, "What shall I do for this people? A little more and **they will stone me**!"

---

15 It is intriguing to compare the people's initial complaint, a verse earlier, with their intensified complaint now. Earlier, the people had used the plural form of verbs when asking for water:

Exodus 17:2

תְּנוּ־**לָנוּ** מַיִם וְנִשְׁתֶּה:

Give **us** water, that we may drink!

Now, though, they use the singular:

Exodus 17:3

לָמָּה זֶּה הֶעֱלִיתָנוּ מִמִּצְרַיִם
לְהָמִית **אֹתִי** וְאֶת־**בָּנַי** וְאֶת
מִקְנַי בַּצָּמָא:

Why have you brought us up from Egypt, to kill **me** and **my** children and **my** livestock with thirst?

The switch in point of view seems to indicate that the people are speaking as one, as if their complaints are so in lockstep with one another that it is a single person voicing them. It is as if nothing else matters but the single, intense desire felt as one by all members of the group.

Things were desperate now. The people's collective despair was turning to rage, and Moses sensed his life was in danger. Something had to give. A grand miracle was in the offing, one that would provide the people with water not just now, but for years ahead. The *tzur* that would give forth torrents of water was about to be revealed. This was the moment God had ordained that water would flow from the rock. But tragically, at that moment, the vehemence of the people left them without eyes to see something as subtle and gentle as a demonstration of the faithfulness of divine care. And so, in the face of the people's desperation, God made a fateful choice: *Hit the rock.*

If the people are threatening to hit you with rocks, then hit the rock, before a rock hits you.

And that's what Moses did. In hitting the rock, his staff became a vehicle for the people's frustrations. The violence latent in their words would find expression in his staff striking the *tzur*.

Strike the Rock Before Rocks Strike You

We often make a crucial error when reading the Torah. We imagine that somehow, when God tells someone to do a particular thing, this means the thing is good, right, or noble in some sort of absolute sense. But sometimes, a situation doesn't present any true "good" option, and what God instructs is the lesser of two evils.

I want to argue that that is the case here. Just because God instructed Moses to hit the rock doesn't mean that this is the way the miracle was supposed to take place. In a more perfect situation, God would have asked Moses to *speak* to the rock, gently, so the rock could be seen as an agent of love; so it could be seen as compassionately responding to the people's needs. Instead, God told Moses to hit the rock, because Moses called 911. Something had to be done. Rocks were about to hit *him*.

And so, an opportunity was lost. The miracle of the rock and the water took place in a compromised form, with violence and apparent compulsion. And that compromised form of the miracle, instead of clearly demonstrating the abiding faithfulness of God as celestial Mother, could instead foster an unfortunate illusion, a lie the people could succumb to, if they so wished—namely, that God is not *really* attentive to our needs, at least not when left to His own devices. He provides only when absolutely forced to by human anger and pressure.

That illusion is not unlike that of a toddler who screams, or bites the mother trying to suckle him, and comes to believe: *Mommy fed me only because I forced her.* That illusion, though understandable, is also tragic. Because when it possesses a child, he fails to understand that his mother's actions are guided by a much more powerful force than whatever miserable attempts he makes to "force" Mommy to feed him. His mother is guided by love.

What's in a Name? Masah and Merivah

The episode with the *tzur* in the book of Exodus ends with Moses giving a new name to the place where it all happened:

וַיִּקְרָא שֵׁם הַמָּקוֹם מַסָּה וּמְרִיבָה, עַל־רִיב בְּנֵי יִשְׂרָאֵל וְעַל נַסֹּתָם אֶת־יְקוָה, לֵאמֹר, הֲיֵשׁ יְקוָה בְּקִרְבֵּנוּ אִם־אָיִן:	[Moses] named the place Masah and Merivah, because of the quarrel of the Children of Israel and because of their testing of God, saying, "Is God among us or not?"	Exodus 17:7

That phrase, "Is God among us, or not?" expresses doubt about something so obvious, so basic and foundational, that it seemingly cannot be denied. God took the people out of Egypt, destroyed their oppressors, and provided them with manna from heaven. God also provided them — hundreds of thousands of them — with water, consistently, in the middle of a parched desert. *And the people wonder: Is God among us or not?* It sounds at least faintly irrational. But that is the tragedy of the child who wails so loudly that she imagines she is forcing her mother to feed her. The illusion is that the mother is just a tool — manipulated, as it were, by the child; *in reality, I'm taking care of myself around here.* The fact that the mother loves the child; that an expression of her — her life-giving milk — is actually *inside* the child, even as the child acts out, is lost on the little one having a tantrum. Yes, to deny that mother is "inside me" is an absurdity. But look, we humans can convince ourselves of all sorts of crazy things. The child who lashes out at his mother is just getting an early, tragic start on that regrettable human tendency.

MOMENT 2: SHATTERED TABLETS

When Moses' staff met the surface of the rock and left behind a shattered scar, that was his first encounter with the *tzur* at Chorev. But it would not be his last. As we saw above, there would be a second chapter in the saga of Moses and the rock. It would happen later in the book of Exodus, after Moses smashed the tablets in the aftermath of the sin of the Golden Calf.

This time, it wasn't water that God had been trying to provide for the people, but laws — divine precepts, carved on two tablets of stone, that would help the people live a meaningful, godly life here in this world. But while Moses was atop the mountain accepting those tablets, the people below started worshipping an idol of their own making, a molten calf fashioned out of gold. God threatened to destroy the people over this profound betrayal. And once again, in a moment of overwhelming crisis, Moses found himself shattering a rock — this time, two of them.

Although these rocks, like the *tzur* at Chorev, embodied a sort of life-giving, divine gift for the people,[16] they were ultimately subjected to violence, like the *tzur* was, because of the people's rebellion. Indeed, it seemed laughable to give the tablets now; the people were guilty of idolatry! The nation's betrayal was so great that a major question loomed: Would they survive? Could their relationship with God be salvaged? Moses went back and forth, negotiating with God over the fate of the people, until finally, he made a daring request:

Exodus 33:18

He said, "Show me, please, Your glory."	וַיֹּאמַר, הַרְאֵנִי נָא אֶת־כְּבֹדֶךָ׃

16 The first rock provided water; the second provided Torah. The Sages of the Talmud (Bava Kama 82a) saw water as a metaphor for the Torah. Both express our Heavenly Parent's care for us here in our physical, terrestrial world, even as our Parent's *actual* presence resides in a world hopelessly beyond our own.

Intriguingly, Rashi comments on the words "Your two breasts are like two fawns, twins of a gazelle" (Song. 4:5) that the words are meant as a poetic description of the two tablets of the Ten Commandments. Evidently, Rashi identifies the giving of these tablets of stone as a "nursing" moment, too.

It always seemed strange to me that Moses would pick now, this moment of profound crisis, to seek his closest encounter with the Divine, an encounter so direct that God Himself would tell him that he could only see God's back, but not His face; that ultimately, Moses would not be able to achieve the full nearness he was seeking, lest he die. Why is *this* the moment to seek such communion with the Master of the Universe? The life of the nation was at stake. Weren't there more pressing matters to attend to? Why would Moses want this *now*?

The answer, I've come to believe, is that Moses saw his request not as a *diversion* from the main task of the moment — finding a way to save the people from the consequences of their sin — but as a way to possibly achieve it. Moses was seeking the essence of God. In effect, he was asking the Master of the Universe: *I need to know who You really are.* All I see is this terrible anger at the people's act of betrayal. Is that all of You? Or is there something more behind this? Can I dare to believe that You still harbor love for them?

Show me Your essence.

The Cleft in the Rock

God answered Moses. What He would reveal to him has since become a constitutive text in Jewish tradition. It is known as the Thirteen Attributes of Compassion:

Exodus 34:6–7

וַיַּעֲבֹר יְקוָה עַל־פָּנָיו, וַיִּקְרָא, יְקוָה יְקוָה קֵל רַחוּם וְחַנּוּן אֶרֶךְ אַפַּיִם וְרַב־חֶסֶד וֶאֱמֶת׃ נֹצֵר חֶסֶד לָאֲלָפִים נֹשֵׂא עָוֺן וָפֶשַׁע וְחַטָּאָה	God passed before him, and proclaimed, "Hashem, Hashem, a merciful and gracious God, slow to anger, abundant in steadfast kindness, who keeps kindness to the thousandth generation, who forgives iniquity, crime, and sin..."

God was telling Moses that divine anger, even if severe, is not His essence. Compassion is. The words of the Thirteen Attributes suggest that God's compassion toward us is virtually inextinguishable. It can be counted on even in our darkest moments. But before God revealed this to Moses, He asked him to do something. He asked Moses to stand in the cleft of the *tzur*. He would need to be *there* when he beheld these truths.

The Heart of the Shattered Rock

We suggested earlier that the Torah seems to want the reader to understand that this *tzur* is the same "rock at Chorev" that Moses struck to get the water. It is the same rock, but now it has a cleft in it — apparently, we surmise, because of the violence done to it by Moses' staff. And, as we noticed earlier, it seems that God is asking Moses to trade places with Him, as it were. In Refidim, it was God who stood on the rock. Now, it would be Moses. God would situate him not just on the rock, but *in* the cleft of the rock, inside its shattered heart. It was as if God were saying:

If you want to know the deepest truth about Me, if you want to perceive the compassion that is the core of My Being — that, like a mother's love, is inextinguishable even for her most wayward child — then yes, sure, I'll show that to you. But first you have to stand in the shattered rock. First, you have to understand the pain that I, the Divine Being, experienced the moment I had hoped to reveal My unbounded love and care for the people. They foiled that revelation with anger, taunts, and rebellion. When you, Moses, can understand the pain of a mother — a celestial Mother — who is unable to convey her love to her child in any way that child can understand, when you can feel the pain of the shattered "breast of the Divine" — then, and only then, will I allow you to perceive how deep the current of divine love truly runs. Then, and only then, will I allow you to see the vulnerable truth that no matter the rejection the child hurls toward the parent, no matter the hurt the child causes — her Mother's love persists all the same.

As Rashi puts it, explaining the opening of the Thirteen Attributes of Compassion:

Rashi on Exodus 34:6, from Rosh HaShanah 17b

"יְקוָה יְקוָה" - מִדַּת רַחֲמִים הִיא. אַחַת קֹדֶם שֶׁיֶּחֱטָא, וְאַחַת אַחַר שֶׁיֶּחֱטָא וְיָשׁוּב.	[The attributes open with] "Hashem, Hashem." This is the attribute of mercy. [The divine name is repeated:] one, [that God is there for us] before a person sins, and the other, after he sins and [seeks to] repent.

The same God who is there for us before sin is there for us after sin, unabashedly waiting for us to come back to Him. That is the great secret, the great vulnerability, of divine compassion. Mother's love is virtually inextinguishable. Even if the child does something inexcusable, the bond between parent and child will still, painfully, endure.

This is a hard truth. It means that the child has the capacity to inflict great pain on the parent — for the parent won't, when push comes to shove, do the easy thing and just walk away. The parent is in it for the long haul. God's compassion may become bruised, but it will not be beaten. It will survive, against all odds, despite the child's determined attempt to ignore or reject it.

MOMENT 3: FORTY YEARS LATER

For forty long years, that rock — the *tzur* struck by Moses, the *tzur* with the cleft in it — continued to provide its water (see Rashi on Num. 20:2). And for all those years in the desert, the people were secure. They had no more water crises. This, despite their self-induced illusion about the rock. The people were free to believe that the mob that nearly stoned Moses had virtually "forced" the Almighty's hand. After all, as we suggested above, Moses' strike on the rock was, in some way, really nothing more than a channeling of the people's own angry demands. The illusion was that these out-of-control demands had produced something valuable, that the people had somehow managed to get water from the rock by their own power. The truth, of course, was otherwise. The consistent care of the *tzur* came from their Creator's love, not the chaos the people were able to create. But that truth was easily overlooked, and the people remained oblivious to it, by and large, as they wandered for years through the desert.

Until finally, in the fortieth and final year in the wilderness, a new moment of truth would arrive.

The most obvious event that would bring about this moment of reckoning was the death of Miriam. With her death, the *tzur*, which the Sages called the Well of Miriam, suddenly stopped giving its water. But in a larger sense, something else triggered it, too. The years of wandering in the desert were coming to a close. The people were poised to the enter the land of Canaan. Because of that, it was now more vital than ever that the people learn the truth about the *tzur*.

Why? Because once the people would enter the land, their lives would change forever. They would no longer be the newborn nation "suckled" by their Creator. They would enter a new stage of maturity, a kind of early adulthood — and their relationship with their Creator would therefore become more complex. Yes, God would still provide for them, but not in the same ways as before. The vehicle for His care would become less glaringly obvious. God would provide sustenance through the gifts of the Land of Israel and rainwater from heaven. In the new arrangement, instead of eating manna from heaven, the people would farm their land and bake bread from the grain they would harvest. And instead of drinking water from the *tzur*, they would construct aqueducts to channel water from rain and from rivers.

In the land, the people would be partners with the Divine in their own nourishment: God provided land and rain; the people worked the land and harvested its produce. But the problem was: *The people needed to be clear about that partnership.* If the people could delude themselves even in the wilderness into thinking that they, with their incessant complaints, somehow forced God's hand and independently brought forth water from the rock — well, then, once they entered the land, it would be even easier to persist in harboring these kinds of delusions. Rather than thanking God, rather than blessing Him for the land through which He bestows divine care upon them, they could imagine that they, with their agricultural prowess, were the ones who were entirely responsible for the bread on their tables. God would be entirely… off the table, if you'll pardon the pun. His love would simply not be a necessary part of the equation.[17]

---

17 As Deuteronomy puts it, the people will all too easily forget about God. They will all too easily forget about the enchanting love bestowed upon them by God's *tzur*:

Deuteronomy 8:11–17

הִשָּׁמֶר לְךָ פֶּן־תִּשְׁכַּח אֶת־יְקֹוָה אֱלֹקֶיךָ...פֶּן־תֹּאכַל וְשָׂבָעְתָּ וּבָתִּים טֹבִים תִּבְנֶה וְיָשָׁבְתָּ:...וְרָם לְבָבֶךָ וְשָׁכַחְתָּ אֶת־יְקֹוָה אֱלֹקֶיךָ הַמּוֹצִיאֲךָ מֵאֶרֶץ מִצְרַיִם מִבֵּית עֲבָדִים...**הַמּוֹצִיא לְךָ מַיִם מִצּוּר הַחַלָּמִישׁ**: הַמַּאֲכִלְךָ מָן בַּמִּדְבָּר אֲשֶׁר לֹא־יָדְעוּן אֲבֹתֶיךָ...וְאָמַרְתָּ בִּלְבָבֶךָ כֹּחִי וְעֹצֶם יָדִי עָשָׂה לִי אֶת־הַחַיִל הַזֶּה:	But beware lest you forget Hashem your God. Lest, when you have eaten and are full, and have built goodly houses, and lived therein…that your heart becomes proud, and you forget Hashem your God, who brought you forth out of the land of Egypt, out of the house of bondage…**who brought you forth water out of the rock of flint**; who fed you in the wilderness with manna, which your fathers didn't know. Lest you say in your heart, "My power and the might of my hand has gotten me all this wealth!"

Without persistent memories of the *tzur*, without a clear understanding of how they were lovingly nursed in infanthood by the one and only Master of the Universe, the people could all too easily lose their spiritual moorings entirely.

The *Tzur,* Redux

And so, in their fortieth year in the wilderness, as the people finally prepared to enter the land, God would seek to reveal the truth about His *tzur*. God would instruct Moses to speak to the rock, and it would give of its water, just as (I'm claiming) was *supposed* to have happened all those years ago. Yes, the people were rebellious, as they were forty years before, and people possessed of a rebellious spirit are not in a welcoming frame of mind to take in lessons about their Creator's love. But in the intervening forty years, the people and God had weathered rebellions. The greatest of these was Korach's, and it was defeated, finally, by Aaron's staff — a symbol of love and human faithfulness, reflecting Aaron's own self-sacrifice and devotion to the very people who sought brazenly to replace him (see our essay on **Parshat Korach**).[18]

Later in Deuteronomy, in the song of *Ha'azinu*, these same concerns would express themselves — but with even more passion and force, distilled into their essence through the power of poetry:

וַיֵּנִקֵהוּ דְבַשׁ מִסֶּלַע וְשֶׁמֶן
מֵחַלְמִישׁ צוּר:...וַיִּשְׁמַן יְשֻׁרוּן
וַיִּבְעָט. שָׁמַנְתָּ, עָבִיתָ, כָּשִׂיתָ.
וַיִּטֹּשׁ אֱלוֹקַ עָשָׂהוּ וַיְנַבֵּל צוּר
יְשֻׁעָתוֹ:

God suckled him with honey out of the stone; oil out of **the flinty rock**.... But [when Israel came to the land, He,] Jeshurun, grew fat and kicked. You have grown fat. You have grown thick. You have become sleek. Then he forsook the God who made him, and belittled **the Rock of his salvation**

Deuteronomy 32:13, 15

18 Korach's rebellion was defeated only by the miraculous flowering of Aaron's staff. I argued in our essay on **Parshat Korach** that it was not coincidental that this miraculous event takes place immediately after Aaron acts boldly and decisively to defend the very people who sought to upend his role as high priest. His integrity and love for the people was beyond dispute. How could anyone really challenge his right to lead anymore? The organic flowering of his staff was nothing but the embodiment of that truth about him. See our essay on **Parshat Korach** for further details.

So now, in the face of another rebellion, God would instruct Moses to take Aaron's staff, and use that to quell the people's murmurings. The people would see the staff and remember a crucial truth: *that they were led by those who loved them.* Aaron, their priest, who helped mediate between them, and the Divine who was entirely devoted to them. And when they would see the *tzur* immediately respond, when gently asked, with overflowing water, they would come to understand a higher truth, too: It wasn't just their terrestrial leader, Aaron, who loved them and would always be there for them; God, their celestial Leader, was entirely devoted to them as well.

This would be one last chance to set things right before the nation graduated from "infanthood," a final chance to teach the people a truth that they should have learned forty years before: Their violence wasn't the thing that forced God to care for them. God, the Creator of this people, was loving and faithful and could be counted upon. In the words of the song of *Ha'azinu*:

Deuteronomy 32:4

הַצּוּר, תָּמִים פָּעֳלוֹ...קֵל אֱמוּנָה וְאֵין עָוֶל	The Rock; His work is perfect...a faithful God, without blemish.

An Opportunity Lost

Alas, Moses didn't do it. Instead of using Aaron's staff to quiet the rebellion through the reassuring example of his brother's love for and dedication to the people, he reached for his own staff instead — a vehicle of might and power, the staff that once turned the entire Nile into blood. He called on *that* staff, and with it, struck the rock once more — as he had done forty years earlier, when the people seemed about to stone him. And as he did this, Moses hurled an accusation at the people:

Numbers 20:10–11

וַיֹּאמֶר לָהֶם, שִׁמְעוּ־נָא הַמֹּרִים! הֲמִן־הַסֶּלַע הַזֶּה נוֹצִיא לָכֶם מָיִם: וַיָּרֶם מֹשֶׁה אֶת־יָדוֹ, וַיַּךְ	And he said to them, "Hear now, you rebels; shall we bring forth water for you from this rock?" And Moses lifted up his

אֶת־הַסֶּלַע בְּמַטֵּהוּ פַּעֲמָיִם	hand,[19] and struck the rock with his staff twice.

Rather than quieting the rebellion with Aaron's staff, Moses sought to confront it, angrily. *You are rebels! Do you really think yourselves deserving of water from that rock?*

And yet, that idea was the opposite of what the people needed to hear right then. It took something they were doing and hardened it into a label. If the people were truly rebels, if that was their identity, then what hope was there for them? How could Mother love someone as awful as them?

But how awful they are, in reality, misses the point. No infant *deserves* their Creator's care. What, after all, has a little child ever done to *earn* that love? A Creator's care isn't earned; it is bestowed on the child simply because... she is His child. Moses' reproof of the people at that moment wasn't what God asked for, and didn't convey the message God wanted to convey.

What Does *Emunah* Really Mean?

We asked earlier, toward the very beginning of this essay, how Moses, in striking that rock, could possibly be accused of evincing a lack of faith. Surely, whether the rock provided water by being spoken to or by being struck — either way, its provision of water to hundreds of thousands of

---

19 It is interesting that the text makes a point of mentioning Moses raising his hand and striking the rock. Why is the raised hand important? Who cares what the motion was that Moses used to start his swing toward the rock? The answer, perhaps, is that Moses's raised hand wasn't a mere technical detail. A raised hand is language used in the Torah to describe a proud victory over enemies. Israel marches out of Egypt with this exact same expression: "with an uplifted hand," victorious over the Egyptians (Ex. 14:8). Likewise, Moses himself raises his hands when he leads the Israelites in victorious battle over the Amalekites (Ex. 17:11; see also Num. 15:30).

Indeed, an uplifted hand is a perfect way to confront your adversary — but what happens when you lift your hand against the *tzur*? Once again, as happened forty years earlier, Moses seems to channel the destructive energy of the rebellious masses toward the *tzur*. God had asked him to do so then. But not now.

people was undoubtedly a miraculous event. So where, exactly, is Moses' supposed lack of faith? Where is his lack of belief? At long last, we are in a position, I think, to answer that question.

The answer is that Moses was actually *not* guilty of showing any lack of faith in God whatsoever. The text never says he was.

No, you're not crazy for thinking that God accused Moses of a lack of faith when he hit the rock. That is, after all, how most translations of the Torah render this verse:

Numbers 20:12	וַיֹּאמֶר יְקֹוָה אֶל־מֹשֶׁה וְאֶל־ אַהֲרֹן, יַעַן **לֹא־הֶאֱמַנְתֶּם בִּי** לְהַקְדִּישֵׁנִי לְעֵינֵי בְּנֵי יִשְׂרָאֵל, לָכֵן לֹא תָבִיאוּ אֶת־הַקָּהָל הַזֶּה אֶל־הָאָרֶץ אֲשֶׁר־נָתַתִּי לָהֶם:	God said to Moses and Aaron, "Because **you didn't trust in Me**, to sanctify Me in the eyes of the Children of Israel, therefore you shall not bring this assembly into the land which I have given them."

But this is one of those situations where you need to read the verse in the Hebrew, not in the English. You have to ask yourself: What does that really important verb, הֶאֱמַנְתֶּם, really mean?

The root comes down to the three Hebrew letters אמן. And yes, although that word does seem to connote the idea of belief or faith in many instances throughout Tanach, this, I would argue, is not the central meaning of the root. You can see this because אמן has other meanings, too. Consider, for instance, what the word means in the book of Esther, when the text tells us that Mordechai took care of his orphaned cousin, Hadassah:

Esther 2:7	וַיְהִי **אֹמֵן** אֶת־הֲדַסָּה, הִיא אֶסְתֵּר, בַּת־דֹּדוֹ, כִּי אֵין לָהּ אָב וָאֵם	He **raised** Hadassah, who is Esther, his uncle's daughter, for she had no father or mother.

The truth is that the root *alef-mem-nun* actually has a deeper, core meaning from which all its various other meanings derive. You see, it is not just a verb, meaning to believe in, have faith, or raise a child. It is also a noun. And when it's a noun, you'd never believe what it means:

RUTH 4:16	NUMBERS 11:12
וַתִּקַּח נָעֳמִי אֶת הַיֶּלֶד וַתְּשִׁתֵהוּ בְחֵיקָהּ וַתְּהִי לוֹ **לְאֹמֶנֶת**. And Naomi took the boy and placed him in her bosom, and she became his **nurse**.	הֶאָנֹכִי הָרִיתִי אֵת כָּל־הָעָם הַזֶּה, אִם־אָנֹכִי יְלִדְתִּיהוּ, כִּי־תֹאמַר אֵלַי: שָׂאֵהוּ בְחֵיקֶךָ כַּאֲשֶׁר יִשָּׂא **הָאֹמֵן** אֶת־הַיֹּנֵק "Have I conceived all this people? Have I brought them forth, that you should tell me, 'Carry them in your bosom, as a **nurse** carries a suckling infant'?"

To be an *omen* is to be someone who nurses a child.

Where Trust Begins

Once you see this core meaning, you realize why the word also means "faithfulness." For where, indeed, does anyone learn the idea of faithfulness from? How do we come to believe that the world is a good place, that anyone in it can possibly be trusted? We learn this from those who raised us and cared for us when we were young and vulnerable, unable to take care of ourselves. We learn this, principally…*from the one who nursed us.*

An *omen* doesn't necessarily denote a biological mother. It denotes someone who takes up the task of nursing an infant, someone who shepherds a child through the first crucial years of its life. That person is the one the child first experiences as being totally, completely, and reliably there for him, night or day, whenever he hungers or thirsts. It is through the young child's experience with an *omen* (whether a mother or nursemaid) that he or she will learn whether trust is even possible in this new realm outside the womb.

Turning Your Back on the Illusion

As the people stood there, in **Parshat Chukat**, on the cusp of entering the land of Canaan, they had a job to do, not unlike the job of a small child on the cusp of graduating out of infanthood. That job is to discover the truth about their caregiver's love. To graduate out of babyhood, a little child needs to learn that you don't get fed just because you screamed or pummeled Mommy. You have words now, and you can use them. You can say: *Mommy, I'm thirsty,* and Mommy will lovingly respond.[20] To believe that all you can do is scream is to believe that you are more helpless than you are. And it is to believe that Mommy, strangely, is helpless, too. She is really just a puppet, dancing to the chaotic beat of your intimidation, while the true provider is *you*. And if that is the case, well, ultimately, you are all alone in a cold, heartless world.

Now that the people were about to enter the land, it was crucial for them to turn their back on this illusion. For if they could not, what kind of society would they build in this new land, so full of promise?

Even if they became a wealthy nation, if they chose to believe that their wealth is purely a function of their own prowess, that they really

---

20 Hence, God's choice to ask Moses and Aaron to speak to the rock. Their role now, as it was forty years earlier, was to channel the collective energy of the people toward the *tzur*. They, representing the people, were to speak gently to the rock, and it would respond. When God instructed Moses to strike the rock forty years earlier, it was because, regrettably, that was the only way he could accurately channel the people's energy. They *were* being angry and rebellious.

I think it is intriguing that there is often a moment in a young child's development where he or she is still nursing, but is also beginning to learn how to speak. Seemingly, this was that moment for the people. They were still receiving water from the rock, but were about to be "weaned"; they were about to enter the land and would be able to provide for themselves. It was a time to learn to use their words, so that they could end their experience of nursing from their celestial Mother in a way that would serve their relationship with God well.

One wonders whether, forty years prior, one of the reasons God, in the end, tolerated their complaints and allowed Moses to hit the rock was because the people were at an earlier stage in their national development. Just as a very young child does not yet have words to communicate with Mommy — all they can really do is scream and cry to make their desires known — maybe that was the stage the people were at back then as well. And yet, even if this was so, one needs to remember that the first story of the *tzur*, forty years prior, took place well before the sin of the spies. Meaning: Then, too, the people were slated to enter the land in only a matter of weeks. Hence, the first story of the *tzur could* have been the crucial transitional moment, too. Had the people been able to rein in their complaints, Moses could have been asked to speak to the rock on their behalf; and, had the rock given its water under *those* circumstances, the transition to a world where the people would leave behind "nursing" and enter the land in an embrace of independence, could have made good progress.

are all alone in this world — they would live a miserable life, *despite* all that wealth. The rich will fear to share their bounty with the weak, because, after all, who can you really trust? *If your Creator doesn't truly care about you, why should anyone else?* Even a land full of milk and honey can eventually become a hard, cold backwater, where each person nervously looks out solely for him- or herself, if the poison of lonely self-interest is allowed to have its way.

God's critique of Moses, at the end of the day, was that he didn't help the people dispel their illusions. They needed to understand that there was an *Omen* in the sky who had their backs. In the words of *Ha'azinu*, קֵל אֱמוּנָה וְאֵין עָוֶל, "a faithful God, without blemish" (Deut. 32:4). And by hitting the rock, rather than allowing it to give of its water freely, Moses didn't make God's faithfulness clear to the people. It wasn't that Moses didn't have enough faith to believe that God could perform a miracle. He surely did. It was that Moses didn't help the people come to understand that God was their *Omen*; that God was faithful to *them*.

What Was Moses Thinking?

What led Moses to lay down Aaron's staff, accuse the people, and hit the rock — with his own staff — instead of speaking to it? Doing this was in direct contravention to what God had asked of him. Why would he do it?

We can't know for sure, but an intriguing possibility suggests itself. The last time the people rebelled at the *tzur*, Moses, the text tells us, feared for his life. This time, forty years later, he no longer appears to be motivated by mortal danger. He doesn't say anything like: "A little more, and they will stone me!" Was this because the people's panic was not as out of control as it was then? Was it because Moses knew Aaron's staff was waiting in the wings, and he could call on it to quiet things if he had to? We can't know. But one way or the other, Moses doesn't feel himself in mortal danger.

What, then, animates his response to the people's complaints? Instead of a sense of self-preservation, it is a sense of moral indignation. He seems anguished and incensed at the people's rebellion:

וַיֹּאמֶר לָהֶם, שִׁמְעוּ־נָא הַמֹּרִים! הֲמִן־הַסֶּלַע הַזֶּה נוֹצִיא לָכֶם מָיִם:	And he said to them, "Hear now, you rebels; shall we bring forth water for you from this rock?"	Numbers 20:10

Why is Moses *so* upset by the people's insubordinate complaints, in a way he wasn't forty years ago? Why does it kindle such outrage in Moses?

The answer, I want to suggest, is that something had changed in Moses since last time. Between last time and this time, Moses had experienced something he could not forget.

He had stood in the cleft of the rock.

Moses had been given an excruciating window into divine anguish, the palpable sense of divine frustration; the pain the celestial Mother feels when her children can't — *won't* — accept her as a loving force in their lives. It wasn't that God explained this in words; rather, Moses had experienced it viscerally, standing there in the shattered *tzur*.

For forty years, Moses carried those haunting memories with him. But now, in the fortieth year, as Moses found himself standing at the rock, once more confronting the bitter, rebellious complaints of a people almost willfully blinding themselves to the idea that their Creator was faithful to them — suddenly, it wasn't a memory anymore. Past was becoming present with burning insistency. And it seemed like an outrage to him. Could those complaints be quieted with Aaron's staff? Yes, of course, but that wasn't the point. *How dare they blindly scream like this! How could they dare treat celestial Mother this way?* And so he accosted them for being rebels, even as he struck the rock, channeling their rebellious complaints, as he had done forty years before.

Ironically, Moses' closest, most profound encounter with God may possibly have been what led him, forty years later, to disobey His words. That was when God had allowed him to glimpse something of the essence of being a mother — the disappointment that ensues when all you want to do is love, and your child turns their back on you. But there is another part of being a mother, too, and perhaps God had also been trying to show *that* to Moses, forty years earlier in the cleft of the rock. God had allowed Moses to perceive the pain of a foiled parent through the *vision* of the shattered rock, but had demonstrated the other, complementary aspect of being a mother through what He *said* to Moses at that moment — namely, the Thirteen Attributes of Compassion. What God had said, in effect, was: No matter how upset Mother might get with the behavior of her child, she is still, in the words of the Thirteen Attributes of Compassion, "merciful and gracious, slow to anger, abundant in steadfast kindness" (Ex. 34:6–7).

Even when there is every reason, in the name of justice, to walk out on this relationship of an ungrateful people to their God, ultimately, I won't do that. I will still be there. I will still be steadfast. Ultimately, Moses was meant to understand and internalize two things: empathy for a parent who is struck by their child, and God's undying compassion and forbearance, even in the face of that violence. But forty years later, he found himself able to relate to only one of them. Suffused with a vivid understanding of divine anguish, Moses found himself defending the God who would not strike back, when God was not asking for any defense at all.

Beyond Retribution

So Moses hit the rock, and for this, he was held back by God from leading the people into the land. A harsh punishment, indeed. But in the end, it may be that God's decision had little to do with punishment or retribution. It was just that the people needed to enter the land differently. If their leader saw them as rebels — if they saw *themselves* as rebels — how could they possibly make the transition to a new life in the land? A new leader, one might hope, could possibly help the people see things differently: that just as God's anger wasn't the full truth of who He was, so too, rebellion wasn't the full truth of who *they* were. They could calm down, and let go of their caustic words. And with that, they would be able to apprehend a truth that had thus far eluded them: Their complaints weren't the secret of their success. They had on their side, and always would, a Parent in heaven whose love was more faithful than the people could possibly imagine.

Balaam and the *Akeidah*

לֹא תֵלֵךְ עִמָּהֶם; לֹא
תָאֹר אֶת־הָעָם, כִּי בָרוּךְ
הוּא׃

Do not go with them; do not curse the nation, because it is blessed.

NUMBERS 22:12

Balaam and the *Akeidah*

IN PIRKEI AVOT, the Sages of the Mishnah contrast two biblical figures that you would never think of contrasting: Balaam, the villain of our parsha and … Abraham.

Avot 5:19

כׇּל מִי שֶׁיֵּשׁ בְּיָדוֹ שְׁלֹשָׁה דְבָרִים הַלָּלוּ, מִתַּלְמִידָיו שֶׁל אַבְרָהָם אָבִינוּ. וּשְׁלֹשָׁה דְבָרִים אֲחֵרִים, מִתַּלְמִידָיו שֶׁל בִּלְעָם הָרָשָׁע. עַיִן טוֹבָה, וְרוּחַ נְמוּכָה, וְנֶפֶשׁ שְׁפָלָה, מִתַּלְמִידָיו שֶׁל אַבְרָהָם אָבִינוּ. עַיִן רָעָה, וְרוּחַ גְּבוֹהָה, וְנֶפֶשׁ רְחָבָה, מִתַּלְמִידָיו שֶׁל בִּלְעָם הָרָשָׁע.	Whoever possesses these three traits has learned from Abraham our father. And anyone who possesses the opposite three traits has learned from Balaam the wicked. A giving eye, a humble spirit, and an unassuming soul: These are the qualities of one who has learned from Abraham. A greedy eye,[1] a haughty spirit, and a boastful soul: These are qualities of one who has learned from Balaam the wicked.

Why would the Sages think of comparing and contrasting these two people? What, if anything, do they have in common?

Of Apples and Cadillacs

Any attempt to contrast two people, even one that draws distinctions between them, begins with an understanding of a certain, unstated

1 The expressions *ayin tova* and *ayin ra'a* in rabbinic literature often refer to the way in which one looks at other people's interests, whether one wishes success for others or enviously desires their failure. This definition is in many ways synonymous with one's degree of generosity or lack thereof. For instance, the Gemara in Bava Batra 64b extends this terminology to describe whether we can interpret the ambiguities in a sale such that the seller acted generously.

commonality. Suppose I ask you: What's the difference between Steven Spielberg and George Lucas? Then, even if I go on to list a whole bunch of differences between them, there must be some commonality underlying my comparison that allows me to contrast them. In this case, they are both storytellers. Specifically, they are both producers of science fiction films. Thus, I may talk to you about how their respective styles of storytelling are different or how the way they chose to pitch their scripts to studios was different. But still, my contrast begins with an underlying commonality. Steven Spielberg and George Lucas are playing in the same sandbox, if you will.

To take this point and boil it down to just one sentence: You can contrast apples and oranges; you can't contrast apples and Cadillacs.

We need to ask, then: Exactly which common sandbox do these two biblical figures occupy? What do Abraham and Balaam have in common that the Sages might think that they are ripe for contrast? Abraham is the grand patriarch of our nation. Balaam is a prophet for hire, who is rented by Balak, king of Moab, to curse the oncoming Israelite army. Adventure ensues, complete with talking donkeys and angelic swords, and Balaam's attempt ultimately fails and he winds up blessing the Israelites instead. This seems like a case of apples and Cadillacs. Abraham and Balaam don't seem to have any nexus for comparison. Abraham isn't trying to defend a nation from invasion. He doesn't seem to be trying to curse people. Yet the Sages seem convinced that there is a basis for comparing these two men. What have the Sages seen that you and I haven't seen yet?

The Evil of Balaam

Besides the question of a basis for comparison, something else seems puzzling in the Sages' statement about Abraham and Balaam, too. If you recall, the Sages, in that teaching, characterized Balaam as a *rasha*, an "evildoer." I think it is worth asking: From where, exactly, do they get such a starkly critical view of Balaam? When you take a quick glance at the text, it doesn't seem to yield such great evil in Balaam, certainly not the kind attributed to him in this mishna. Sure, he is a prophet for hire, and he is willing to harm the Israelites at Balak's request — but, as he keeps on telling Balak: He can't curse Israel unless God goes along with it. In the end, he is true to his word about that, and he blesses the camp of Israel because that's what God demands of him. So why do the Sages say he embodies arrogance and greed? He seems to be a person who follows the word of God. Why do they label him a *rasha,* casting him as categorically evil?

These two questions will occupy us for the balance of this essay. I think that if we can answer the first question — why do the Sages contrast Abraham and Balaam in the first place? — it will put us in a position to answer the second: What convinced the Sages of Balaam's great evil?

Finding the Links

Let's start with our first question: Why do the Sages contrast these two figures? Why do they feel they occupy a common sandbox?

I want to suggest to you that the Sages are actually building off of a close reading of the biblical text. When reading the story of Balaam, they saw things that persistently reminded them of Abraham, of all people. After enough of these cues accumulated, they became convinced that the Torah itself saw Balaam as an Abraham-like figure.

What did they see?

If we start at the very beginning of the Balak story, do we find anything there that might remind us of Abraham?

At the very beginning of the Balaam story, Balaam finds himself accosted by messengers of Balak, king of Moab, who are seeking to gain Balaam's consent to leave home and go on a journey to aid the king. The messengers relay words of Balak that are full of praise for Balaam. Here's what Balak says:

כִּי יָדַעְתִּי, אֵת אֲשֶׁר-תְּבָרֵךְ מְבֹרָךְ, וַאֲשֶׁר תָּאֹר, יוּאָר:	I know that those whom you bless will be blessed and those whom you curse will be cursed.	Numbers 22:6

Well, that phraseology sure does sound familiar, doesn't it? It reminds us of God's reassuring words to Abraham. It is as if the beginning of the Balaam story matches up... with the beginning of the Abraham story.

In a way, in the Abraham story, God is doing a version of what Balak would later do. He is a Heavenly King asking someone to leave home and go on a journey to be of service to Him. And in this context, the

Almighty speaks of blessings and curses, just as Balak, this earthly king, would later do:

Genesis 12:3

וַאֲבָרְכָה מְבָרְכֶיךָ, וּמְקַלֶּלְךָ, אָאֹר	I will bless those who bless you, and those who curse you, I will curse.

In both cases, our protagonists — Abraham in one case, Balaam in the other — seem to be the source of special blessings, and curses, that can and will affect others. Even the language the Torah uses to describe Balaam's capacity with curses and blessings seems to mirror the language we find with Abraham: In each case, the word for blessing appears twice, as does the word for curse.

BALAAM	ABRAHAM
כִּי יָדַעְתִּי, אֵת אֲשֶׁר־תְּבָרֵךְ מְבֹרָךְ, וַאֲשֶׁר תָּאֹר, יוּאָר:	וַאֲבָרְכָה מְבָרְכֶיךָ, וּמְקַלֶּלְךָ, אָאֹר
I know that those whom you **bless will be blessed** and those whom **you curse will be cursed**. (Num. 22:6)	**I will bless those who bless you**, and those who curse you, **I will curse**. (Gen. 12:3)

We find here the beginnings for a basis of comparison between these two biblical figures.

It should be noted, by the way, that for all the similarities in language here, the text also creates a powerful contrast between Abraham and Balaam. These two people are very emphatically not doing the same thing. In the case of Balaam, we are told that Balaam is the one who bestows blessings and curses: Balaam is active. However, in Abraham's case, he is passive. It is not he who bestows the blessings; rather, it is God. So while the biblical language seems to link these two men, it also at the same time presents them as kind of inverses of one another — interestingly, just as we find the Sages doing in the Mishna.

But that's only the beginning. There's more.

Abraham's Journey and Balaam's Journey

So that's a first link between Balaam and Abraham. But it is not the last. For as it turns out, the Heavenly King, God, asked Abraham to go on two great journeys — one at the beginning of his story, right when we are first introduced to him, and one at the end. The first journey was to the land of Canaan; the second was to Mount Moriah, where he was asked to offer up his son Isaac, in the story we now know as the *Akeidah* (the Binding of Isaac). And, wouldn't you know it, the parallels between Balaam and Abraham seem to link Balaam's journey not just to Abraham's first journey, but to Abraham's second one as well. Consider, for example, these words, which describe how Balaam prepared himself to travel at Balak's behest:

וַיָּקָם בִּלְעָם בַּבֹּקֶר וַיַּחֲבֹשׁ אֶת־אֲתֹנוֹ	Balaam woke up in the morning and saddled his mule.	Numbers 22:21

Well, does that remind you of anything, perchance, in the Abraham narrative? Does the text ever tell us about Abraham rising in the morning? Does it ever tell us about Abraham saddling his animal of choice? It most certainly does. When God tells Abraham to take his son, the son that he loves, and offer him up on a mountain that He will show him, Abraham begins his journey in almost exactly the same way:[2]

BALAAM	ABRAHAM
וַיָּקָם בִּלְעָם בַּבֹּקֶר וַיַּחֲבֹשׁ אֶת־אֲתֹנוֹ Balaam woke up in the morning and saddled his mule. (Num. 22:21)	וַיַּשְׁכֵּם אַבְרָהָם בַּבֹּקֶר וַיַּחֲבֹשׁ אֶת־חֲמֹרוֹ Abraham woke up early in the morning and saddled his donkey. (Gen. 22:3)

2 Indeed, Rashi cites the Sages of the Talmud (Sanhedrin 105b) as making this connection between Balaam and Abraham as well.

Moreover, we often forget a little detail about Balaam's story, but it's there: When he went on his journey, he took two lads with him, just as Abraham once did:

BALAAM	ABRAHAM
וְהוּא רֹכֵב עַל־אֲתֹנוֹ, **וּשְׁנֵי נְעָרָיו עִמּוֹ׃**	וַיִּקַּח אֶת־**שְׁנֵי נְעָרָיו אִתּוֹ**
[Balaam] was riding on his donkey, and **his two lads were with him.** (Num. 22:22)	And [Abraham] took **his two lads with him.** (Gen. 22:3)

And, dear reader, lest you are tempted to chalk all this up to coincidence, know that the parallels between the men and their respective journeys continue still further. Consider, for example, the role that angels play in Abraham's and Balaam's respective travels.

After God grants Balaam permission to travel with Balak's messengers, and Balaam sets off on his journey, an angel comes along and blocks his way:

Numbers 22:26

וַיּוֹסֶף מַלְאַךְ־יְקוָה עֲבוֹר,
וַיַּעֲמֹד בְּמָקוֹם צָר, אֲשֶׁר אֵין־
דֶּרֶךְ לִנְטוֹת יָמִין וּשְׂמֹאול׃

And the angel of God again moved forward, and stood [blocking his way] in a narrow path where there was no room to turn right or left.

Well, in the story of the Binding of Isaac, an angel showed up at a crucial moment, too. God commanded Abraham to take Isaac and offer him up as an offering. But then, an angel of God came along... and blocked that outcome from actually occurring. Here are the two, side by side:

BALAAM	ABRAHAM
וַיּוֹסֶף **מַלְאַךְ-יְקוָה** עֲבוֹר, וַיַּעֲמֹד בְּמָקוֹם צָר, אֲשֶׁר אֵין־דֶּרֶךְ לִנְטוֹת יָמִין וּשְׂמֹאול: And the **angel of God** again moved forward, and stood [blocking his way] in a narrow path where there was no room to turn right or left. (Num. 22:26)	וַיִּקְרָא אֵלָיו **מַלְאַךְ יְקוָה**...אַל־תִּשְׁלַח יָדְךָ אֶל־הַנַּעַר, וְאַל־תַּעַשׂ לוֹ מְאוּמָה And an **angel of God** called out to him.... "Don't send your hand against the boy and don't do anything to him." (Gen. 22:11–12)

The echoes are striking. And remember: It's not just that the two stories happen to share a few common phrases or events. These commonalities also just happen to progress in precisely the same order in each story:

BALAAM	ABRAHAM
וַיָּקָם בִּלְעָם בַּבֹּקֶר וַיַּחֲבֹשׁ אֶת־אֲתֹנוֹ וַיֵּלֶךְ עִם־שָׂרֵי מוֹאָב: וַיִּחַר אַף אֱלֹקִים כִּי־הוֹלֵךְ הוּא, וַיִּתְיַצֵּב מַלְאַךְ יְקוָה בַּדֶּרֶךְ לְשָׂטָן לוֹ, וְהוּא רֹכֵב עַל־אֲתֹנוֹ **וּשְׁנֵי נְעָרָיו עִמּוֹ**. וַתֵּרֶא הָאָתוֹן אֶת־**מַלְאַךְ יְקוָה נִצָּב בַּדֶּרֶךְ וְחַרְבּוֹ שְׁלוּפָה בְּיָדוֹ** וַתֵּט הָאָתוֹן מִן־הַדֶּרֶךְ וַתֵּלֶךְ בַּשָּׂדֶה. וַיַּךְ בִּלְעָם אֶת־הָאָתוֹן לְהַטֹּתָהּ הַדָּרֶךְ:	**וַיַּשְׁכֵּם אַבְרָהָם בַּבֹּקֶר וַיַּחֲבֹשׁ אֶת־חֲמֹרוֹ וַיִּקַּח אֶת־שְׁנֵי נְעָרָיו אִתּוֹ** וְאֵת יִצְחָק בְּנוֹ, וַיְבַקַּע עֲצֵי עֹלָה, וַיָּקָם וַיֵּלֶךְ אֶל־הַמָּקוֹם אֲשֶׁר אָמַר־לוֹ הָאֱלֹקִים. ... וַיִּשְׁלַח אַבְרָהָם אֶת־יָדוֹ וַיִּקַּח אֶת־הַמַּאֲכֶלֶת לִשְׁחֹט אֶת בְּנוֹ: **וַיִּקְרָא אֵלָיו מַלְאַךְ יְקוָה מִן־הַשָּׁמַיִם**, וַיֹּאמֶר "אַבְרָהָם אַבְרָהָם" וַיֹּאמֶר "הִנֵּנִי." וַיֹּאמֶר "אַל תִּשְׁלַח יָדְךָ אֶל־הַנַּעַר וְאַל־תַּעַשׂ לוֹ מְאוּמָה, כִּי עַתָּה יָדַעְתִּי כִּי־יְרֵא אֱלֹקִים אַתָּה, וְלֹא חָשַׂכְתָּ אֶת־בִּנְךָ אֶת יְחִידְךָ מִמֶּנִּי."

Balaam **woke up in the morning** and **saddled his mule** and departed with the Moabite dignitaries. But God was incensed at his going; so an angel of God took a position in his way as an adversary. He was riding on his mule, with **his two lads with him**, when the mule caught sight of **the angel of God standing in the way, with his drawn sword in his hand.** The ass swerved from the road and went into the fields; and Balaam beat the ass to turn her back onto the road. (Num. 22:21–23)	**So early next morning, Abraham saddled his ass** and took **his two lads with him** and his son Isaac. He split the wood for the burnt offering, and he set out for the place of which God had told him.... And Abraham picked up the knife to slay his son. **And an angel of God called to him from heaven**: "Abraham! Abraham!" And he answered, "Here I am." "Don't send your hand against the boy and don't do anything to him. For now I know that you fear God, since you have not withheld your son, your favored one, from Me." (Gen. 22:3, 10–12)

In light of these parallels, drawing comparisons between Balaam and Abraham, as the mishnah does, is starting to feel not quite as odd; a lot less like apples and Cadillacs. For some as yet unexplained reason, it feels like the Torah itself is trying to connect these two figures. The question though is: Why? What about these two men bears comparison to one another?

A Tale of Two Journeys

A clue, perhaps, comes from the "point of contact" here. Most of the parallels we have seen between Balaam and Abraham seem to revolve around *journeys*. For Abraham, there were two journeys, and for Balaam only one — but in each case there were journeys.

Intriguingly, in the case of Abraham, although one journey (to Canaan) happens at the beginning of his story and the other (to go offer up his son as an offering) occurs at the end, each comes with a directive from God that is almost exactly the same:

GOD TO ABRAHAM IN	GOD TO ABRAHAM IN
וַיֹּאמֶר, קַח־נָא אֶת־בִּנְךָ, אֶת־יְחִידְךָ, אֲשֶׁר אָהַבְתָּ, אֶת־יִצְחָק, **וְלֶךְ לְךָ** אֶל־**אֶרֶץ** הַמֹּרִיָּה, וְהַעֲלֵהוּ שָׁם לְעֹלָה He said, "Please, take your son, your only one, whom you love, Isaac, **and go forth** to **the land** of Moriah, and offer him up as an offering." (Gen. 22:2)	וַיֹּאמֶר יְקוָה אֶל־אַבְרָם, **לֶךְ־לְךָ** **מֵאַרְצְךָ** וּמִמּוֹלַדְתְּךָ וּמִבֵּית אָבִיךָ, אֶל־**הָאָרֶץ** אֲשֶׁר אַרְאֶךָּ: "**Go forth** **from your native land**, from your birthplace, and from your father's house, to **the land** that I will show you." (Gen. 12:1)

The similarity in language invites us to think of the second journey as an extension of the first. Reading these two stories together confirms the truth of this connection. In the first story, Abraham is asked to leave his home, his birthplace, and his father's house behind; in the second story, he is being asked to give his child, Isaac, back to God. In the first story, Abraham is asked to leave behind everything that ties him with his past. In the second story he is asked to leave behind his future.

In any case, if Abraham is somehow to be seen as on one long journey, a journey which culminates with his trek up the mountain with Isaac, it would seem that Balaam's journey up a mountain (in his case to curse the Israelites) is meant to be seen by the reader as running parallel, somehow, to Abraham's journey. But the question, again, is: *Why*? The Torah seems to be telling us that Balaam is on an *Akeidah*-like journey. But what about his mission was *Akeidah*-like?

It's Not Just Whether You Say "Yes"

Well, Abraham was being tested in the *Akeidah*. Perhaps the Torah is suggesting that Balaam was undergoing some sort of test, too. But a test of what?

To wrap our minds around this question, I think we need to return to the story of the *Akeidah* and try to understand the nature of the test it imposed on Abraham. On an overt level, we might say that the test was: Will Abraham give up what is most precious to him, and thereby prove his fealty to God? But on a deeper level, it seems to me, there was another test. A more basic one.

The demand God is making of Abraham is unsettling. Abraham waited a lifetime for a child — and now, unimaginably, God wants Abraham to take a knife to him, to send that child back to God in heaven. Every fiber in Abraham's being must have wanted to rebel against that command. Imagine God instructed you to do something you desperately did not want to do. What exactly would be the nature of this test? The obvious answer is: Would you do it or not? And yes, at face value, that is certainly true. But I think you would also be faced with a more subtle and even more basic test: *Would you even allow yourself to fully and accurately hear those instructions in the first place?*

By way of explanation, allow me to share a midrashic teaching with you. It is a story the Sages tell about the *Akeidah* — and I suspect that the point of their little story is to illustrate the idea I am suggesting here.

Who Did You Mean Again?

The midrash I want to point you to imagines a conversation, so to speak, that God has with Abraham at the beginning of the *Akeidah* story. In the biblical text itself, of course, God does have a conversation with Abraham at this point in the story — but, since God does all the talking, it hardly merits being called a conversation at all:

Genesis 22:2

וַיֹּאמֶר, קַח־נָא אֶת בִּנְךָ, אֶת־
יְחִידְךָ, אֲשֶׁר־אָהַבְתָּ, אֶת יִצְחָק,
וְלֶךְ־לְךָ אֶל אֶרֶץ הַמֹּרִיָּה,
וְהַעֲלֵהוּ שָׁם לְעֹלָה

He said, "Please, take your son, your only one, whom you love, Isaac, and go forth to the land of Moriah, and offer him up as an offering."

But the midrash (*Tanchuma, Vayera* 22) fleshes out the conversation, and imagines that, at each descriptive phrase, Abraham offered a response. For example, when God said to Abraham, "Take your son," Abraham replied: "*Which son would you like me to take?*" After all, Abraham had two sons, Isaac and Ishmael. To this, God replied: "Your only one." But Abraham persisted, protesting: "*Each is 'the only son' to his mother.*" And so God clarified the request further: "The one that you love." At that point, Abraham responded: "*But I love them both!*" And finally, the Master of the Universe gave the ultimate clarification: "Isaac."

The sense we get from the midrash is that Abraham is almost playing a game with God. He seems to know, deep down, who God is referring to — that God wants him to offer up Isaac — but he doesn't like the answer. He doesn't *want* God to be talking about Isaac. And so he engages in what amounts to a desperate back-and-forth, seeking to forestall, somehow, the inevitable conclusion.

Indeed, as we read the rest of the midrash, the Sages seem to amplify this theme. They go on to relate other conversations one might imagine that Abraham, as well as Isaac, might have had on the way up the mountain to carry out the *Akeidah*. Only this time, their interlocutor was not God, but ... Satan.

You'll Never Guess Who I Met on My Way up the Mountain...

The midrash suggests that Satan appeared to Abraham in the guise of an old man and struck up a conversation with him. The conversation quickly progressed from mere small talk to more weighty matters.

The disguised Satan asks Abraham where he happens to be going. Evasively, Abraham responds that he's going to pray to God. But the old man won't let Abraham alone. He points out all the accouterments that Abraham has with him and he slyly inquires about them:

וּמִי שֶׁהוֹלֵךְ לְהִתְפַּלֵּל, לָמָּה אֵשׁ וּמַאֲכֶלֶת בְּיָדוֹ וְעֵצִים עַל כְּתֵפוֹ?

[Really now! You're only going to pray?] Someone going to pray — for what does he need fire and a knife in his hand, and wood on his shoulder?

Again, Abraham responds evasively. Sure, I'm going to pray, but maybe I'll stick around on top of the mountain for a day or two and we'll slaughter an animal, bake some food, and eat it.

Having forced Abraham into ever more strained evasions of the real truth, the Satan sees his opening and pounces:

אָמַר לוֹ, "זָקֵן, לֹא שָׁם הָיִיתִי כְּשֶׁאָמַר לְךָ הַקָּדוֹשׁ בָּרוּךְ הוּא ,קַח נָא אֶת בִּנְךָ? וְזָקֵן כְּמוֹתְךָ יֵלֵךְ וִיאַבֵּד בֵּן שֶׁנִּתַּן לוֹ לְמֵאָה שָׁנָה?!"

Satan retorted, "Old man, wasn't I there when God told you, 'Take your son'? An old man like you is really going to go and destroy the son finally given to him at the age of one hundred?"

In the Sages' narrative, Satan then plays the ultimate mind game with Abraham. He attempts to confuse Abraham about who it was who issued the decree to take Isaac up that mountain and offer him up as a sacrifice. He attempts to suggest to Abraham that it wasn't God who issued that command, but Satan:

"וְאִם תֹּאמַר יִהְיֶה לְּךָ בֵּן אַחֵר, תִּשְׁמַע מִן הַמַּשְׂטִין, וּתְאַבֵּד נְשָׁמָה שֶׁתִּתְחַיֵּב עָלֶיהָ בַּדִּין." אָמַר לוֹ, "לֹא מַשְׂטִין הָיָה, אֶלָּא הַקָּדוֹשׁ בָּרוּךְ הוּא יִתְבָּרַךְ הָיָה! לֹא אֶשְׁמַע מִמְּךָ."

"Perhaps you think that [once you kill Isaac], you will have another son, but [don't delude yourself with that thought]; you must have been talking to a seducer (Satan), because in reality, one who murders someone is liable to be killed." [To this, Abraham replied], "It wasn't a seducer [Satan] talking to me; it was God Himself! I will not listen to you."

Abraham ultimately rebuffs Satan. But to do so, he needs to play a confusing game of Who's Who with the old man who accosts him. He needs to keep straight the fact that it was God, not Satan, who instructed him to offer Isaac up on the mountain — a task made harder by the fact that Abraham is, at this very moment, in discussion with someone who is actually Satan in disguise!

Finding no luck in seducing Abraham with lies, Satan, according to the midrash, tries his luck with Isaac instead. This time, he appears in the guise of a strapping young lad, and begins, again, with the same innocent question:

אָמַר לוֹ: "לְאָן אַתָּה הוֹלֵךְ?"

He said to Isaac: "Where are you going?"

Isaac, too, responds evasively, telling Satan that he's on his way to learn Torah. To this, Satan replies with the same sardonic wit he used with Abraham:

"בְּחַיֶּיךָ אוֹ בְּמִיתָתְךָ?"

"[Really now? Going to learn Torah, are you?] While you're living or while you're dead?"

Then, having softened Isaac up, Satan moves in for the kill. He appeals to Isaac's sense of compassion for his own mother:

"עָלוּב בַּר עֲלוּבָה, כַּמָּה תַעֲנִיּוֹת נִתְעַנֵּית אִמְּךָ עַד שֶׁלֹּא נוֹלַדְתָּ, וְהַזָּקֵן הַזֶּה הִשְׁתַּטָּה וְהוּא הוֹלֵךְ לְשָׁחֳטֶךָ!"

"Oh, unfortunate son of an unfortunate mother! How many fasts did your mother fast until you were born, and now this old man has gone crazy and is going to slaughter you!"

But Isaac, too, withstands Satan's challenge. He answers the young man standing beside him this way:

אָמַר, "אַף עַל פִּי כֵן, לֹא אֶעֱבֹר עַל דַּעַת יוֹצְרִי וְעַל צִוּוּי אָבִי."

[Isaac] said, "Despite all this, I will not violate my Creator's will or the command of my father."

Who Is That Angel in the Bright Red Suit?

What did the Sages want us to understand by telling us about these elaborate, and somewhat fantastical, discussions Abraham and Isaac had on the way to the *Akeidah*? I think the answer can be gleaned if we ask ourselves a deceptively simple question:

Who, exactly, is Satan?

In the popular imagination, Satan conjures images of pitchforks and bright red suits. But to understand what the midrash means by Satan, I think you need to look a little more carefully at his disguises. When Satan stops Abraham, he's dressed up as an old man; but then, when he moves on to Isaac, he appears as a strapping young lad. Clearly, he is taking on the appearance of the one he's talking to. Isaac is a strapping young lad, while Abraham is a wizened old man. So Satan looks like each, in turn, when he talks to them.

Why? Because, in the eyes of the midrash, what Satan really *is* — what this great opposing force, that causes us to come to sin in our lives really comes down to — is a *part* of ourselves, namely, our fears.

Indeed, such a view of Satan would seem to have a precedent: A similar view of Satan seems to emerge from another well-known midrash that speaks to us about the events leading up to the Golden Calf. The biblical text tells us that when Moses was delayed coming down Mount Sinai, the people asked Aaron to make a god for them because "this man, Moses, we have no idea what became of him." In explanation, Rashi (Ex. 32:1) cites a midrashic teaching that Satan surreptitiously showed the Israelites an image of a dead Moses atop the mountain.

Again, the Sages seem to be using the idea of Satan as a way of talking about our deepest fears — what can be seen as our ultimate internal catalyst to sin. The people feared Moses would die atop the mountain. After all, that was why they sent Moses in the first place: As the Torah itself attests, they were too afraid to speak with God directly, fearing that any mortal man would die if they encountered the Divine. In suggesting that Satan showed the people an image of a dead Moses in heaven, the Sages seem to be saying that the catalyst for the people's worship of the calf was their fear that a human could not withstand the encounter with God. In the absence of a human who could make the connection for them, they sought something akin to a machine, a god of their own making, who could represent them in an encounter with the Almighty and who could not be killed (see also Ramban on Ex. 32:1).

A Shifting Disguise

To return to the Sages' discussion of Satan with respect to Abraham and Isaac, I would surmise that Satan appears differently to Abraham and Isaac because they each have their own set of dreaded fears. The way the midrash talks about Abraham's internal struggle with those fears is in terms of a conversation with himself. Abraham sees what amounts to a reflection of himself, an externalization of his fears, and has a conversation, so to speak, with those fears. He is, in fact, an old man who waited, hoped, and prayed for a child for a hundred years, who desperately wishes for that child to survive and carry on his legacy. So how will he deal with that?

What would Isaac's deepest fear be? The midrash surmises it might be that his father has perhaps lost his mind. Would God really tell him to sacrifice me? And so, in entertaining those fears, the midrash portrays Isaac as having a discussion with a mirror image of himself.

For both Isaac and Abraham, their real test, the midrash suggests, is how they will deal with their fears. In each case, fear wants them to believe that the command God has issued is not, in fact, real, that Abraham didn't hear from God what he in fact heard. Were Abraham or Isaac to give in to Satan, each would be giving in to the part of themselves that wants to believe that reality is other than it is. Each would be capitulating to a convenient but patently false illusion, foisted upon them by none other than themselves.

The Ultimate Test: Saying Yes to an Inconvenient Truth

All told, the midrash suggests that the test Abraham must pass is a more subtle one than we might have supposed. Before Abraham must decide whether to comply with God's command to offer up his son, he must actually believe the truth of the command in the first place. He must acknowledge the terribly inconvenient truth of what is really being asked of him. It would be so very convenient for Abraham to imagine that the command to give Isaac back to Heaven was issued by an impostor. Abraham's ultimate challenge is to keep himself anchored, despite all his fears, hopes, and desires, to what he knows is the awful truth: *This is absolutely God's message. Every fiber of my being wants to deny that. But I will acknowledge this to be true, and will faithfully carry out what God is asking of me.*[3]

Balaam and Balak Play "Broken Telephone"

We are in a position now, I think, to go back to our original questions about Balaam and Abraham, and to understand why the Sages, and the biblical text itself, seemed to nudge us into thinking that Balaam made his own *Akeidah*-like journey. It may well be that, deep down, Balaam struggled with a very similar test to Abraham's. Yes, of course Balaam obeys whatever he allows himself to hear God saying to him. But that's not the same as saying he obeys whatever God *in fact* says to him. The question is: To what extent is Balaam willing to lie to himself?

To see how this *Akeidah*-like struggle plays out for Balaam, consider the beginning of the story, where the Torah details a curious series of exchanges between Balak and Balaam. Balak sends messengers to Balaam seeking to recruit him to curse the Israelites. Balaam tells them to spend the night so he can confer with God. And God, right on cue, comes to Balaam with a set of instructions:

---

3 A similar interpretation is advanced in Rabbi Shagar's approach to the *Akeidah*; see "My Faith: Faith in a Postmodern World," in *Faith Shattered and Restored: Judaism in the Postmodern Age* (Maggid Books, 2017) 21–39.

Numbers 22:12

לֹא תֵלֵךְ עִמָּהֶם; לֹא תָאֹר אֶת־הָעָם, כִּי בָרוּךְ הוּא:	"Do not go with them; do not curse the nation, because it is blessed."

Please take a moment to reread those words, and as you do, ask yourself: *Has God been clear to Balaam about His wishes, or has He been ambiguous?*

The Almighty really didn't leave Balaam that much wiggle room there. He has said "no" in every conceivable way you can imagine: (a) don't go with them, (b) don't curse the nation, and (c) they are blessed. It is hard to see any room for argument. But listen to how Balaam communicates God's words back to Balak. He wakes up in the morning, goes to the messengers of Balak, and tells them:

Numbers 22:13

לְכוּ אֶל־אַרְצְכֶם, כִּי **מֵאֵן יְקוָה** לְתִתִּי לַהֲלֹךְ עִמָּכֶם:	Go back to your land, because **God has withheld Himself** from allowing me to go with you.

Now, how accurate a reflection of God's words would you say *that* is?

It's *kind of* accurate. But Balaam paints a much fuzzier picture of God's stance than we, the reader, have been given to understand. The most straightforward thing for Balaam to have done would be to explain to the messengers basically what God told him — tell them God said no, and *why* He said no. Namely, the mission is utterly futile: "*God said absolutely not. This whole plan of cursing the Israelites is never going to happen. They're just blessed. Go home; this is a waste of time.*"

Instead, though, Balaam fudges it. He says that God refused to let him go and that's it. The implication is that he's been given no reason for the refusal, and perhaps, no reason exists. God is being … capricious, maybe even unfair. It's like when your friend asks you to come play and you come back with: My mom said no. Mom actually said: Its past your bedtime, you have homework for tomorrow, and you didn't do your chores. So, while saying that Mom said no is not technically inaccurate, it's not the whole story.

Moreover, even the word for "no," in Balaam's telling is … well, telling. That word, מֵאֵן, which sometimes means "refusal," often conveys a lingering sense of unresolved tension. A comparable use of the word that comes to mind is in the Joseph story, where Joseph mightily resists the attempts of Potiphar's wife to seduce him:

וַיְמָאֵן, וַיֹּאמֶר אֶל־אֵשֶׁת אֲדֹנָיו, הֵן אֲדֹנִי לֹא־יָדַע אִתִּי מַה־בַּבָּיִת, וְכֹל אֲשֶׁר־יֶשׁ־לוֹ נָתַן בְּיָדִי. אֵינֶנּוּ גָדוֹל בַּבַּיִת הַזֶּה מִמֶּנִּי, וְלֹא־חָשַׂךְ מִמֶּנִּי מְאוּמָה כִּי אִם־אוֹתָךְ, בַּאֲשֶׁר אַתְּ־אִשְׁתּוֹ

He refused, and he said to his master's wife, "Behold, with me here, my master gives no thought to anything in the house, and all that he has, he has given into my hands. There is no one in this house greater than I, and he did not keep anything from me, except for you, as you are his wife."

Genesis 39:8–9

Me'en doesn't just mean that Joseph refused her. The word suggests a kind of tormented holding oneself back. This inner struggle of Joseph also is conveyed by the cantillation markings in the biblical text. When Joseph "refuses," a *shalshelet* appears above the word *vayema'en*. The *shalshelet* is one of the rarest of all cantillation notes, and it conveys, tonally, the idea of wavering back and forth. Similarly, Balaam — with his מֵאֵן — appears to be signaling to Balak's messengers that God was wavering. *Yes, He may certainly have said no, but look, He was just "holding Himself back"; I suspect that… perhaps God could be persuaded.*

And, as it turns out, that implication is not lost on Balak's messengers. Except that Balak's messengers may be able to perceive a truth about Balaam that Balaam himself is actually blind to. Look at how they report Balaam's words back to Balak:

וַיָּקוּמוּ שָׂרֵי מוֹאָב, וַיָּבֹאוּ אֶל־בָּלָק, וַיֹּאמְרוּ, **מֵאֵן** בִּלְעָם הֲלֹךְ עִמָּנוּ:

The officers of Moav got up and came to Balak and said, "Balaam **has withheld himself** from coming with us."

Numbers 22:14

Did you notice how that very word מֵאֵן, to "withhold oneself," meanders into their report? Only they don't use that word to describe *God*; they use it to describe *Balaam*. The messengers seem to have discerned that when

Balaam claimed that God "withheld Himself," Balaam actually revealed more about his *own* state of mind than God's. It is as if they are telling Balak: Sure, Balaam said "no," but he may yet be persuaded.

Perceiving that Balaam is vacillating, the king of Moab decides to try again. And this time, he sweetens the pot:

Numbers 22:15–17

וַיֹּסֶף עוֹד בָּלָק שְׁלֹחַ שָׂרִים רַבִּים וְנִכְבָּדִים מֵאֵלֶּה. וַיָּבֹאוּ אֶל־בִּלְעָם, וַיֹּאמְרוּ לוֹ, כֹּה אָמַר בָּלָק בֶּן־צִפּוֹר, אַל־נָא תִמָּנַע, מֵהֲלֹךְ אֵלָי, כִּי־כַבֵּד אֲכַבֶּדְךָ מְאֹד	Balak again sent officers, greater and more honorable than the others. They came to Balaam and said to him: "Thus says Balak ben Tzipor, 'Do not hold yourself back from coming to me, for I will honor you greatly.'"

And here's where something subtle happens. Balaam sees that Balak is looking to seduce him with promises of honor and wealth. And he seems to respond by assuring the messengers that he can't be bought; his only allegiance is to God. But even in his rejection of Balak's entreaty, one detects the undercurrents of Balaam's own ambivalence. So much so, that at some level, Balaam's rejection isn't so much a rejection as it is an invitation:

Numbers 22:18–19

אִם־יִתֶּן־לִי בָלָק מְלֹא בֵיתוֹ כֶּסֶף וְזָהָב, לֹא אוּכַל לַעֲבֹר אֶת־פִּי יְקוָה אֱלֹקָי, לַעֲשׂוֹת קְטַנָּה אוֹ גְדוֹלָה: וְעַתָּה, שְׁבוּ נָא בָזֶה גַּם־אַתֶּם הַלָּיְלָה, וְאֵדְעָה מַה־יֹּסֵף יְקוָה דַּבֵּר עִמִּי:	"If Balak were to give me a whole house full of silver and gold, I cannot transgress that which God, my God, asks of me, not in a small way or a great way. So now, wait here tonight, and let's see what God will tell me again."

Of course, it sure *sounds* righteous of Balaam to say that he can't transgress what God says, even in the slightest bit. But his mention of an entire houseful of gold and silver *does* seem oddly explicit — almost as if this measure of wealth might be something, despite Balaam's denials, that he is actually angling for. And the real kicker is what Balaam says next. He tells the messengers to hang around another night — because look, who knows? Maybe the Master of the Universe will change His mind.

Tellingly, when Balaam does ask God again, surprisingly, God *does* change His mind. The Almighty allows Balaam to go with the messengers, with the caveat that, once he arrives at the designated place, Balaam must absolutely say whatever God tells him and nothing else (see Numbers 22:20). At face value, that seems quite strange — but on second thought, maybe it is not so surprising, after all. For remember: God had earlier made clear what He wanted, and Balaam had, in return, made clear that he wasn't prepared to accept the truth that this is what God actually wanted. And so God chose to play along with that: If Balaam is going to ignore God's expressed desires, then so be it — here's how we will play it: *Go, if you must, but you absolutely have to do what I say once you get there.*

Indeed, the Midrash (Bamidbar Rabbah 20:12) derives from God's eventual choice to allow Balaam to go with the messengers a basic truth about the way the Master of the Universe chooses to interact with mankind:

Bamidbar Rabbah 20:12

בדרך שאדם רוצה לילך, בה מוליכין אותו	In the path that a person wants to walk, so Heaven guides him.

How We Become Vulnerable to Self-Delusion

Getting back to Balaam's suggestion to the messengers that they stick around for the night to see what God will tell him — that supposition that perhaps God will change His mind, that there are conflicting forces at play in God's nature, is more of a wish than anything else. But the important thing to notice is that Balaam doesn't recognize it as such. If you could go back in time and interview Balaam at this moment, he might well be offended by any suggestion that he was playing fast and loose with God's words: *Didn't I tell those messengers that no matter how much money is on the table, I absolutely cannot contravene God's words?* But it is precisely Balaam's smugness, his sense of his own incontrovertible righteousness, that makes him so vulnerable to self-delusion. Balaam blinds himself to the way that his own inner desires are manipulating his choices and thus falls ever more deeply under their sway. He tells the messengers to spend the night because maybe God will change His mind, and in so doing, willfully ignores the truth of God's adamant opposition, without ever being honest with himself that this is what he's doing.

And it is here, I think, that we arrive at why the Sages of the Mishnah were so willing to castigate Balaam as an evildoer. He failed his own little version of an *Akeidah*-test. And how did he fail it? Through self-deception.

The Sandbox of Balaam and Abraham

In the end, Balaam and Abraham really *are* playing in the same sandbox. Each undertakes a great journey in which they must go, bidden by God, to do something that stands in opposition to their greatest desires. Moreover, each has enough fealty to God that they would not even consider contravening God's words. But that is not their real struggle. Their real struggle is to admit that God's words really are what they are in the first place. If you can see the truth for what it is, despite your desperate desire for things to be otherwise, then you are an Abraham. If you are unable or unwilling to see that, you are a Balaam.

Ironically, what makes Balaam's evil so dangerous is that he's so convinced of his righteousness. Yes, Balaam is right about the fact that he will not act against God's words, but only once he convinces himself that God is saying what He absolutely, clearly, is actually saying — which may never happen. And therein lies Balaam's losing struggle. Despite all evidence to the contrary, Balaam clings to the notion that God doesn't mean what He says He means, that God is ambivalent, that He can be persuaded. And in so doing, Balaam projects upon God his own struggle with unseen desires. He crafts God ... in his own image.

Of Humility and Transparency

What proclivities push one toward the Balaam side of the ledger? And what tools does one need to cultivate to be an Abraham? The Sages weren't shy about telling us:

Avot 5:19

כָּל מִי שֶׁיֵּשׁ בְּיָדוֹ שְׁלֹשָׁה
דְּבָרִים הַלָּלוּ, מִתַּלְמִידָיו שֶׁל
אַבְרָהָם אָבִינוּ. וּשְׁלֹשָׁה דְּבָרִים
אֲחֵרִים, מִתַּלְמִידָיו שֶׁל בִּלְעָם

Whoever possesses these three traits
has learned from Abraham our father.
And anyone who possesses the opposite
three traits has learned from Balaam

הָרָשָׁע. עַיִן טוֹבָה, וְרוּחַ נְמוּכָה, וְנֶפֶשׁ שְׁפָלָה, מִתַּלְמִידָיו שֶׁל אַבְרָהָם אָבִינוּ. עַיִן רָעָה, וְרוּחַ גְּבוֹהָה, וְנֶפֶשׁ רְחָבָה, מִתַּלְמִידָיו שֶׁל בִּלְעָם הָרָשָׁע.

the wicked. A giving eye, a humble spirit, and an unassuming soul: These are the qualities of one who has learned from Abraham. A greedy eye, a haughty spirit, and a boastful soul: These are qualities of one who has learned from Balaam the wicked.

In the Sages' view, the crucial Abrahamic character trait is humility. It allows for a certain kind of transparency in how one deals both with others and with oneself and one's own hidden desires and fears. Conversely, arrogance must be avoided at all costs. Because look, if you're arrogant, ultimately, everything is about *you*. Moreover, arrogance is a double-whammy: Not only does the arrogant person put a premium on fulfilling his own desires, he lacks the humility to see that this is what he's doing. Because he is convinced that his saintliness is beyond reproach, the arrogant person blinds himself to the unseen biases that shape his decisions.

And therein lies the arrogant man's true susceptibility to evil. Because, look, all of us have desires. We want what we want, and what *we* want isn't always what God wants. But it is one thing to have desires that may diverge from God's will and to face those desires squarely — a perfectly fine, honest, and even noble endeavor; and it is quite another thing not to admit that you have such desires in the first place. That's the dangerous part. Anyone who finds themselves at *that* end of Balaam and Abraham's sandbox, anybody who cloaks unseen desires in the mantle of pure self-righteousness ... is dangerously prone to acting with real, unchecked malice. For once someone is convinced of their own saintliness, the last guardrails on their conduct — their recognition of the reality of their own fears and desires — have been gingerly plucked away. With this gone, their unknowing transformation into the ugly puppet of those hidden fears and desires will likely not be long in coming.

When Bad Things Happen to Good People

וַיֹּאמֶר יְקֹוָה אֶל־מֹשֶׁה, "עֲלֵה אֶל־הַר הָעֲבָרִים הַזֶּה, וּרְאֵה אֶת־הָאָרֶץ אֲשֶׁר נָתַתִּי לִבְנֵי יִשְׂרָאֵל. וְרָאִיתָה אֹתָהּ וְנֶאֱסַפְתָּ אֶל־עַמֶּיךָ גַּם־אָתָּה, כַּאֲשֶׁר נֶאֱסַף אַהֲרֹן אָחִיךָ."

God said to Moses, "Go up this Mountain of Avarim, and see the land which I have given to the Children of Israel. You shall see it, and then, you too shall be gathered in to your people, as Aaron your brother was gathered."

NUMBERS 27:12–13

When Bad Things Happen to Good People

Part I: Moses and the Mountain of Crossing: The Beginning of the End

Parshat Pinchas marks, in a way, the beginning of the saddest episode in the entire Torah.

Back in **Parshat Chukat**, Moses hit a rock which God had asked him to speak to and, in response, the Almighty told Moses that He would not be allowed to lead the people into the Promised Land. In **Parshat Pinchas**, God begins to make good on that promise. The Almighty tells Moses to ascend a mountaintop and to look out from there at the land he would not be allowed to cross into:

וַיֹּאמֶר יְקֹוָה אֶל־מֹשֶׁה, עֲלֵה אֶל־הַר הָעֲבָרִים הַזֶּה, וּרְאֵה אֶת־הָאָרֶץ אֲשֶׁר נָתַתִּי לִבְנֵי יִשְׂרָאֵל. וְרָאִיתָה אֹתָהּ וְנֶאֱסַפְתָּ אֶל־עַמֶּיךָ גַּם־אָתָּה, כַּאֲשֶׁר נֶאֱסַף אַהֲרֹן אָחִיךָ:	God said to Moses, "Go up this Mountain of Avarim, and see the land which I have given to the Children of Israel. You shall see it, and then, you too shall be gathered in to your people, as Aaron your brother was gathered."	Numbers 27:12–13

Later, in **Parshat Va'etchanan**, Moses recounts how he had pleaded with God for his story to end differently. But God told him no in no uncertain terms:

Deuteronomy 3:26–27

וַיִּתְעַבֵּר יְקוָה בִּי לְמַעַנְכֶם וְלֹא שָׁמַע אֵלָי. וַיֹּאמֶר יְקוָה אֵלַי, רַב־לָךְ! אַל־תּוֹסֶף דַּבֵּר אֵלַי עוֹד בַּדָּבָר הַזֶּה: עֲלֵה רֹאשׁ הַפִּסְגָּה, וְשָׂא עֵינֶיךָ יָמָּה וְצָפֹנָה וְתֵימָנָה וּמִזְרָחָה, וּרְאֵה בְעֵינֶיךָ, כִּי־לֹא תַעֲבֹר אֶת־הַיַּרְדֵּן הַזֶּה:

And God said to me, "Enough; speak no more to Me of this matter! Go up to the mountaintop, and lift up your eyes westward, and northward, and southward, and eastward, and see with your eyes — for you shall not pass over this Jordan."

And so it was. The very last paragraphs of the Torah, in **Parshat Vezot HaBerachah**, tell the actual story of Moses' final ascent to the summit of Mount Nevo. From the top of the mountain, God showed him the land. And there, Moses died.

Beyond Sadness

How are we to feel about all this?

My first impulse is to say: Sad. *Very* sad. I know that when, on Simchat Torah, we read the text's description of Moses' final, lonely ascent up that mountain, I feel like crying. It feels strange because our tradition mandates that we celebrate when we finish reading the Torah. But the dancing on the holiday feels to me oddly out of step with what we read in these last verses.

But here's what I want to consider with you: *Is it more than just sad?* It sounds a little heretical to say it, but it feels like this also might be the most… *unfair* moment in the entire Torah. Here is Moses, arguably the most righteous, spiritually accomplished person who has ever lived. A man whom the Torah itself eulogizes simply as "a servant of God" (Deut. 34:5); perhaps even *the* archetypal servant of God. A man who put himself on the line time and time again for the people he led so faithfully. And *this* very man, what does he really want at the end of his life? What is the *only* thing that matters to him? He's not looking to be applauded, or even recognized, for his accomplishments. All he wants is to finish his mission; to cross into the Promised Land, to feel underneath his feet the land he worked so hard to bring the people of Israel to. But it is *this* which God denies to him. It seems utterly inexplicable.

And it's more than that. I want to ask not just about the *event* of Moses' death, but about the way the Torah writes about that event — here in

Parshat Pinchas, and later in **Parashot Va'etchanan**, **Ha'azinu**, and **Vezot HaBerachah**. Because, remember — this book wasn't written by some hostile journalist who had it in for God, some curmudgeon who didn't like how the Master of the Universe handled the whole Exodus thing. The book was written by God. And yet, how does this ending make you feel about the great Writer in the sky?

Here you are, the reader of this Torah. You're rooting for Moses throughout the whole book. He's your guy. And you're rooting for him because God wrote the book in a way that *made* you root for him. And yet, the Almighty chose to tell you, at the very end of this book, how seemingly mean He was to Moses, denying him entrance to the land on the basis of what seemed to be a triviality: He hit the rock. Isn't it a little strange that God would close out the book with a story that casts Himself, the Master of the Universe, in such an apparently unfavorable light?

I Know What You're Thinking

Now, I know what you're thinking. Or, at least, I know what you're thinking if you read my previous essay, a few dozen pages ago, on **Parshat Chukat**. You're thinking:

Wait a minute, Fohrman, you spent a whole essay making sense out of the Moses-hit-the-rock violation. And there, you argued that it wasn't a triviality, how it was really a big deal! So why are you making such a big tzimmes about Moses' death seeming unfair? He did something really significantly wrong, and God punished him for that!

And to this, dear reader, I say: I hear your point. But still, even if you accept the argument I laid out in that **Parshat Chukat** essay; even if that argument is absolutely airtight and correct in every detail — still, the straightforward text of the Torah makes you *feel* terrible about what happens to Moses. It seems like God wants us to read the Torah and feel sad about Moses' fate. God's decree about his death seems so harsh, even if, behind the scenes, the very sophisticated reader can begin to make out something of a divine rationale for all this.

And so, at the very least, a kind of meta-question persists: *Because* the simple reading of the Torah's text seems to portray Moses' transgression in hitting the rock as relatively trivial, the reader, when finishing reading the Torah, can't help but be struck by the Almighty's apparent capriciousness. The Torah seems designed to make you scratch your head once you reach the last page and ask: *Why in the world would God write the book and make Himself look so bad?*

A Mountain with a Stark Name

And the truth is, the picture the text paints of God seems to get even worse. As I mentioned, it is in **Parshat Pinchas** that God first tells Moses to ascend the mountain and look upon the land he will not cross into:

Numbers 27:12

וַיֹּאמֶר יְקוָה אֶל מֹשֶׁה, עֲלֵה אֶל־הַר הָעֲבָרִים הַזֶּה וּרְאֵה אֶת־הָאָרֶץ אֲשֶׁר נָתַתִּי לִבְנֵי יִשְׂרָאֵל:	God said to Moses, "Go up this Mountain of Avarim, and see the land which I have given to the Children of Israel."

And now, look at the name of the mountain Moses is to ascend. Instead of calling it Mount Nevo, as it is later called in **Parshat Vezot HaBerachah**, **Parshat Pinchas** calls it **הַר הָעֲבָרִים** (Har Ha'avarim, or the Mountain of *Crossing*—from the Hebrew root **עבר**. But given the context, that seems like a bit of a provocative name to give this mountain. Because Moses had desperately wanted to cross into the land. His language elsewhere, in **Parshat Va'etchanan**, uses that very word, "crossing," to signify what it was that he wanted so badly:

Deuteronomy 3:25

אֶעְבְּרָה נָּא וְאֶרְאֶה אֶת הָאָרֶץ הַטּוֹבָה אֲשֶׁר בְּעֵבֶר הַיַּרְדֵּן	"Please let me **cross over** and see the good land that is on the other side of the Jordan."

To name this mountain "Mount Crossing"... I don't know, it just feels like a taunt: *You wanted to cross, didn't you? Well, why don't you die right here, on the Crossing Mountain!* This is the mountain that is the final, insurmountable barrier for Moses, the mountain that stands in the way of his achieving his most hoped-for aspiration. God may as well have called it "The Mountain of Everyone-but-Moses-Crossing." Why would God see fit to add this little cherry on top to His denial of Moses' request?

It's Not a Bug, It's a Feature

So I would like to suggest the general outline of a theory here. The theory is that this sadness, this poignancy, this apparent unfairness at the very end of the Torah — to borrow the parlance of Silicon Valley — is not a bug. It is a feature. It's intentional. This is how God *wants* you to feel when you're reading the final episode of the Torah.

In other words, the text is *trying* to make you uncomfortable with what you're reading. And therefore, as a reader, your goal is not to try to pretend it all makes perfect sense to you. Your job, instead, is to read this episode, and as you do, acknowledge the sadness and poignancy that you feel; acknowledge even that nagging sense of unfairness that you feel — and live with that unresolved discomfort. As you read of Moses' lonely ascent of Mount Nevo, you're meant to feel some of the same discomfort that Moses himself might have felt as he walked his last journey. You are meant to imagine: What would it be like to be Moses at that moment? What would it be like to be a "servant of God" and make that trek up the mountain, knowing that your final, heartfelt, request — which seemed to you to be so eminently reasonable — was denied by God? What would *that feeling* have been like? Your job is to feel some of *that*.

Let me put this another way, which will start to open up the issue I really want to talk to you about here: It is fashionable, in some circles, to believe that the great vulnerability of religion is the question, Why do bad things happen to good people? If God is really so wonderful, the argument goes, then how come wonderful people suffer so much? Presumably, either God can't do anything about it or He doesn't care to do anything about it. These seem to be the only two available options. And either conclusion threatens our picture of an all-powerful and compassionate deity.

It is likewise fashionable to believe that the Torah *must* be somehow trying to get us to avert our eyes from this terrible question. The Torah must be hoping, as it were, that it won't dawn on its reader to ask this question because the reader's faith could not withstand the encounter, were the question actually acknowledged. And that, dear reader, is what I'm arguing *against* here. The question of bad things happening to good people, I believe, is not *external* to the Torah at all. It is, by design, the climactic question of the book. The Torah, at the very end of its story, is trying to force the reader into grappling with this issue. It is trying to do that by creating a visceral crisis in the mind of its reader: How could God do this to Moses?

But I want to be clear about the nature of this crisis. I don't believe that it is so much a philosophical crisis as it is an emotional or spiritual one. It's not that the Torah is challenging the reader to figure out the answer to *why* bad things happen to good people. The Torah is not giving you an answer to the conundrum, at least not in any overt way.[1] But that is the whole point. The crisis, in the Torah's view, isn't meant to be *figured out*. It's meant to be experienced and lived through.

What does it mean for us to experience and live through this question? We aren't Moses, after all.

Well, the Torah, whatever else it is — spiritual guidebook, halachic lawbook, teller of our historical tradition — is also literature. And literature bids us to identify with its characters and to learn from their experiences. The Torah is asking us to identify with Moses and to begin to see things through his eyes. His experience is meant to become our vicarious experience. We aren't meant to figure out an answer to why bad things happen to good people, but to experience, as *he must have,* what it is like to maintain a relationship with God, *without* having the answer as to why God appears to be so very unfair to you. It may seem that it is not possible to maintain a relationship with God under those circumstances. The example of Moses, though, shows us that such a thing, somehow, *is* possible. And that, I believe, is the Torah's final lesson to us.

How is it possible? To understand that, I think we need to look not just at the end of the Torah, but at its beginning. I think we will find the contrast between the two instructive.

---

1 The Torah, seemingly, is not really bothered by the crisis from a philosophical point of view. *Why* that is so is a wonderfully intriguing question. I will try to explore this a bit later in this essay.

Part II: An Earlier Struggle

Moses, in the Torah's final, climactic story, isn't the first person in the Torah who must have had to struggle with a divine decree that seemed absolutely inscrutable to him. The very first people we ever meet — Adam and Eve — would have undergone a similar struggle too, only on a more basic, elementary level.

Think about it from their perspective:

I've been put in this wonderful garden. There are all these trees with luscious fruit. But for some strange reason, there's one tree whose fruit I can't have. And that tree just happens to be named the Tree of Knowledge of Good and Evil. Now why in the world can't I have its fruit? Seemingly, I eat from this tree, and I get ... what? An understanding of good and evil. I get to start deciding what's right and what's wrong. Moral choice. It's the most elevated thing in the world. What could be better than having that? Are you telling me that it's wrong, somehow, to have such splendid knowledge? Why in the world would God make this tree, of all trees, off-limits to me?

And that argument *seems* eminently reasonable. But in reality, the name of the tree hints toward the point of the restriction. There is a difference between the Creator's way of looking at good and evil and a creature's perception. It's not so much that our *values* are different — we were, after all, created in the image of God, and part of that means that we share God's values: We, like the Almighty, have an affinity for things like justice and compassion. But still, our *perspectives* are different. They *have* to be. We live in the world. We are part of this game called life. God, though, is *outside* that game. He is the Maker of it. And a maker's perspective is just different. It is not good for us, therefore, to be the ultimate arbiters of good and evil. We don't have the necessary perspective.

To borrow one of my favorite analogies: Imagine a Monopoly board, brought to you courtesy of Parker Brothers. There's Little Hat and Little Shoe, making their way through the squares on the board. You bend your ear and listen to their conversation. It turns out Little Hat is complaining to Little Shoe. Evidently, he's feeling constrained by the rules of the game. Little Hat says he doesn't think Parker should make those rules;

they should make the rules. *They* should be in charge of good and evil on this board of theirs.

So, how well do you think that's going to work out for them? Little Hat rolls a seven. It looks like that should land him on the go-to-jail square. But just then, Little Hat decides that it's time for a new rule: *Whenever you roll a seven, you get to advance to Free Parking and collect $500*. Little Shoe, as you might imagine, doesn't take kindly to that, and when he rolls a nine, he makes up a new rule too: *Whoever rolls a nine, gets to take from the other player whatever money they collected on the last turn.*

It's pretty evident that if Little Hat and Little Shoe get to make the rules, the game will quickly descend into chaos. The game's creator, who lives outside the game, is objective and gets to decide how the game is played. The determination of what is restricted and what's permitted is up to him.

As for Little Hat and Little Shoe, they may not very much like restrictions they don't understand. Living within the game, they may not grasp the value of these restrictions the way their creator does. They may not understand how, in the larger scheme of things, the game is enhanced by them. And so, as they continue to make their way around Tennessee Avenue and Park Place, they may well find themselves frustrated with restrictions that, for all they know, seem to be randomly placed upon them.[2]

And so, the central challenge facing Little Hat and Little Shoe is not unlike the central challenge facing Adam and Eve back in the Garden. It is this: *Can you accept an inexplicable decree that you don't like from your Creator, without concluding that He hates you or doesn't care about you?* Can your relationship with your Creator survive this?

---

2 To extend the analogy even further, perhaps a bit fancifully, we might imagine that, in a deep way, coping with those frustrations might just be the central challenge for Little Hat and Little Shoe. They may think the game is about passing Go and collecting $200 every week, building as many hotels as possible on their properties and charging their opponent ever more exorbitant prices to stay there. But their *true* objective on the board, in, at least, my fanciful recreation of their game, might just be: finding a way to maintain their relationship with Parker in the face of Parker's unexplained — and, to them, maddeningly capricious — vision of right and wrong.

The Tools to Succeed

Back in the Garden, God had primed Adam and Eve to be able to succeed in this challenge. The Creator did this with what amounts to a two-step command:

Genesis 2:16–17

וַיְצַו יְקוָה אֱלֹקִים עַל־הָאָדָם
לֵאמֹר, מִכֹּל עֵץ־הַגָּן אָכֹל
תֹּאכֵל: וּמֵעֵץ הַדַּעַת טוֹב וָרָע,
לֹא תֹאכַל מִמֶּנּוּ

And Hashem, God, commanded the man, saying, "From all the trees of the Garden you shall eat; yes, eat! But from the Tree of Knowledge of Good and Evil, you may not eat from it."

The first command given to Adam and Eve was *not* to stay away from the Tree of Knowledge of Good and Evil. The first command was not a restriction at all. It was a positive mandate to "eat; yes, eat" of the fruit of all the other trees. The fruit of those trees had specifically been described in a previous verse as being luscious, delicious to eat, and beautiful to look at (Gen. 2:9). The bounty of those other trees — these were gifts given to the first humans from the Creator. And the imperative to eat from those trees meant the Creator really wanted us to have that gift. By eating from all of those trees, by tasting all of those wonderful flavors, the first humans were meant to understand something crucial: *Their Creator loves them.* Their Creator would take care of them. They can trust their Creator.

Every day that Adam and Eve would return to those other trees and take another bite of their inviting fruits, every pear, kiwi, or passion fruit they would taste for the first time, would reinforce that truth. *God loved them, God was there for them, and God would take care of them.*

In other words, the positive command at the beginning of the sentence was meant to create the conditions for Adam and Eve to be able to accept the negative command at the end of the sentence. Given visceral evidence, through God's first, positive command, that your Creator loves you, can you accept the negative command that follows? Can you accept the existence of a restriction that you don't understand from your Creator without concluding that His apparent love for you was just a sham?

In this, though, Adam and Eve failed. They were too shaken by the inexplicable restriction, and their faith in their Creator faltered. They ate from the tree and found themselves banished from the garden.

What Makes Faith Possible

In a sense, then, I want to argue that the end of the Torah mirrors its beginning. Just as Adam and Eve had the tools to find a kind of faith in God that would allow them to weather the storm of a restriction they could not, for the life of them, understand, so would Moses have those very same tools.

For when God tells Moses to ascend Mount Nevo, a human protagonist faces a divine decree that they find inexplicable. And the question is: Can Moses accept it? For he does, indeed, have the tools to accept it. He can draw on his previous experience with God to find the faith he needs to accept what would otherwise seem to be divine caprice.

Indeed, like Adam and Eve, Moses, too, had evidence that God loved him. For long before he was told to ascend Mount Nevo to look upon the land he would not enter, Moses was told to ascend a different mountain: Sinai. There, he longingly made a request of God — a request that ostensibly broke all the tacit rules that govern relationships between humans and the Almighty. He asked to know God's innermost ways; and then he asked — seemingly — to literally behold the Divine:

Exodus 33:12–13, 18

וַיֹּאמֶר מֹשֶׁה אֶל־יְקוָה, רְאֵה אַתָּה אֹמֵר אֵלַי הַעַל אֶת־הָעָם הַזֶּה... וְאַתָּה אָמַרְתָּ יְדַעְתִּיךָ בְשֵׁם, וְגַם־מָצָאתָ חֵן בְּעֵינָי: וְעַתָּה, אִם־נָא מָצָאתִי חֵן בְּעֵינֶיךָ, הוֹדִעֵנִי נָא אֶת־דְּרָכֶךָ וְאֵדָעֲךָ... וַיֹּאמַר, הַרְאֵנִי נָא אֶת כְּבֹדֶךָ:

And Moses said to God, "See, You say to me, 'Bring up this people' ...and You have said, 'I have known you by name, and you have also found grace in My eyes.' Now, if I have found grace in Your eyes, make known to me, please, [the secret of] Your ways, that I may know You...." And he said, "Show me, please, your Glory."

The bottom line is that Moses asked for a close encounter with the Master of the Universe. But as God reminded him at that moment, humans can't withstand the experience of seeing the Almighty in any direct way and live to tell the tale. Nevertheless, God told Moses that He would find a way to show him what He could. He would shield Moses in the cleft of a rock and allow him to glimpse something of the Divine, even if He could not directly reveal His "face" (Ex. 33:19–23). And God made clear to Moses why He would allow this. It was a gift of love:

וַיֹּאמֶר יְקוָה אֶל־מֹשֶׁה, גַּם־אֶת הַדָּבָר הַזֶּה אֲשֶׁר דִּבַּרְתָּ, אֶעֱשֶׂה, **כִּי־מָצָאתָ חֵן בְּעֵינַי**	God said to Moses, "Even this thing that you have spoken, I will do — **for you have found grace in My eyes**."	Exodus 33:17

So, forty years later, Moses would hear a command from God to ascend another mountain, Mount Nevo. And when he did, he faced a challenge: Would he be able to accept God's denial of the thing he wanted most, without losing faith in the Master of the Universe? But what Moses has going for him now is that this is a *déjà vu* moment. As he's commanded to ascend Mount Nevo to look out upon the land — and then, to die — he can find it within himself to recall another time, forty years earlier, when he was commanded to go up a mountain. Moses can, and seemingly does, marshal his past experience of God loving him to accept what Adam could not or would not accept: *God's denial of my request doesn't mean His love of me is a sham. I can maintain a relationship with the Almighty, even in the face of this inexplicable command.*

The Beginning of the Book Prepares Us for Its End

Looking at the similarities between the end of the Torah and its beginning, I find myself wondering whether the Torah's beginning — the case of Adam and Eve — is, in a way, meant to pave the way for the reader to be able to accept the fate of Moses at the end of the book. Indeed, it is easier, emotionally at least, for the reader to come to grips with how God treats Adam and Eve. We, the reader, are less invested in the fates of Adam and Eve. We don't know much about these two humans in the third chapter of Genesis, where the story of the Tree of Knowledge plays itself out. They were just created, and they seem more blank slates than righteous or heroic people. So we don't feel quite as badly about them facing a decree from God they don't understand. Moreover, the restriction they faced — avoiding a tree they may have otherwise wished to eat from — seems intuitively like something that God may well have had His reasons for, even if Adam and Eve themselves may have found it inexplicable.

Perhaps once the reader finds him- or herself able to accept the fate of these first humans, they prime themselves for a much more difficult challenge, the challenge that appears at the end of the book. There, Moses faces a restriction that is much more visceral and torturous, when he's told he may not cross into the Promised Land. Moreover, we, the readers, know Moses well, having traveled with him from the pages of Exodus all the way through Deuteronomy. We're on his side. We feel his angst. His anguish is our anguish. Still, we as readers are perhaps meant to draw on the first story of the book, the Adam and Eve story, for a paradigm that may help us grapple with the death of Moses: God had His reasons back then; and so, despite the palpable rebellion of our hearts, *we are forced to acknowledge that perhaps the Almighty has His reasons now, too.*

And so, perhaps the Torah wants Moses to be our guide. Because these kinds of questions are not, let's face it, of merely academic interest. They interest any of us who play this game we call life. We aren't all that different from Little Hat and Little Shoe, wondering about the inexplicable ways of Parker. And so, if the Torah is meant to guide us, and if Moses is our teacher — maybe he is our teacher not only through his life, but also through his death. Perhaps he not only makes *known* to us the Torah, with all its myriad laws and commands, but he also helps us confront the great *unknown,* when we find ourselves facing divine decisions we desperately wish went the other way. At these times, we, like he, must yield to the Creator His right to run this world as He sees fit — and we, like Moses, can find the ability to do that, if we can draw on some sort of reservoir of belief that God is a loving being.

None of this is easy, though. Finding faith in God when we want a "yes" and we instead seem to get a hard, resounding "no" is really hard. And part of the reason why Moses is such a good teacher here is that the Torah doesn't pull its punches when it comes to telling us about the difficulty of his experience. Indeed, as I want to show you now, the example of Moses shows us just how hard this quest can really be.

Part III: Moses and the Secrets of Divine Justice: A Tale of Two Mountains

OK, let's get back to Moses' story now. Above, I suggested that when we read the story of God commanding Moses to ascend to his death atop Mount Nevo, we should read this event almost as if it is a *déjà vu* moment, a reexperiencing of an earlier event — the time, forty years earlier, when God commanded Moses to ascend a different mountain, Mount Sinai. God loved him then; perhaps Moses can find the strength to believe that God loves him just as deeply now.

So it sounds like all stardust and roses, right? God reveals His love to Moses at Sinai, and this helps him the next time he's on a mountain, facing his death. *Very sweet.* The only thing is, the Sages of the Talmud had something to tell us about that moment in which God revealed His love for Moses at Sinai, the moment He granted Moses a glimpse of His essence. And what the Sages have to say about it will cause a chill to tingle down your spine.

Moses' Secret Question

The Talmud in Berachot (7a) tells us that when Moses requested that close encounter with God at Sinai; when He asked God to reveal to him the secret of His ways, to really know Him (Ex. 33:13) — what Moses was *really* after was the answer to maybe the greatest theological conundrum of all time. They say Moses was asking about the very conundrum you and I have been wrestling with in this essay:

"הוֹדִיעֵנִי נָא אֶת דְּרָכֶיךָ": אָמַר לְפָנָיו, רִבּוֹנוֹ שֶׁל עוֹלָם, מִפְּנֵי מָה יֵשׁ צַדִּיק וְטוֹב לוֹ וְיֵשׁ צַדִּיק וְרָע לוֹ,

[When Moses asked God], "Make known to me, please, [the secret of] Your ways," [this is what] He was saying: "Master of the Universe! Why is it that [sometimes] there is a righteous person and [things are] good for him, and [other times] there is a righteous person and [things

Berachot 7a

יֵשׁ רָשָׁע וְטוֹב לוֹ וְיֵשׁ רָשָׁע וְרַע לוֹ?	are] bad for him? [Why is it that sometimes] there is a wicked person and [things are] good for him, [and sometimes] there is a wicked person and [things are] bad for him?"

To be sure, much is puzzling about the Sages' contention here. Why would they think Moses was asking this of God? And why would they think he was asking this of God at this particular moment? All good questions. But if you just stand back and look at this statement from the Talmud, I find myself wondering: *Did the Sages notice the same link between the two Moses-on-the-Mountaintop stories that we did?* For indeed, is it just a coincidence that when God first told Moses to ascend one mountain — Sinai — the Sages are telling me that Moses was *asking* about bad things befalling good people, and, later, when God told Moses to ascend another mountain, Mount Nevo, there Moses would *experience*... a bad thing befalling a really good person (himself)? There, God was denying Moses' request to see the land and was instead asking him to go up a mountain and die there, alone in the barren wilderness.

But what are we to make of that confluence? If the Sages *were* suggesting a link between Moses' experience on these two mountains, and if they further proposed that Moses had actually been asking God about bad things happening to good people, what did they want us to make of all that?

I think we may get a glimpse of their intent if we keep in mind how, according to the biblical text, God answered that request. Seemingly, although God did His best to accommodate Moses — He allowed the Divine Presence to pass over Moses, as God sheltered him in the cleft of a rock — still, God held back. He did not *completely* grant Moses the totality of the encounter he was seeking. God says to him:

Exodus 33:20–23	וַיֹּאמֶר, לֹא תוּכַל לִרְאֹת אֶת פָּנָי, כִּי לֹא־יִרְאַנִי הָאָדָם וָחָי... וְרָאִיתָ אֶת־אֲחֹרָי, וּפָנַי לֹא יֵרָאוּ:	He said, "You won't be able to see My face, because man cannot see Me and live. ...You shall see my back, but My face shall not be seen."

God seemed to be telling Moses that a total encounter with the Divine is not possible in this world. Human beings, composed of a body delicately attached to a soul, are not built to withstand the intensity of such an encounter. That is the *peshat*, the simple meaning of the verses. But now, let's take that *peshat*, and superimpose upon it the *derash*, the rabbinic spin the Sages are giving to this story, when they suggest that Moses was really trying to understand why bad things happen to good people. When you do that, it sounds like the Sages were saying that why bad things happen to good people is a divine secret, and, like the visage of God Himself, it is not accessible to human beings in this world.

Consistent with this line of thought, I should tell you that the Talmud in Berachot relates, in the name of R. Meir, that God actually *denied* Moses' request to understand why bad things happen to good people. *As much as I like you, Moses, there are certain things that just aren't accessible to you in this world.* Why bad things happen to good people is emblematic of those secrets.

Or, to put it a little more sharply, it is as if the Master of the Universe was saying something like this: *Moses, you want to know why bad things happen to good people? I'd show you if I could. But I'd have to kill you first.*

I'd Have to Kill You First

And this, friend, opens the door to an enchanting possibility. Because one day, long after this episode at Sinai, God *does* "kill" Moses. He causes him to die just before he can complete his life's mission and set foot, finally, in the Land of Israel. And when the Almighty does this, He arranges the episode of Moses' death in a way that seems to recreate the moment when Moses tried to encounter Him closely atop Mount Sinai: Once again, God summons Moses to ascend a mountain, all alone; and once again, He bids Moses to travel to the very top. The first time around, the Talmud says, Moses had asked about why bad things happen to good people, but that question had been left unanswered. The second time around, perhaps, Moses will get his answer.

It is as if, back at Sinai, God was saying to Moses: *I can't show you what you're asking for while you're still alive. But... when you're no longer alive, I can show you.* And indeed, in the transition into death, perhaps God *does* show him.

I'd like to suggest that *this* is the point of R. Meir's teaching. In the story of the death of Moses, God intentionally engineered a moment of "bad things happening to good people," visible for all to see. God, in effect, was saying to Moses:

I haven't forgotten about the question you asked Me all those years ago. I'm going to give you its answer, now. But I'm not going to give you the answer in words. I'm going to *show* it to you. You'll come to know it through your own experience.

So God does exactly that. He engineers an event that seems absolutely outrageous from the standpoint of justice — an event that would seem absolutely outrageous to all who would witness it, including Moses. *Really* bad things are happening to a *really* good person, all brought to you courtesy of the Master of the Universe. But from God's perspective, it is all … a teaching moment. This is the moment Moses learns the truth, the truth that was inaccessible to him as a mortal human being. At some level, Moses' death before he enters the land isn't a punishment. It is a revelation. It is an answer to the question that most troubled him. Through the mystery of his own death, Moses comes to understand why bad things happen to good people.

To say a little more about this, perhaps Moses comes to understand a truth that God had once tried to teach Adam and Eve, when the Master of the Universe put that special, divine tree off-limits to them, a tree that somehow related to knowledge of good and evil. Good and bad — these are the kinds of things that people *inside* the game would sometimes see very differently from how the Creator, who occupies a position *outside* the game, sees them. It is all a matter of perspective, just like Parker would have said to Little Hat and Little Shoe.

The prospect of your own death before entering the land, Moses, the prospect of that looks absolutely terrible to you while you're alive, there on earth. It looks terrible to everyone around you. But when you are with Me, in My world in the heavens, when you share My perspective, you may come to look at the circumstances of your death very differently.

Indeed, we asked above why God would call the mountain Moses would die upon the Mountain of Crossing. Well, at the end of the day, it *is* a mountain of crossing. It's just not the mountain of crossing *horizontally* into Israel; it is the mountain of crossing *vertically*. Moses' ascent up that mountain is the beginning of his ascent to a place beyond time and space, the point at which he would cross into the next world.

MATOT-MASEI

Of Gilead and Gal-Ed

וְיָאִיר בֶּן־מְנַשֶּׁה הָלַךְ
וַיִּלְכֹּד אֶת־חַוֺּתֵיהֶם,
וַיִּקְרָא אֶתְהֶן חַוֺּת יָאִיר.

Ya'ir son of Manasseh went and
captured their villages, and
called them Chavot Ya'ir.

NUMBERS 32:41

MATOT-MASEI

Of Gilead and Gal-Ed

PARSHOT MATOT-MASEI BRING THE book of Bamidbar to a close, and at the end of **Parshat Matot** we read a little-known vignette. Truth to tell, it might be considered the most trivial of episodes. It is a story that seems to have almost no lasting significance or memorable implications. The story I'm thinking of concerns the conquest, and naming, of an obscure parcel of land on the east side of the Jordan River:

Numbers 32:39–41

וַיֵּלְכוּ בְּנֵי מָכִיר בֶּן־מְנַשֶּׁה גִּלְעָדָה, וַיִּלְכְּדֻהָ וַיּוֹרֶשׁ אֶת־הָאֱמֹרִי אֲשֶׁר־בָּהּ: וַיִּתֵּן מֹשֶׁה אֶת־הַגִּלְעָד לְמָכִיר בֶּן־מְנַשֶּׁה, וַיֵּשֶׁב בָּהּ: וְיָאִיר בֶּן־מְנַשֶּׁה הָלַךְ וַיִּלְכֹּד אֶת־חַוֺּתֵיהֶם, וַיִּקְרָא אֶתְהֶן חַוֺּת יָאִיר:

The children of Machir the son of Manasseh went to Gilead, and they conquered it and drove out the Amorites who were there. Moses gave Gilead to Machir the son of Manasseh, and they settled there. And Ya'ir the son of Manasseh captured their villages and called them Chavot Ya'ir.

I want to suggest to you, though, that hidden within this seemingly trivial vignette lies something of great consequence, indeed. This "little" episode involving Ya'ir's conquests is actually the final chapter in an epic story, a tale whose origins begin all the way back in the book of Genesis, when the family of Israel was in its infancy.

Let's try to reconstruct that story.

The Origin Story of Gilead

The story of Gilead in the Torah is rooted in an episode that appears to have given this land its name. It is the account of the Covenant of Gal-Ed, which was made between Jacob and his father-in-law, Lavan. Let's refresh our memory about what happened there.

Jacob had spent years working for his father-in-law, Lavan. That arrangement had started back when Jacob was an unmarried man, but now he had a family and he was looking to leave, go back to Canaan, and start an independent life for himself. For his part, Lavan always seemed to have another excuse to hang on to him. But finally, in Genesis 31, Jacob just picks up in the middle of the night and leaves. As he sets out on his journey, though, Jacob was unaware of one important thing: Rachel, his wife, had secretly stolen her father's teraphim, figurines that Rashi suggests were some sort of idols.[1]

Three days later, Lavan finds out that Jacob and his family have fled, and he chases after him. Eventually, Lavan overtakes Jacob, and accuses him of betrayal: *"Why did you run away without telling me, without giving me a chance to kiss my daughters goodbye?"* (Gen. 31:28). And then Lavan asks about the missing teraphim:

Genesis 31:30	"לָמָּה גָנַבְתָּ אֶת־אֱלֹהָי?"	Why did you steal my gods?

When Lavan launches this accusation at him, Jacob is at first incredulous. He has no idea Rachel has taken these teraphim, and, thinking that his family could not possibly be in possession of Lavan's stolen property, he makes a rash declaration. He promises that the thief — if found among his family — should die for his crime:

Genesis 31:32	עִם אֲשֶׁר תִּמְצָא אֶת־אֱלֹהֶיךָ, לֹא יִחְיֶה! נֶגֶד אַחֵינוּ, הַכֶּר־לְךָ מָה עִמָּדִי, וְקַח־לָךְ	Whoever you find with your gods shall not live! In front of our brethren, recognize what I have of yours, and take it.

1 In support of this theory, Lavan will later describe them as "his gods." While the text doesn't make clear Rachel's motivation, Rashi opines that Rachel did it to distance her father from idolatry. Rashbam, on the other hand, theorizes that Lavan used the teraphim as an instrument of divination, and Rachel feared that if her father remained in possession of them, he might be able to quickly realize, through their power as an oracle, that Jacob and his family had absconded (see Rashi and Rashbam on Gen. 31:19).

In the end, Lavan makes a comprehensive search of Jacob's property, searching for his lost teraphim. The text tells us that he enters Leah's tent and can't find them, and then he enters Rachel's tent, and still can't find them. But all the while, Rachel is quite literally sitting on the teraphim. The text tells us she has hidden them in the cushion of her camel's saddle, which she is now using as a chair of sorts, inside her tent. When her father approaches, Rachel evades detection by telling her father that "the way of women" is upon her (31:35) and she can't rise to greet him as she might have customarily done. She thus ensures that her father won't look in the one place the teraphim could actually be found: In the cushion that is right beneath her.

Lavan ultimately leaves the scene without his teraphim, but he is not quite satisfied that the matter is closed. Just before they part, he and Jacob make a covenant together — and the symbol for that covenant becomes a pile of stones, in Hebrew, a **גל**, *gal*. That pile of stones gets named **Gal-Ed** — literally "the pile is a witness" (Gen. 31:48). Interestingly, Gal-Ed is spelled the same way in Hebrew — **גלעד** — as **Gilead**, the name of the mountain that Jacob and Lavan were encamped upon when they made this covenant (Gen. 31:25). This, actually, is the first time the Torah refers to the land of Gilead (the same land Ya'ir would later conquer in the book of Numbers). Seemingly, that pile of stones became a touchstone; that is, the name of the place apparently derives from the name Jacob ultimately grants to that heap of stones.

In any case, Jacob swears to the agreement he and Lavan make at Gal-Ed, and, as part of that agreement, the two somberly vow that God Himself will judge between them regarding their unresolved claims — chief of which is the matter of the missing teraphim. All of which leads the reader to wonder…

Did God ever answer that call to pass judgment?

Losing Rachel

Jacob, you will recall, had promised that anyone found to have the teraphim would die. In the moment, perhaps, that was nothing but an astonished declaration of innocence. But, chillingly, Rachel *does* die young. She passes away tragically while giving birth to Benjamin, not long after the story of Gal-Ed takes place. And so the reader is left to wonder: Was that a coincidence?

Rashi, citing a midrashic teaching, asserts that it wasn't:

Rashi on Genesis 31:32, from Bereshit Rabbah 74:4

ומאותה קללה מתה רחל בדרך

It was because of that very curse [spoken by Jacob] that Rachel died [in childbirth] on the road.

So the Midrash attributes Rachel's death to Jacob's words at Gal-Ed. But if you actually look carefully at those words, I want to suggest that this teaching of the midrash is actually just the tip of a much larger iceberg.

Here is what Jacob actually said to Lavan:

Genesis 31:32

עִם אֲשֶׁר תִּמְצָא אֶת־אֱלֹהֶיךָ, **לֹא יִחְיֶה**!

Whoever you find with your gods **shall not live**!

Now, in that statement, Jacob made a curious choice of words: "Whoever you find with your gods *shall not live*." That's not the most straightforward way to make his point. He could have just said: "Whoever you find with your gods *will die*." It leads one to wonder: Could "not living" perhaps imply something even more severe than "dying"?

What I'm getting at here is the concept of legacy and continuity. When a person dies, their children can carry on their legacy, ensuring that they are never truly forgotten. In the case of Rachel, if Jacob's fearsome, unintended vow were to be realized in full — that is, if Rachel were to actually not just die, but "not live" — that would mean that her legacy would need to be lost as well.

Rachel is survived by her sons, Joseph and Benjamin. To really lose Rachel, Jacob would need to lose Joseph and Benjamin, too. Here, then, is what I'm wondering about: *Did Jacob's unintended curse end up extending even to Rachel's progeny?*

A Closer Look at the Text of Gal-Ed

Now, this may sound like a pretty big leap to make. *The midrash tells us that Jacob lost Rachel because of Gal-Ed; now, you're telling me that in Gal-Ed lay a threat that was even bigger than this?* And sure, dear reader, I understand your skepticism. But keep in mind that, as a matter of fact, Jacob *does* come dangerously close to losing each of these sons. Joseph, of course, was nearly erased from Jacob's life by the infamous events of the sale of Joseph. And later, as the ramifications of the sale of Joseph play out, Jacob would come within a hair of losing Benjamin, too. You'll recall that, toward the end of Genesis, Benjamin gets framed on charges of theft, and Judah and the brothers are very nearly forced to return to Jacob without him.[2]

I'm wondering, then: In the Heavenly calculus of justice, might the potential loss of both these children somehow be related to the curse of Gal-Ed? Might the near loss of Joseph and Benjamin somehow be related to Jacob and Lavan's mutual call, at Gal-Ed, for God to be their judge?

And let me be straight with you here: I'll admit that such a possibility would probably never have occurred to me. Or, if someone had suggested it to me, I would have likely politely dismissed the ideas as the product of their overactive imagination. But, dear reader, I've become convinced that this possibility is not just a possibility, but a strong probability, maybe even a near certainty. What did the convincing for me is some very odd language in the biblical text of the story of teraphim, Jacob and Lavan, and Gal-Ed.

I want to share that with you.

We Found This. Do You Recognize It?

When Lavan first accuses Jacob of stealing his idols, Jacob protests his innocence with these words:

עִם אֲשֶׁר **תִּמְצָא** אֶת־אֱלֹהֶיךָ, לֹא יִחְיֶה! נֶגֶד אַחֵינוּ, **הַכֶּר**־לְךָ	Whoever you **find** with your gods shall not live! In front of our brethren,	Genesis 31:32

2 When Joseph becomes second in charge to Pharaoh in Egypt and the brothers are unaware of his true identity, he demands that Benjamin be brought to him — and when Benjamin finally arrives, Joseph arranges to have Benjamin framed on charges of theft. As a consequence, the brothers are very nearly forced to leave Benjamin behind in Egypt. Would that have occurred, Jacob's family would have permanently lost the two children of Rachel. The last remnants of her legacy would have been lost to the people of Israel forever.

מָה עִמָּדִי, וְקַח־לָךְ	**recognize** what I have of yours, and take it.

Now, we've already considered how Jacob uses לֹא יִחְיֶה in that declaration. But I want to focus on other words now, specifically, the confluence of **תִּמְצָא** and **הַכֶּר**. Because it turns out that these are not just random words Jacob happens to employ here. These words become quite important years later, when they recur verbatim. Only the second time around, Jacob wasn't the one to speak these words. He was the one to hear them spoken by others.

What I'm referring to here is, arguably, the worst moment in Jacob's life:

Genesis 37:32

וַיְשַׁלְּחוּ אֶת־כְּתֹנֶת הַפַּסִּים, וַיָּבִיאוּ אֶל אֲבִיהֶם, וַיֹּאמְרוּ, "זֹאת **מָצָאנוּ. הַכֶּר־נָא**: הַכְּתֹנֶת בִּנְךָ הִוא, אִם לֹא":	[Joseph's brothers] sent the coat, and they brought [it] to their father. They said, "**We found** this. **Please recognize** it: Is it your son's coat, or not?"

It just so happens that, when the brothers show Joseph's bloody coat to Jacob, trumped-up evidence that Joseph has been killed by animals somewhere in the desert, they use the exact words that Jacob once used to protest his innocence to Lavan. Or, to put that a little differently: A generation later, Joseph's brothers would take the brother that their father loved even more than them, and cast him into a pit. But when it comes time for an alibi, the brothers falsely profess to their father an innocent lack of knowledge of what became of his beloved son, Joseph. At that point, their words unmistakably echo Jacob's own expression of innocent ignorance regarding what became of things that had been precious to his own father (-in-law), Lavan.

It really jumps out at you when you put the two texts side by side:

STORY OF GAL-ED	SALE OF JOSEPH
״עִם אֲשֶׁר **תִּמְצָא** אֶת אֱלֹהֶיךָ, לֹא יִחְיֶה. נֶגֶד אַחֵינוּ, **הַכֶּר**־לְךָ, מָה עִמָּדִי, וְקַח־לָךְ״	וַיְשַׁלְּחוּ אֶת־כְּתֹנֶת הַפַּסִּים, וַיָּבִיאוּ אֶל־אֲבִיהֶם, וַיֹּאמְרוּ, ״זֹאת **מָצָאנוּ**. **הַכֶּר**־נָא: הַכְּתֹנֶת בִּנְךָ הִוא, אִם־לֹא״
"Whoever you **find** with your gods shall not live! In front of your brethren, **recognize** what I have of yours, and take it." (Gen. 31:32)	[Joseph's brothers] sent the coat, and they brought [it] to their father. They said, "We **found** this. Please **recognize** it: Is it your son's coat, or not?" (Gen. 37:32)

Might the repetition of language be a coincidence? Perhaps. But here's the thing: It's not just this. It happens again. The more closely you look at the events surrounding the disappearance of Joseph from Jacob's life, the more you'll see resonances of that covenant at Gal-Ed. I'll show you what I mean.

Of Brothers and Bread

After leaving him in the pit, the text tells us that Joseph's brothers were breaking bread together. But it just so happens that there is one other time in the Torah when brothers sit down to break bread together. When did that occur? It occurred, of all places, in the story of Gal-Ed:

SALE OF JOSEPH	STORY OF GAL-ED
וַיֵּשְׁבוּ **לֶאֱכָל־לֶחֶם**	וַיִּקְרָא לְאֶחָיו **לֶאֱכָל־לָחֶם**, וַיֹּאכְלוּ לֶחֶם
[The brothers] sat down **to eat bread.** (Gen. 37:25)	[Jacob] called to his family (litrally "brothers") **to eat bread**, and they ate bread. (Gen. 31:54)

And the breaking bread at Gal-Ed wasn't any old meal. Take a look at the context of Jacob's meal with his "brothers," the sons of Lavan, and you'll find that this occurs immediately after the solemn proclamation of the covenant between them. The two sides declare the covenant, swear to its terms, then break bread together (see Gen. 31:51–54). The context suggests that their choice to eat a meal together served as a kind of ratification of the terms of Gal-Ed that the two sides had agreed to. So in a very real way, it was this "breaking bread" between brothers — between Jacob and Lavan's children — that ratified the Gal-Ed covenant and put it into effect. Now, in the sale of Joseph, that very covenant seems to be coming back to haunt Jacob.

Teraphim and Torn-Up Pieces

The connections go further. Consider how, exactly, Rachel evaded detection by her father when he went searching through her tent for the missing teraphim:

Genesis 31:34

וְרָחֵל לָקְחָה אֶת־הַתְּרָפִים וַתְּשִׂמֵם בְּכַר הַגָּמָל, וַתֵּשֶׁב עֲלֵיהֶם

Rachel had taken the teraphim. She placed them in the saddle pillow (בכר) of the camel, and sat on them.

If you look carefully at Rachel's words, you can detect an elaborate series of double entendres that seem to foreshadow the loss of her own child, years later. The wordplay begins with the word for Lavan's idols, the **teraphim**. Does that word happen to remind you of anything later on in the Torah, in the story of the sale of Joseph? If it doesn't, stop looking at how the word is spelled — listen to how it *sounds*, phonetically. Teraphim just happens to evoke the exclamatory declaration that Jacob makes when he sees the bloody coat:

Genesis 37:33

טָרֹף טֹרַף יוֹסֵף!

Yosef has been torn apart!

It is as if teraphim, a noun in the Jacob and Lavan story, becomes a series of verbs in the Joseph story: *taroph, toraph!* And, in a remarkable extension of the wordplay, keep in mind that Jacob uses a *double* form of that word for "torn up," טרף טרף (*taroph toraph*! Well, take two *tarophs* and put them together in Hebrew and what do you get? Why...you get teraphim![3]

Of Firstborn Children and Camels

But what does Rachel *do* with those teraphim? Well, the text in the verse I quoted above tells us that she puts them בְּכַר הַגָּמָל, in the pillow of her camel's saddle. And think about what a remarkably vivid piece of detail the text gives us here! She didn't simply put them underneath her couch, bed, or chair; she put them ... *in the pillow of her camel's saddle.* בְּכַר, it should be noted, is a highly unusual word. It is not found with this meaning anywhere else in the entire Tanach. It feels like the text is trying to tip us off to some idea with this highly unusual phraseology.

Indeed, here, too, wordplay is afoot. To detect what the text has got up its proverbial sleeve with the word בְּכַר, this time, do the opposite of what we just did with teraphim: Forget how the word *sounds*; just pay attention to how it is *spelled*.

What else does ב־כ־ר spell?

Yes, you got it. It spells בְּכֹר — *bechor*, the word for firstborn son. Add it all up, and when the verse says that Rachel took the teraphim and placed them *bechar hagamal*, it is as if it is saying that she was doing something quite curious; she was placing her *bechor*, her firstborn son, Yosef, "on the camel."

On the camel? What in the world could that mean?

Well, if that's what you're saying to yourself right about now, keep in mind that, years later, in the story of the sale of Joseph, when Rachel's firstborn child is carted away from the land of Canaan by the Ishmaelites, bound for a new life as a slave in Egypt — he just happened to have been hoisted up onto ... a camel:

וַיִּשְׂאוּ עֵינֵיהֶם וַיִּרְאוּ, וְהִנֵּה	And behold, a caravan of Ishmaelites	Genesis 37:25

3 In Hebrew, the suffix *im* indicates the plural form of a noun.

אֹרְחַת יִשְׁמְעֵאלִים בָּאָה מִגִּלְעָד, **וּגְמַלֵּיהֶם** נֹשְׂאִים נְכֹאת וּצְרִי וָלֹט, הוֹלְכִים לְהוֹרִיד מִצְרָיְמָה:	was coming from Gilead, **their camels** bearing gum, balm, and ladanum, headed to take [the cargo] down to Egypt.

The text is thus telling us something chilling: In deceiving her father by hiding his teraphim under the pillow of her camel's saddle, Rachel has created the possibility for a future event that resonates with her act. In effect, she has personally hoisted her own *bechor*, Joseph, up onto the Ishmaelite's waiting camel. *Rachel's actions will reverberate a generation later in the loss of her own child.*

And her actions will reverberate as well, in the excuse the brothers employ to disguise what *really* happened to Joseph that fateful day. For, although the truth of the matter was that Joseph was hoisted up onto those camels and carted down to Egypt, that's not what Jacob would be given to understand. Instead, as we mentioned earlier, Jacob would be confronted with false evidence: a bunch of bloody clothes, presented to him by Joseph's brothers. And thus, in a stark way, what goes around comes around, for Rachel, too, had hidden teraphim from her father with talk of blood-stained clothes:

Genesis 31:35

וַתֹּאמֶר אֶל אָבִיהָ, "אַל־יִחַר בְּעֵינֵי אֲדֹנִי, כִּי לוֹא אוּכַל לָקוּם מִפָּנֶיךָ, כִּי דֶרֶךְ־נָשִׁים לִי"	[Rachel] said to her father, "Don't be angered, for I cannot stand before you, for the way of women is upon me."

In effect, Rachel was saying to her father that it was not worth his while asking her to stand up; all he would find beneath her is a bunch of blood-stained rags.

The Long Arm of Gal-Ed Returns

Finally, there's one more thing we should notice about the sale of Joseph that reminds us of Jacob's covenant with Lavan at Gal-Ed. To see it, I need to call your attention to an apparently trivial detail concerning the moment Joseph is sold as a slave. After the brothers left Joseph in the pit, during the meal they ate together, the text tells us that the brothers spied something in the distance. They spotted a caravan of Ishmaelites approaching their position. It is that caravan that will eventually haul Joseph down to Egypt. Now, here's my question for you: Can you recall where this caravan had come from? Do you happen to remember its origin point?

I'd excuse you for not remembering. It is, as I said, an apparent triviality. There seems little reason for the Torah to even bother mentioning it. But mention it the Torah does, and once you notice this origin place, it may well make your blood run cold:

וְהִנֵּה אֹרְחַת יִשְׁמְעֵאלִים בָּאָה **מִגִּלְעָד**.	Behold, a caravan of Ishmaelites was coming **from Gilead**.	Genesis 37:25

The caravan that would find Joseph and cart him down to Egypt came from … Gilead, of all places! It is as if the long arm of Gal-Ed has returned — returned to claim its next victim. First, it took Rachel away from Jacob. Now, it will take Rachel's child, Joseph, from him, too.

Putting It All Together

All in all, a remarkable confluence of events emerges. Nearly everything that happened on the fateful day that Lavan and Jacob sealed their covenant at Gal-Ed reverberates once more in the sale of Joseph:

How Gal-Ed Finds Its Echo in the Sale of Joseph

THE COVENANT AT GAL-ED	THE SALE OF JOSEPH
Finding; Recognizing	
עִם אֲשֶׁר **תִּמְצָא** אֶת־אֱלֹהֶיךָ, לֹא יִחְיֶה. נֶגֶד אַחֵינוּ, **הַכֶּר**־לְךָ, מָה עִמָּדִי, וְקַח־לָךְ	וַיֹּאמְרוּ, "זֹאת **מָצָאנוּ**. **הַכֶּר**־נָא: הַכְּתֹנֶת בִּנְךָ הִוא, אִם לֹא":

<table>
<tr><td>“Whoever you find with your gods shall not live! In front of your brethren, recognize what I have of yours, and take it.”
(Gen. 31:32)</td><td>[Joseph’s brothers] said, “We found this. Please recognize it:. Is it your son’s coat, or not?”
(Gen. 37:32)</td></tr>
<tr><td colspan="2">Brothers Eating Bread Together</td></tr>
<tr><td>וַיִּקְרָא לְאֶחָיו לֶאֱכָל-לָחֶם,
וַיֹּאכְלוּ לֶחֶם

[Jacob] called to his family (literally “brothers”) to eat bread, and they ate bread.
(Gen. 31:54)</td><td>וַיֵּשְׁבוּ לֶאֱכָל-לֶחֶם

[The brothers] sat down to eat bread.
(Gen. 37:25)</td></tr>
<tr><td colspan="2">Taroph Toraph and Teraphim</td></tr>
<tr><td>וְרָחֵל לָקְחָה אֶת־הַתְּרָפִים

Rachel took the teraphim,
(Gen. 31:34)</td><td>”טָרֹף טֹרַף יוֹסֵף!“

“Taroph toraph Yosef!” (Yosef has been torn apart!)
(Gen. 37:33)</td></tr>
<tr><td colspan="2">A Bechor on a Camel</td></tr>
<tr><td>וַתְּשִׂמֵם בְּכַר הַגָּמָל, וַתֵּשֶׁב
עֲלֵיהֶם

[Rachel] placed [the teraphim] in the saddle pillow (bechar) of the camel, and sat on them.
(Gen. 31:34)</td><td>וְהִנֵּה אֹרְחַת יִשְׁמְעֵאלִים בָּאָה
מִגִּלְעָד, וּגְמַלֵּיהֶם נֹשְׂאִים נְכֹאת
וּצְרִי וָלֹט, הוֹלְכִים לְהוֹרִיד
מִצְרָיְמָה:

And behold, a caravan of Ishmaelites was coming from Gilead, their camels bearing gum, balm, and ladanum, headed to take [the cargo] down to Egypt.
(Gen. 37:25)</td></tr>
</table>

Duplicitous Blood-Stained Clothes	
לוֹא אוּכַל לָקוּם מִפָּנֶיךָ כִּי־דֶרֶךְ נָשִׁים לִי I cannot get up from before you, because **the way of women is upon me**. (Gen. 31:35)	" וַיִּטְבְּלוּ אֶת־הַכֻּתֹּנֶת בַּדָּם: And they dipped Joseph's coat **in blood.** (Gen. 37:31)
Gal-Ed and the Caravan from Gilead	
עַל כֵּן קָרָא שְׁמוֹ גַּלְעֵד: That's why its name is called **Gal-Ed**. (Gen. 31:48)	וְהִנֵּה אֹרְחַת יִשְׁמְעֵאלִים בָּאָה מִגִּלְעָד Behold, a caravan of Ishmaelites were was coming from **Gilead**. (Gen. 37:25)

Beyond the Loss of Joseph

So it really *does* seem like the Sages were on to something when they spoke of a curse of Gal-Ed having lasting consequences. Jacob had promised that whoever was found with the missing teraphim would "not live," and he and Lavan had both called upon God to judge between them. Heartbreakingly, an element of that judgment seems to come in the form of Rachel's early death — and then, later on, in the sale of Joseph. The first event deprives Jacob of Rachel. And the second deprives him of Rachel's legacy.

But, as I suggested above, if Jacob is to truly lose Rachel through the mysterious curse of Gal-Ed, it would not be enough to merely take away Joseph from him. Benjamin, Rachel's other child, would have to go, too.

As I mentioned above, Jacob came quite close to losing Benjamin forever when Joseph, then disguised as a high Egyptian official, demanded that Benjamin be brought to him, and then framed him on charges of stealing his special silver goblet (see Gen. 44:1–5). Seemingly, at this moment, the script for the loss of Benjamin has been written: Joseph would pretend to keep Benjamin as a slave as punishment for this staged theft, and the brothers would be forced to return to Canaan without him. We might wonder: Does the Torah intend for the reader to perceive this episode, too, as part of the terrible vengeance of Gal-Ed? Is this the moment that the long-standing curse of Gal-Ed is finally to reach its awful climax?

Lavan's Chase, Redux

I think that a closer look at the verses confirms this hypothesis. As the sons of Jacob set off on their return journey to Canaan, Joseph puts his scheme into action. He instructs his servant to chase after his brothers and overtake them:

Genesis 44:4

Get up, chase after those men, and overtake them.	קוּם, רְדֹף אַחֲרֵי הָאֲנָשִׁים, וְהִשַּׂגְתָּם

Now, does that language remind you of anything? Have you perhaps encountered anything like it earlier in the book of Genesis?

You have. It is the language the Torah uses to describe Lavan chasing after Jacob a generation earlier, when he thought someone in Jacob's household had taken his teraphim. Put the texts side by side, and you'll see exactly what I mean:

A GENERATION LATER, JOSEPH'S SERVANT CHASES AFTER JOSEPH'S BROTHERS	**LAVAN AND HIS MEN CHASE AFTER JACOB**
קוּם רְדֹף אַחֲרֵי הָאֲנָשִׁים, וְהִשַּׂגְתָּם Get up, **chase after those men**, and **overtake them**. (Gen. 44:4)	וַיִּקַּח אֶת־אֶחָיו עִמּוֹ וַיִּרְדֹּף אַחֲרָיו...וַיַּשֵּׂג לָבָן אֶת יַעֲקֹב [Lavan] took his brethren with him and **chased after** him. Lavan **overtook** Jacob. (Gen. 31:23–25)

After the chase, Joseph's servant conducts a search of the brothers' possessions, just as Lavan once searched the family of Jacob's possessions. The details of the search correspond in an eerie way, too: Just as Lavan began his search with the eldest and proceeded to the youngest (he started by riffling through the belongings of an older sister, Leah, and only afterward, got to Rachel and her belongings), so did Joseph's servant take account of age in his search for the goblet:

וַיְחַפֵּשׂ, בַּגָּדוֹל הֵחֵל וּבַקָּטֹן כִּלָּה – וַיִּמָּצֵא הַגָּבִיעַ בְּאַמְתַּחַת בִּנְיָמִן:	He searched from oldest to youngest — and found the goblet in Benjamin's sack.	Genesis 44:12

Cast of Characters

Once again, the long-reaching hand of Gal-Ed has returned, and is threatening to complete its task. Not only will Joseph be taken, but Benjamin will be lost, too. But something startling is happening. It turns out that the very brother who was lost to Gal-Ed the first time around, (i.e., Joseph) is engineering what amounts to the kidnapping of the last remaining child of Rachel, threatening to take him away from Jacob's family forever. It is as if Joseph, now disguised as a high Egyptian official... has taken up the mantle of Lavan, of all people. Once a victim of the curse of Lavan, Joseph has now become a latter-day manifestation of him. In holding Benjamin prisoner, it is Joseph who stands to deprive the family of Jacob of the last vestiges of Rachel's lineage.

And now let's take that thread and pull on it a little. If Joseph, in the story of Benjamin's capture, is now playing the role of Lavan a generation earlier, back when Lavan chased after Jacob in the land of Gilead... who in the Joseph story would you say is now playing the role of Lavan's adversary, Jacob?

Well, let's figure that out. Jacob, back in the Lavan story, was the family leader. It was he who confronted Lavan in the face of Lavan's accusations of theft. And yet, Jacob had done so tragically. For Jacob remained unaware that someone in his camp possessed the stolen teraphim; and thus, Jacob's own words led him, unwittingly, to put his beloved Rachel in jeopardy.

So, does that remind you of anyone in the later story?

It sure does. In the later story, it is Judah who follows an almost identical path. He is the de facto leader of the brothers and, like Jacob, he speaks up to try to defend the family against the accusations of theft leveled against them. But he, too, is unaware of a crucial fact: Benjamin is in possession of a "stolen" goblet. And like Jacob before him, Judah, through his own words, unwittingly puts Benjamin, the precious child Judah had pledged to protect,[4] in jeopardy.

In words that are a virtual replay of Jacob's, Judah tells the disguised Joseph, this latter-day incarnation of Lavan, that the person found to have the stolen goblet will die:

JACOB SPEAKING TO LAVAN	JUDAH SPEAKING TO JOSEPH
עִם **אֲשֶׁר תִּמְצָא** אֶת־אֱלֹהֶיךָ **לֹא יִחְיֶה**!	**אֲשֶׁר יִמָּצֵא** אִתּוֹ מֵעֲבָדֶיךָ **וָמֵת**, וְגַם אֲנַחְנוּ נִהְיֶה לַאדֹנִי לַעֲבָדִים:
"Whoever **you find** with your gods **shall not live**!" (Gen. 31:32)	"Whoever of your servants, **is found** with [the goblet] shall die, and we, too, will be slaves to you." (Gen. 44:9)

4 Indeed, Judah had "inherited" the role of Benjamin's guardian from Jacob himself. He had heroically taken on this role with the words:

אָנֹכִי אֶעֶרְבֶנּוּ מִיָּדִי תְּבַקְשֶׁנּוּ,

I will be accountable for him; you may seek him from me (Gen. 43:9),

These are words that, chillingly, echo Jacob's own words, when he sought to defend himself against Lavan's accusations:

"טְרֵפָה לֹא־הֵבֵאתִי אֵלֶיךָ; אָנֹכִי אֲחַטֶּנָּה; **מִיָּדִי תְּבַקְשֶׁנָּה**. גְּנֻבְתִי יוֹם וּגְנֻבְתִי לָיְלָה:

That which was torn by animals I have not brought to you; I bore the loss; ***from my hand you would seek it****, be it stolen by day or stolen by night?* (Gen. 31:39).

It is a haunting moment of *déjà vu*. Just as Jacob once did, Judah has unwittingly sentenced to death the very person he most wishes to protect. The curse of Gal-Ed seems poised to claim its final victim.[5]

Judah Flips the Script

It seems as if the march of Gal-Ed's curse is inexorable, unstoppable. In the end, though, something — or better, *someone* — does stop it. At the last moment, the nightmare loss of both Benjamin and Joseph is averted. That heroic "someone" is Judah.

As we mentioned above, Judah trods the same ground as staked out a generation earlier by his father, Jacob. But he refuses to succumb to the same tragic ending. Instead, against all odds, he finds a way to flip the script. And in doing so, he saves Rachel's last remaining child from the menacing jaws of Gal-Ed.

Faced with the seemingly unavoidable loss of Benjamin, Judah summons the courage to make an impassioned speech to the high Egyptian official who, in reality, is his long-lost brother, Joseph. In that speech, he does not resort to any kind of deception or subterfuge. To the contrary, he risks everything and lays out the excruciating truth.[6]

---

5 For more textual evidence linking the potential loss of Joseph and Benjamin to Jacob's curse of Gal-Ed, see the addendum below.

6 It is interesting that Judah defeats the curse of Gal-Ed through nothing but truthful words — excruciatingly truthful words. Perhaps it is fitting that this is so. The curse of Gal-Ed initially came about because both Rachel and Jacob had acted with subterfuge toward their father (or father-in-law) simultaneously. Jacob had picked up in the middle of the night and fled, without Lavan's knowledge, and Rachel had at the very same time, slipped away with her father's teraphim. In back-to-back verses, the Torah characterizes each of these as an act of theft, using the identical word, *ganav* (see Gen. 31:19 and 31:20). Later, when Lavan calls Jacob on these things, he defends himself, unaware that his wife has stolen the teraphim, and unwilling to see his own middle-of-the-night departure as in any way duplicitous. Of course, all is not black and white. There are exculpatory factors that would contribute to Jacob's defense: He had no reason to suspect that Rachel took the teraphim, and he was worried Lavan would try to stop him if he told him he was leaving. Nevertheless, neither of these factors keep the text of the Torah itself from describing his act, and Rachel's act, as anything other than

He tells the disguised Joseph how he personally took responsibility for Benjamin and pledged to bring him back safely to his father. He tells him that his father has already lost one of the children of his beloved wife, Rachel; he couldn't possibly allow him to lose Rachel's last, remaining child.

And it is here that Judah confronts perhaps the most painful truth of all: His father loves Benjamin most of all, like he once loved Joseph most of all. His soul is bound up with Benjamin. Jacob loves Benjamin so, because of his undying love of Rachel, a love that dwarfs the feelings Jacob had for Judah's own mother, Leah.

Faced with these truths, Judah musters the strength to change course radically. He turns his back on the decision he and his brothers made years ago. Yes, there was a time when Judah was willing to sell a child of Rachel into slavery rather than face these truths about his father's love. But today would not be that day. He implores Joseph to take him as a slave instead of Benjamin:

Genesis 44:34

אֵיךְ אֶעֱלֶה אֶל־אָבִי וְהַנַּעַר
אֵינֶנּוּ אִתִּי? פֶּן אֶרְאֶה בָרָע
אֲשֶׁר יִמְצָא אֶת אָבִי!

How will I go up to my father if the boy is not with me? Lest I see the evil that will find my father!

Judah offers to sacrifice his own future for the welfare of a rival brother. And that shining act had lasting consequences. In one fell swoop, it not only brought Benjamin back into the family of Israel, but it brought Joseph back, too. Judah's words inspire a tearful Joseph to reveal his true identity and to reconcile with his shocked brothers.

Gal-Ed was a formidable foe. It had methodically threatened to erase any remnant of Rachel among the family of Israel. But in the end, Judah, the man who was once, actually, the prime architect of the sale

---

a kind of theft. When Jacob then joins with Lavan in swearing to their respective positions at Gal-Ed, and inviting God Himself to judge between them, the stage is set for the Almighty to undertake a kind of audit of Jacob's position, as uncomfortable as the consequences of that may be. The bottom line is that the curse of Gal-Ed came about through (perhaps even well-intentioned) acts of subterfuge. It is intriguing that the curse is put to rest by Judah through radical acts of truth telling.

of Joseph (see Gen. 37:26) — is the one who ensures that Rachel's legacy will still shine brightly among Israel's tribes. He emerges victorious against the curse of Gal-Ed.

Bookends

If we stand back, though, and survey the nature of Judah's "victory" against the hidden hand of Gal-Ed, we find something incomplete. Judah had been able to undo only one facet of the curse that Jacob unwittingly set in motion. In a moment reminiscent of Lavan's chasing of Jacob, Judah had been able to stand in the breach, and stop a disguised Joseph from capturing Benjamin and taking him away from the family of Israel forever. *That*, Judah had been able to forestall. He had been able to bring back Benjamin, and Joseph, for that matter, into the family once more. But the other part of Gal-Ed's insidious legacy — the terrible crime of the sale of Joseph, in which Rachel's firstborn child was originally lost — there is no way to undo that terrible event and its eternal stain. Judah himself engineered that sale. Try as he might like, Judah has no way to undo what happened that fateful day, when he and the brothers cast Joseph in the pit and spied the caravan of Ishmaelites coming from afar, coming from Gilead.

Judah can't undo that. But perhaps his descendant could. At least symbolically.

That descendant was Ya'ir.

A Man with a Veiled Past

We heard about Ya'ir a while ago, all the way back at the beginning of this essay, when we looked at the story of Gilead in the book of Numbers:

Numbers 32:39–41

וַיֵּלְכוּ בְּנֵי מָכִיר בֶּן־מְנַשֶּׁה
גִּלְעָדָה, וַיִּלְכְּדֻהָ וַיּוֹרֶשׁ אֶת־
הָאֱמֹרִי אֲשֶׁר־בָּהּ. וַיִּתֵּן מֹשֶׁה
אֶת־הַגִּלְעָד לְמָכִיר בֶּן־מְנַשֶּׁה,
וַיֵּשֶׁב בָּהּ. וְיָאִיר בֶּן־מְנַשֶּׁה הָלַךְ
וַיִּלְכֹּד אֶת־חַוֹּתֵיהֶם, וַיִּקְרָא
אֶתְהֶן חַוֹּת יָאִיר׃

The children of Machir the son of Manasseh went to Gilead, and they conquered it and drove out the Amorites who were there. Moses gave Gilead to Machir the son of Manasseh, and they settled there. And Ya'ir the son of Manasseh captured their villages and called them Chavot Ya'ir.

If you recall, we were perplexed by the text's attention to the details of Ya'ir's conquests. We asked: What was so important about this man, Ya'ir? Why were his conquests of these villages of such note that they needed to be singled out?

The key to answering these questions can be found in a sly little trick the text seems to employ when it relates to us Ya'ir's identity.

This fellow, Ya'ir, who exactly *was* he? As it turns out, his identity isn't quite as simple as it seems. Because in the above verse in the book of Numbers, we are introduced to Ya'ir as a child of Manasseh. And, if you were a reader of the book of Numbers, and you happened on that verse, you'd be excused for thinking that Ya'ir was a member of the tribe of Manasseh. After all, according to the text, he is "Ya'ir, the son of Manasseh." But mysteriously, another book in Tanach suggests that Ya'ir *wasn't* actually a member of the tribe of Manasseh at all.

As it turns out, the book of Chronicles fleshes out a more expansive picture of Ya'ir's lineage — and therein, we learn to which tribe Ya'ir really belonged:

I Chronicles, 2:21–22

וְאַחַר בָּא **חֶצְרוֹן** אֶל בַּת־מָכִיר
אֲבִי גִלְעָד, וְהוּא לְקָחָהּ וְהוּא
בֶּן־שִׁשִּׁים שָׁנָה וַתֵּלֶד לוֹ אֶת־
שְׂגוּב. וּשְׂגוּב הוֹלִיד אֶת **יָאִיר**,
וַיְהִי־לוֹ עֶשְׂרִים וְשָׁלוֹשׁ עָרִים
בְּאֶרֶץ הַגִּלְעָד:

And afterward, **Chetzron** went in to the daughter of Machir, the father of Gilead, whom he took to wife when he was sixty years old; and she bore him **Seguv**. And Seguv fathered **Ya'ir**, who had twenty-three cities in the land of Gilead.

What Chronicles adds is the fact that Ya'ir had a grandparent, a paternal grandfather — namely, Chetzron — from the tribe of Judah. Since the Torah assigns tribal affiliation through patrilineal descent, that places Ya'ir squarely as a member of the tribe of Judah. Here is how Chronicles presents Ya'ir's family tree:

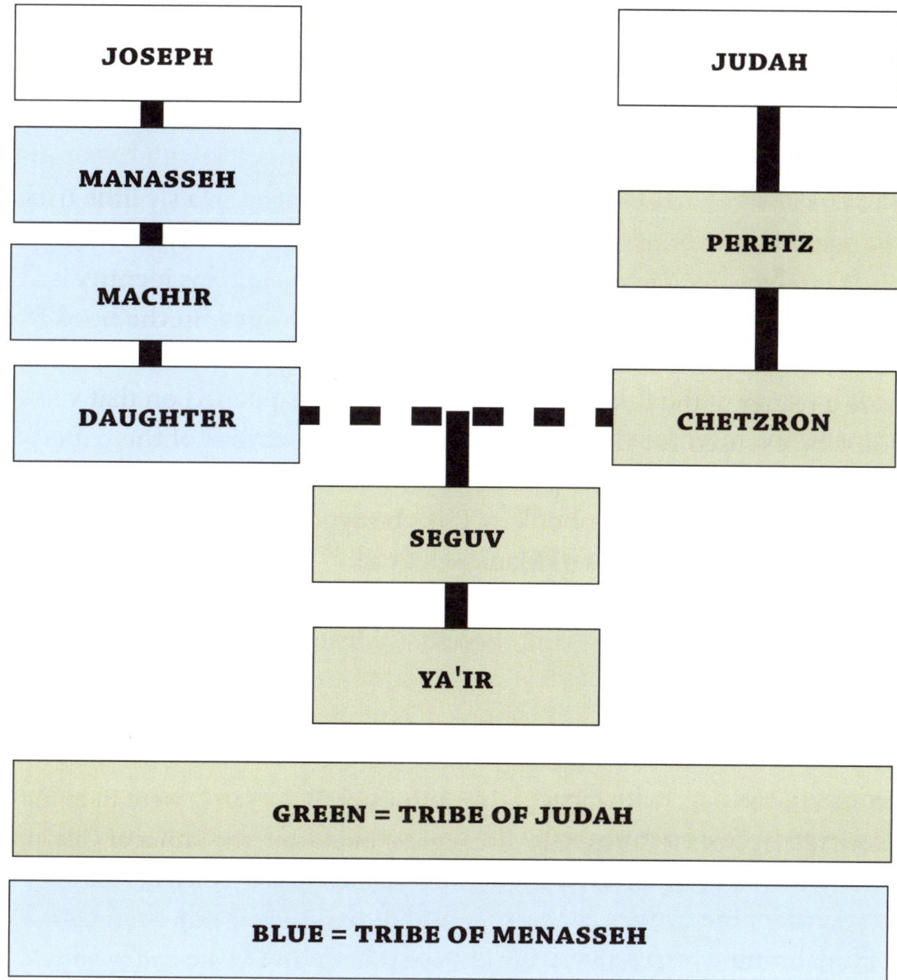

Why then, does the book of Numbers call Ya'ir a child of Manasseh if he's clearly a card-carrying member of the tribe of Judah? Ah, dear reader, I'm glad you asked. Allow me to suggest a theory.

Judah, Joseph, and Gilead: The Triangle Closes

When the book of Numbers relates to us the tale of Ya'ir's conquest, it wasn't just any old land that Ya'ir had conquered. He had conquered **Gilead**, a land with a storied and painful past for the family of Israel. That makes all the difference in the world. Judah's role, as we've seen, was not inconsequential in the story of Gal-Ed. Neither was Joseph's. And now, at the end of Numbers, in Ya'ir's conquest, all three of these participants, Gilead, Joseph, and Judah, intersect one more time.

Centuries after Judah emerged victorious against the menace of Gal-Ed's curse, a descendant of Judah picks up Judah's baton for one last relay in the race against the legacy of Gal-Ed. Ya'ir captures the land of Gilead — Gal-Ed's namesake, and the place where the confrontation with Lavan and the covenant at Gal-Ed actually occurred. But *how* Ya'ir does this — *under whose banner he does it* — symbolically rights an old wrong, an ancient stain on the name of Judah.

As we saw earlier, Judah brought the family of Israel together, and restored Joseph and Benjamin, the children of Rachel, to its ranks. He could not, however, undo the actual sale of Joseph. That sale, in hindsight, had cataclysmic reverberations. Joseph was the first Israelite slave in Egypt. That sale catalyzed the family's descent to Egypt for what would become hundreds of years of slavery. Ya'ir can't reverse that; no one could. But he could do the next best thing. And he would do it at a very propitious moment.

Centuries earlier, when the long arm of Gal-Ed took Joseph down to Egypt, it marked the moment when the family of Israel first began to *leave* the land of Canaan. Now, as the book of Numbers winds down, Israel was beginning its process of *return,* and the conquest of Gilead, on the west side of the Jordan, helped begin that process. But it wasn't just a geographical victory. Ya'ir's act would be the final rebuff of Gal-Ed. For this child of Judah didn't just conquer Gal-Ed. He conquered it *as a child of Manasseh,* on behalf of the tribe of Manasseh. And in so doing, this latter-day child of Judah would help redeem the ghosts of his father's past.

Indeed, Joseph had been captured by a caravan from Gilead, in an act that had the spiritual fingerprints of Gal-Ed all over it. Now, a child from Judah — the very person who orchestrated that capture — would in turn, capture that very land on behalf of the children of Joseph. You see, Ya'ir, who hailed from Judah, resisted the time-honored dictum that "to the victor go the spoils." He chose *not* to claim the land for the tribe of Judah, as might have been his right. No, the land would go to Manasseh, child of Joseph. And this victory would be Ya'ir's legacy. Indeed, he would be known to all, through the language of the book of Numbers, as a child of Manasseh, for evermore.

And one last thing, dear reader, before I let you go: Consider what the book of Numbers tells us about the particular family that would possess Gilead. It would be the family of Machir, no less. *Machir* — מכיר — it's quite a name. It doesn't seem like a coincidence that Manasseh, child of

Joseph, would name his own child Machir — a name so evocative of the sale, the *mechirah* (מכירה) of Joseph. In assigning his conquest to the family of Machir — indeed, in linking *himself* so closely to Machir, Ya'ir, this scion of Judah, acts, perhaps, with ultimate solidarity toward the children of Joseph and their blackest moment, and turns his back on the divisive legacy of Gal-Ed for evermore.

Addendum

In the above paragraphs, I've cited some of the textual evidence that links the potential loss of Joseph and Benjamin to Jacob's ill-fated curse of Gal-Ed. But there is a great deal more evidence as well. I'll cite it briefly here.

Right after Lavan fails to find the missing teraphim, Jacob gives a detailed response to what he sees as his father in law's unfounded accusations. He highlights what he sees as his surpassing integrity during the many years he worked for Lavan. Of course, unbeknownst to him, that integrity is undermined by the fact that his family *does* possess the stolen teraphim. And, wouldn't you know it? The text of Jacob's impassioned defense is riddled with foreshadowing of future tragedy. Here is the text of that response, with highlights to indicate that foreshadowing:

Genesis 31:38–39

זֶה עֶשְׂרִים שָׁנָה אָנֹכִי עִמָּךְ, רְחֵלֶיךָ וְעִזֶּיךָ לֹא שִׁכֵּלוּ וְאֵילֵי צֹאנְךָ לֹא אָכָלְתִּי. טְרֵפָה לֹא־הֵבֵאתִי אֵלֶיךָ. אָנֹכִי אֲחַטֶּנָּה; מִיָּדִי תְּבַקְשֶׁנָּה. גְּנֻבְתִי יוֹם וּגְנֻבְתִי לָיְלָה:	These twenty years that I have been with you, **your sheep** and goats **have never miscarried**, and I did not eat from the rams of your flock. I never brought you a torn-up animal. Whether an animal was **stolen by day or stolen by night**, I was considered guilty, **and you sought [payment] from my hand**.

- רְחֵלֶיךָ וְעִזֶּיךָ לֹא שִׁכֵּלוּ, Jacob tells Lavan: *Rechelecha*, your sheep, never miscarried. But that word also spells out the name of our matriarch Rachel.[7] Read that way, the verse would have the additional meaning:

---

7 Rachel is not the only one alluded to in this verse. Jacob refers to רְחֵלֶיךָ וְעִזֶּיךָ, your sheep (*rachel*) *and your goats*, together, never miscarried. Was Rachel ever married to someone who looked like a goat, together with whom she never miscarried? Indeed, Jacob had once dressed up in goat skin when he came before his

Rachel shelcha, **your Rachel**, never miscarried. That is a particularly poignant statement in light of the fact that while Rachel never did miscarry, she *almost* did, in the birth of Benjamin, where the live birth cost her own life.

- Jacob tells his father-in-law that he never brought a ***terefah***, a torn up' (**טְרֵפָה**) animal to him and excused himself from having to pay for it. But later in his life, Jacob would have evidence that his own son, Joseph, was "torn up": **טָרֹף טֹרַף יוֹסֵף** — *Joseph has been torn up*! (Gen. 37:33).
- Jacob protests that "**גְּנֻבְתִי** יוֹם **וּגְנֻבְתִי** לָיְלָה"; whether an animal was **stolen** *by day, or* **stolen** *by night,* he would always be responsible for it. Later, though, Jacob's own child, Joseph would tell his fellow prisoners in jail: **כִּי־גֻנֹּב גֻּנַּבְתִּי** מֵאֶרֶץ הָעִבְרִים, **I have been stolen** *from the land of the Hebrews!* (Gen. 40:15).
- **אָנֹכִי אֲחַטֶּנָּה; מִיָּדִי תְּבַקְשֶׁנָּה**, Jacob says at Gilead: "*That which was torn by animals I have not brought to you; I bore the loss;* **from my hand you sought it**." Later on, Judah will say a phrase that literally *rhymes* perfectly with this, when he promises himself to Jacob as a guarantor for the safety of Benjamin: **אָנֹכִי אֶעֶרְבֶנּוּ; מִיָּדִי תְּבַקְשֶׁנּוּ** — "*I will be accountable for him; you may seek him from me*" (Gen. 43:9). In the end, Judah's redemption of that pledge to Jacob constitutes the moment he heroically stops the insidious progress of Gal-Ed's curse, as we will show below.

Here are the parallels in the original Hebrew:

---

father Yitzchak to receive the blessing intended for his hairy brother Esau (Gen. 27:16).

<table>
<tr><th>GILEAD</th><th>JOSEPH</th></tr>
<tr><td rowspan="3">זֶה עֶשְׂרִים שָׁנָה אָנֹכִי עִמָּךְ רְחֵלֶיךָ
וְעִזֶּיךָ לֹא שִׁכֵּלוּ וְאֵילֵי צֹאנְךָ לֹא
אָכָלְתִּי. טְרֵפָה־לֹא הֵבֵאתִי אֵלֶיךָ
אָנֹכִי אֲחַטֶּנָּה מִיָּדִי תְּבַקְשֶׁנָּה
גְּנֻבְתִי יוֹם וּגְנֻבְתִי לָיְלָה:
(Gen. 31:38–39)</td><td>טָרֹף טֹרַף יוֹסֵף
(Gen. 37:33)

גֻּנֹּב גֻּנַּבְתִּי מֵאֶרֶץ הָעִבְרִים
(Gen. 40:15)</td></tr>
<tr><th>BENJAMIN</th></tr>
<tr><td>אָנֹכִי אֶעֶרְבֶנּוּ מִיָּדִי תְּבַקְשֶׁנּוּ אִם־
לֹא הֲבִיאֹתִיו אֵלֶיךָ וְהִצַּגְתִּיו לְפָנֶיךָ
וְחָטָאתִי לְךָ כָּל הַיָּמִים:
(Gen. 43:9)

וַאֲנִי כַּאֲשֶׁר שָׁכֹלְתִּי שָׁכָלְתִּי:
(Gen. 43:14)</td></tr>
</table>

Maggid Books
The best of contemporary Jewish thought from
Koren Publishers Jerusalem Ltd.